3945

THE LAST BEST HOPE

ALSO BY ROD MCQUEEN

The Moneyspinners (1983)
Risky Business (1985)
Leap of Faith (1986)
Both My Houses (with Sean O'Sullivan, 1986)
Blind Trust (1987)

THE LAST BEST HOPE

How to Start and Grow Your Own Business

Rod McQueen

Canadian Cataloguing in Publication Data
McQueen, Rod, 1944–
   The last best hope: how to start and grow your own business

Includes bibliographical references and index.
ISBN 0-7710-5630-3

1. New business enterprises – Canada – Management.
2. Entrepreneurship – Canada.   I. Title.

HD62.5.M38 1995   658.1'1   C95-931755-4

Typesetting by M&S, Toronto

Printed and bound in Canada on acid-free paper

McClelland & Stewart Inc.
The Canadian Publishers
481 University Avenue
Toronto, Ontario
M5G 2E9

1 2 3 4 5   99 98 97 96 95

CONTENTS

FOREWORD

When my wife, Sandy, and I returned to Canada in 1993 after living in London, England, and Washington, D.C., for most of the previous six years, we were surprised by the despairing mood of our country. The recession, the GST, and Brian Mulroney had all conspired to make Canadians grumpy. So, it was a treat for me, as senior writer at *The Financial Post*, to interview the CEOs of the fifty best-managed private companies, as chosen by accounting firm Arthur Andersen & Co.

That group, their successors in 1994, and the many other entrepreneurs I interviewed over the next two years restored my faith in Canada. Their individual drive, unbridled enthusiasm, and hopes for success led me to write this book. May their ups and downs serve as both a guide and an inspiration for others who might want to realize their dreams and start their own businesses.

Many people helped along the way. My agents, Bruce Westwood and Linda McKnight of Sterling Lord Associates, offered wise advice and counsel. Avie Bennett, Douglas Gibson, and Pat Kennedy at McClelland & Stewart were supportive and creative throughout. I am also indebted to three readers who commented constructively on the draft manuscript: Gary Curtis of Balmoral Partners Ltd., Gordon Sharwood of Sharwood & Co., and Nick Ross of Ernst & Young. Finally, there's Willy and George, the two barn cats whose antics awoke me daily at 4 A.M. so that I could write for three hours before breakfast and my day job. I'd say thanks, but they'd know I didn't mean it.

Rod McQueen
May 1995

Fanning the Fire

*"If everybody else has faith in me,
how come I haven't got faith in myself?"*

– Rick Padulo, Padulo Integrated

Rick Padulo's first job in the advertising business couldn't have been more modest. At eighteen, while still in school, he began working for his brother Joe as a research assistant – a grand label for someone who collared shoppers in Montreal to ask questions about buying habits and brand preferences. Photo shoots for clients weren't very glamorous either. There was no jetting off to Jamaica for exciting days on the beach with models, followed by pina coladas on soft evenings around the hotel pool. Instead, his first assignment was a day trip to the nearby Eastern Townships. To make matters worse, Padulo was expected to use his own Volkswagen as transportation and bring a rake to gather leaves for the photo, which would be used in a financial-services brochure.

But by the time he was twenty-three, Padulo had moved up the ladder and landed four major accounts, worth about

$4 million in annual billings. In 1977, like a lot of other Montrealers fleeing the rise of separatism, he moved to Toronto. Padulo worked at the Morris Saffer Agency and by the mid-eighties had achieved sufficient success and profile that he was attracting the attention of others. A number of firms began chasing after him to come work with them.

Padulo was tempted to switch agencies, so he sought advice from his brother and father. Both had ideas for his future, but Padulo had another option in mind: going out on his own. So, in 1985, Padulo launched Padulo Integrated. Today it's a unique hybrid of seven companies with 120 employees, is among the top ten agencies in the country, and enjoys better than 50-per-cent annual growth in billings and profits.

Of all the personal aspects stopping most people from launching a new business, personal confidence – the question so aptly captured by the phrase "how come I haven't got faith in myself?" – is the first hurdle. One way many people go "on their own" is to buy into a franchise organization. While that's certainly an effective approach for some, in fact a franchise is just another way of working for a boss. You will be putting your own money at risk, but you're buying into a larger business, one where all the thinking has been done for you. Although buying a franchise is discussed in Chapter Six, for the most part this book focuses on something else – having your own idea, getting under way, then growing that enterprise just as far as your ambition and the fire in your belly will take you.

Emmie Leung was born in China and moved at age six to Hong Kong with her family. Tradition, respect, and hierarchy meant that the family was dominated by two grandmothers who had grown up in an era in which their feet were bound to keep them at home. Leung had no desire to remain similarly controlled. For her, North America would supply freedom and opportunity. She came to Canada in 1972 and spent four difficult years in Winnipeg at the University of Manitoba, struggling with the weather, the language, the courses, and the loneliness. She graduated in 1976 in honours business administration, thinking that the worst was behind her – until she spent a year looking for work at a time when there were no jobs.

For Leung, the problem became an opportunity. As she pounded the pavement, she kept seeing wastepaper in dumpsters and decided that other people's garbage could be her gold. "If no one will make me a boss," she concluded, "I'll make myself a boss." In 1977, Leung started International Paper Industries Ltd. in Vancouver and bought used cardboard for sale as salvage. At first, the only markets were overseas, because there were no Canadian buyers. Over time, however, she virtually invented the Blue Box recycling program and curbside pickup of waste in British Columbia. Today International Paper does $13 million in sales a year and has eighty-six employees. "You have to tell yourself you can succeed and you will succeed," says Leung.

Start-up tip: *If you can dream it, you can do it.*

Not everyone has achieved the profile Rick Padulo had in his community when he began his own business, nor does everyone command the financial clout he did. Padulo invested $150,000 of his own money, borrowed another $150,000 from a private backer, and hired twelve employees for his Toronto-based company. Don't let a lack of resources stop you. You can also begin with absolutely no money in your pocket just like Kimberley Thomas, who created her business in the family room of her home in Richmond Hill, Ontario. Her story, fully detailed in Chapter Three, tells how a good idea became JoeJobs Inc. and supplied work for scores of others in her neighbourhood.

The advice Thomas gives about starting a business not only comes from the heart; but she suggests *using* the heart. "Do what you love. If you don't love it, you won't be able to do it, because it's going to take everything you've got," she says. "I just have a lot of faith. I'm helping a lot of people stay at home with their kids. Believe you can succeed and you will."

So whether you're an Emmie Leung, a Rick Padulo, or a Kimberley Thomas, all you have to do is be convinced you have a plan, then launch that plan, and keep working until you succeed.

Start-up tip: *Plan the work; work the plan.*

Looking back at the early days of his own start-up, Padulo isn't reluctant to admit, "It was scary." When he opened the doors, his father telephoned to ask, "How do you like your first day of unemployment?" Padulo's first big account was retail chain Suzy Shier. As it turned out, the firm won awards and quickly established its reputation with Padulo's "What's Suzy wearing?" campaign. In addition to the profile that followed such industry-wide attention, Padulo realized that he needed to occupy a niche no one else did, so he created what he calls a transaction-based company. "I realized at Saffer that we were getting pigeonholed. As good as retail [advertising] was, it was too much of a confining thing. Once we'd covered each [retail] category, there was nothing more to cover. At Padulo, I was going to worry about my client's business and profitability. That alone changed the way we thought about business in a communication company. The idea was to become a customer-driven service company, a collaborative partner with the client, whether the client was a manufacturer, a retailer, a financial institution, or a politician looking for votes. We weren't an ad agency, we were a service company." A *service* company – not a bad way for any small business to describe its role in the nineties.

Padulo's big breakthrough came in 1994 when the Canadian Imperial Bank of Commerce invited him to pitch a television campaign for the bank. Instead, his team decided to go for broke. In three short weeks, Padulo created an entirely new approach to all of the bank's outreach advertising, an approach that sprang from both his personal-service methods and gung-ho professional attitude. The resulting presentation included not just TV, as requested, but tied that with print, radio, direct mail, items for use in the branches (such as brochures and posters), as well as a 1-800 number so that customers could call in with ideas, questions, and complaints. Padulo won out over BBDO Canada, the bank's ad agency for the previous eighty-seven years. The crux of the program, called Personal Vision, downplays the repayments on a new car loan and celebrates instead the customer's capacity to realize a dream involving the freedom such a vehicle would bring. Says Padulo, "We all have a dream."

Fulfilling your dream in business begins by following three secrets from Margot Franssen, who bought Canadian rights to The Body Shop from its British owners. First, not having a business degree makes life easier because, rather than becoming confused by academic learning, you trust your instincts. Second, "The whole thing is about love and work," says Franssen. "Don't try and squeeze everything into nine-to-five." And third, don't worry about launching with little or no money. "Nothing to risk," Franssen says, "means you can be creative."

Franssen also believes that adversity can be turned into an opportunity. Poor inventory control that caused a shortage of containers in the early days of her business meant that in-store staff had to ask customers to bring back their containers for refills. The public viewed this as an environmentally conscious move and applauded the approach. Blind luck came into play too. The green colour adopted for all the stores seemed to

match the environmental concerns with which The Body
Shop became synonymous. In fact, in the beginning, that particular green was the only colour that would cover the mould
they found when they set out to paint the first store. "People
think we're remarkably clever, and we're not at all," says
Franssen.

Your hobby can also become your business. Leonard Lee of
Ottawa liked working with hand tools and thought others
would like to buy good tools too. But before the former trade
commissioner gave up his day job at the Department of
Industry, he decided to make and sell wood-burning stoves on
the side. Beginning in the mid-seventies, Lee and his teenaged
son, Robin, would pound away on cast iron every evening, and
his wife, Lorraine, would lug the creations to the post office
for shipment to buyers. Lee's thinking was that, if potbellied
stoves sold reasonably well, something like fine hand tools
might have an even broader market appeal.

The stoves were popular; so, in 1978, Lee emptied his
savings account, slapped two mortgages on his house, and
started Lee Valley Tools Ltd. A loan from his brother resulted
in a third mortgage and more debt, but the three mortgages
also provided money for a showroom, a warehouse, and a catalogue that listed fifteen hundred tools. "My theory was to
come on the market looking as if we'd always been there.
When you're just a little fish, sometimes it helps to puff up
your gills," Lee says. In addition to his marketing savvy, Lee's
guts, daring, and flair for presentation have paid off. He has
opened stores in Toronto, London, Calgary, Edmonton, and
Vancouver, selling woodworking and gardening tools (the firm
designs and manufactures about one-third of its offerings), as
well as other products such as wooden Adirondack chairs and
kitchen hardware.

The monthly catalogues, mailed to about 150,000 Canadian
households and featuring eight thousand items, not only com-

prise 50 per cent of sales but also bring pre-sold shoppers into the stores. "A new catalogue is like a piston," Lee says. "The catalogue sells, the stores deliver." Since Lee added gardening tools to the line in 1989, they have come to account for about 20 per cent of sales and half the growth in the company. "The future for firms like ours and Canada as a whole is in design and intellectual-property innovation," says Lee. "Canada's muscle power is high priced, so we have to sell our brain power. If Canadian firms don't design their products, they'll have a short life span."

Indeed, such capacity to innovate must be a key component of any entrepreneur's talents. A Statistics Canada survey released in 1994 showed that the kind of innovation practised by Lee is one of the core characteristics for success. Of the fifteen hundred small firms studied, more than half said they had introduced some innovation recently. But, as the next chapter will show, there is a lot more required of you than the capacity to innovate. Above all other characteristics, as Rick Padulo says, you have to believe in yourself and your dream. "Have confidence in yourself. Be flexible," says Emmie Leung. "Equip yourself with a road map. Daydreaming with a purpose equals vision."

Summary:

1. Define a need and fill it.
2. Have a plan. Follow it.
3. Trust your instincts.
4. Be resourceful.
5. Never give up. True character means refusing to accept defeat.

CHAPTER I

The Nature of
the Entrepreneur

*"You'll have trouble being successful if you
don't have a lot of common sense."*

– Geoff Martin, Vas-Cath Inc.

In 1957, when Austrian-born Frank Stronach started his
company, supplying car parts from a small coach house in
Toronto, he was just looking for personal freedom and a
place in his adopted land. He had no idea where his work
would lead, but along the way he managed to build a business
in which other like-minded individuals could also become
plant managers and share in the profits. Today, Magna International is a $3.5-billion multinational with seventy factories
and twenty thousand employees. "Countries like Canada
have real choices to make," says Daniel Drache, professor of
political economics at York University in Toronto. "If they
want to be players they have to have leverage. One Frank
Stronach isn't enough," he adds. "You need forty Frank
Stronachs or you'll just have a wilderness of single instances.

Innovation requires support of all kinds, but change must come from the business community."

Like Stronach, you don't need to have the twenty-year plan in place right at the beginning. What you do need is the desire to work your way through every obstacle placed in your path; you also need the willpower to change your life. Think about successful people you know in business, and they probably possess common sense about people and about the business world. Sometimes such knowledge comes naturally; many entrepreneurs can trace their interest in business to an early age when they had a newspaper route or did babysitting in the neighbourhood. They say that the reason they understand business as adults and can make sensible decisions is because they had business role-models when they were young. They grew up in a family where one or both of their parents were in business; perhaps a favourite aunt or uncle ran a small firm. Husband-and-wife team Jane and Geoff Martin of Vas-Cath Inc. – a manufacturing firm in Mississauga, Ontario – both come from families that were in business. Says Geoff: "Because of our backgrounds, we started with a little bit of an edge."

The top four reasons to launch your own business:
1. To be your own boss.
2. To fulfil a dream.
3. To be able to choose where you work and live.
4. To avoid constraints on your talent or creativity.

Within the very core of a budding entrepreneur burns the desire to gain control over your own life. A good education, an understanding of the basic rules of accounting, inventory control, and administration are helpful – but the lack of formal training need not prevent a person from going into business. Poor grades certainly marked the school career of Tim Moore, who failed Grade 3, missed his Grade 10 math, and failed

Grade 12. "I can't tell you how many people told me I'd never amount to anything," says Moore, who eventually graduated from the University of Western Ontario and went on to McGill University for postgraduate studies.

There he ran out of money, so he started a moving business with a pickup truck, no insurance coverage, and no cartage licence. "I was a bandit, a pirate," Moore confesses. "Everything was cash. It was a matter of survival." Today he is president of AMJ Campbell Van Lines, Canada's largest moving company, with $60 million in annual revenue and three thousand employees. "You have to be able to communicate successfully and motivate people," says Moore. "As long as your goals are reasonable, you can do anything you want."

Start-up tip: *Formal education might get you a job, but self-education in your chosen field is the way most people get rich.*

Like Moore, many entrepreneurs have spotty academic records. Surveys have shown that 29 per cent of successful entrepreneurs never went to university and another 27 per cent started but didn't finish. What they do have, however, is street smarts, commitment, and a desire to control their life. One of the reasons why formal education is so difficult may be that many entrepreneurs have learning disabilities that mean they cannot, for example, comprehend the numbers so necessary in the minds of some people – like bankers. Linda Lundström, the successful clothing designer who launched her Toronto-based business in 1974, freely admits that she still suffers from a mental block about business terms and their meaning. "To this day," she says, "I don't know the difference between a debit and a credit."

Lundström has been a mentor to countless potential entrepreneurs and believes that she has come to understand the core values and characteristics that are required. According to her, entrepreneurs are basically unemployable, so they must start their own company. No one else will hire them! They also refuse to accept defeat and are driven to work so hard that they will almost ruin their health. Lundström says that entrepreneurs often come from families where there was an entrepreneur who was also an alcoholic, a problem that meant that household responsibilities were thrust onto a child at an unusually early age.

An entrepreneurial person may also have a helping attitude that values people and does community-service work with no expectation of commercial gain. "That's the heart and soul of the company," she says. "That's what makes you want to get out of bed and go to work some mornings." Finally, entrepreneurs are optimists. Entrepreneurs don't blame governments, the economy, or anyone else for their problems. "You're getting a curve ball thrown at you every day," says Lundström. "The sooner you see it as an opportunity, the better."

So, how do you know if you're one of those who can be successful with a start-up? Among the most important prerequisites are your disposition and the need for a high energy level. Says Emmie Leung, "I have a positive attitude. And I can't sit still." Every business consultant and successful company president will point to one particular aspect over another as *the* ingredient for success, but you'll need to be able to answer yes to a majority of the following questions before launching a new business. Try this self-analysis to see if you have the commitment required to be an entrepreneur:

Have you got what it takes?
1. Do you possess lots of energy?
2. Do you enjoy meeting people?
3. Are you a good organizer?
4. Are you a leader rather than a follower? Are you a doer rather than a watcher?

5. If you fail at something, do you try again, perhaps using a different approach?
6. Do you learn from your mistakes?
7. Can you *see* yourself running a business? Is this something you really want to do?
8. Have you got an idea that you believe in?
9. Do you believe in yourself?
10. Do you have the support of your spouse, your children, and other close members of your family who will be affected?

Of motivations there are many. Greed can be a driving factor, but the business you go into should also be something you *want* to do. Financial need can be an equally compelling reason if, for example, a spouse suddenly departs or dies and the family income shrinks. Time on your hands, a desire for personal or professional independence, or simply a hope to accomplish something with your life are all legitimate forces for change. Finally, you'll need to be a risk-taker. The core of being an entrepreneur is to do something few others have the guts to do. That does not mean, however, that you should do something totally foolish. You must take calculated risks. Bill Zeckendorf, a real-estate developer in the sixties and seventies, put it best when he said, "I don't care how large a deal is, I don't care how complicated a deal is, I don't care how risky a deal is, I ain't got any of my money in it."

Emmie Leung also urges potential entrepreneurs to ask, "Do people need your service? Do they need your product? Can you deliver at a price they can afford or can I deliver it at a price that's lower than my competition?" She warns, "You must be prepared to sacrifice, including personal life and vacations."

Most of all, you must be able to spot and act on opportunities that are right under your nose. Oakville, Ontario, interior designer Marte Belisle had been working from an office, until she decided that commuting was a waste of time. At home, however, she soon found that she couldn't "turn off." There wasn't enough space for her to have a separate room as an office, so the work was always visible and beckoning her. Belisle decided that the answer was an office-furniture system that could be hidden away behind folding panels. "It was important to be able to close it at the end of the day and have a life of my own beyond my business life," she says. Belisle designed the system with her own needs in mind – shelves, good lighting, computer accessories, filing space, and doors that could hide everything.

It was 1990, and Belisle realized that a lot of other people were beginning to work from home. If such an office system could help her, maybe the product could be sold to others too. But first she had to learn about wood, hardware, lighting, and all the other constituent parts of her system. In order to carry out the sort of self-education required by every entrepreneur, Belisle visited numerous potential suppliers, always asking them to sign a confidentiality agreement so they couldn't steal her idea. Because the design wasn't new, she couldn't get a patent. Instead, she got the protection of an industrial design registration. Belisle used a patent agent (less expensive than a patent lawyer) to obtain the registration, and by 1993, she had a custom-built system ready for display at a trade show. The design was functional, the materials top quality, and everything could be hidden behind pocket doors when work was done (the chair back folded down and the chair slipped into the kneehole). Even the name of the firm seemed perfect, Cocoon Inc. The price of the unit, however, was a steep $7,500, plus the cost of the chair. Interest was limited; most homepreneurs couldn't afford it.

The self-education continued. Belisle took her design to the Canadian Industrial Innovation Centre in Waterloo, Ontario.

For about $500, the centre did a market survey and confirmed
that there was nothing like her idea already available. The
centre then offered to redesign the unit as a less-expensive,
ready-to-assemble system that could be shipped flat to the customer. The National Research Council was willing to share
costs of such projects under development, so Belisle split the
$20,000 redesign costs with the NRC and, after four months,
the centre came up with an eight-foot system that now sells for
$4,995 and a six-foot unit for $3,995.

Throughout the redesign, Belisle continued to play a key
role in her project. "I had all the control," she says. "There
were parts of this [system] that I knew better than they did."
The centre also proved to be a networking bonanza that put
her in touch with potential manufacturers. "They opened so
many doors that would have normally been closed to me."
Belisle contracted out both the manufacturing and the sales of
the units and began shipping them in March 1994. "If there's
one thing I've learned it's to ask questions. Every question is a
good question. It's okay to ask them all."

Start-up tip: *Everyone will experience failure; the person who
is successful is the one who presses on regardless.*

Throughout the early going, your outlook must be sunny.
Just as the best salespeople are always "up" and make their customers feel good, so must you make the people you deal with
feel good. Equally important is the adage for successful selling,
known as the ABCs of selling, Always Be Closing. That means
you must be persistent without being offensive, constantly
trying to convince the potential customer to act in response to
your knowledge, belief, drive, and determination. Think how
often you've bought something or taken a decision not only
because the arguments were well put but also because the seller
demonstrated competence and earned your trust through the
sheer force of a happy personality. You should have just such a

positive frame of mind whether you're dealing with a customer, a potential supplier, or your next landlord.

Still, you can't just smile your way to success. You need a disciplined approach. Each successful entrepreneur must be able to manage herself or himself, have a plan, stick to it, and also be able to manage others. One of the keys in the early going is to set a daily goal and strive to achieve it. Your goal might simply be to make ten phone calls that morning, or visit a potentially important customer, but without such a specific, regular objective, you'll find that disappointment can set in, because you will seem to be making no progress. After a few dud days, discouragement takes over.

Discouragement is difficult to avoid. Customers can be rude or suppliers can act too busy to deal with a small enterprise. Often you'll feel very alone, because not everyone will wish you well in your venture. In fact, some people would much rather you failed, because that would validate their own inability to try something new. The successful entrepreneur must be convinced the cause is right no matter how noisy are the naysayers. A partner will help buttress your bad days, but if you are linking with someone else, make sure that you seek out someone who complements you. Their strengths should offset your weaknesses. Your goals, however, should be the same.

You may be aided and abetted in these initial efforts by something else, something outside yourself. "I believe entrepreneurs are being visited by divine inspiration," says Linda Lundström. "I also believe an entrepreneur can visualize something and make it happen." Like many new entrepreneurs, her initial investment came from members of her family, $10,000 borrowed from her parents. But even with start-up funds in hand, if there is no vision, your efforts won't amount to much.

Start-up tip: *Decide your path: if you don't know where you're going, any old route will do.*

Once, while driving on Toronto's Gardiner Expressway, Lundström was thinking about the parkas she planned to add to her clothing line. This was her first attempt to make coats, and Lundström required machinery she had ordered without any idea where the money would come from, as well as material from suppliers who might not be able to ship. "I was filled with doubt," she says. "My bankers were breathing down my neck." Nothing unusual there, she thought, just the normal tightrope walk of a struggling entrepreneur. A bird-dropping suddenly splattered on her windshield. Although many would find such an incident annoying, Lundström took it as a positive sign from on high that all would be well.

Next, a truck came onto the highway and pulled in front of her vehicle. The name painted on the truck was Laparkan Trading – almost the very name she had in mind for her own new jacket, La Parka. Another happy harbinger! But what, she suddenly thought, if someone had beat her to the punch? What if her idea wasn't so new after all and some other firm was already making and selling a similar product? Back at the office she looked up Laparkan in the telephone book, called, and was elated to discover that the firm shipped parcels to Guatemala. Today, Lundström's firm employs ninety people and does $10 million in annual sales – and two-thirds of that is the result of La Parka.

At the core of someone like Linda Lundström, or someone like you who wants to be an entrepreneur, there must be that deep-rooted capacity to believe and the desire to make something happen. That talent to see what others cannot is a prerequisite for success, because you must battle all odds to fulfil that vision. "Entrepreneurs will fight tooth and nail for something they really believe in," says Lundström. "An entrepreneur absolutely refuses to accept failure."

Inspiration can come from anywhere. Platforms abound

with speakers' tips about the required inner strength. Among the most enduring public figures and feel-good artists is Shirley MacLaine, who tells audiences across North America, "We're in a transformational decade. We create each new reality by causing it or allowing it." For an optimist like MacLaine – and an optimist is what you need to be – failure isn't, and can't be, a possibility. "Destruction is a new beginning. A harmony lurks under the chaos," she says.

According to John Rieschi, president and CEO of Transact Data Services Inc. of Mississauga, the nature of an entrepreneur leads directly to joy in the job. "You're able to turn on a dime. You're able to come to work and make a decision without going through a large bureaucracy."

That doesn't mean you've always wanted to go into business. "Nobody at age six ever says, 'I want to be a corporate executive.' Management comes to you late," says William Brown, who has run big businesses and is now CEO of Columbia Health Care Inc., a chain of occupational-therapy clinics in British Columbia and Ontario. "You may have technical skills, but you need conceptual skills and must understand how to marshal human talent. People have to be under a bit of stress – not too much, but enough to make them achievers."

Among the toughest characteristics for an entrepreneur to develop are problem-solving and conflict-resolution techniques. According to Greig Clark, founder of College Pro Painters, before people can solve a problem they first have to take ownership of that problem. "As soon as they say, 'It's not my problem, it's your problem,' they lose control and become victims," he says. "The next step in solving a problem or conflict is to examine your own contribution to that problem." If an employee brings you a problem, try to get that person to recommend a solution. If you can get to the point where your people are solving their problems, then that just leaves you with your own dilemmas to solve!

Being an entrepreneur will also sometimes require being able to swallow your anger or overlook your disappointment with people who let you down. While you don't want to be naïve – after all, business requires you to be tough at times – you always want to leave an open door. You never know when you'll need to go back. The saying "Don't get mad, get even" might work in politics, but in business – particularly if you are in a small community – you need all the help you can get. It's harder to make and keep a friend than an enemy. It's also easier to keep a customer than have to look for a replacement client. You don't need to either forgive or forget, but getting even can waste a lot of time, and that's a precious commodity you can't afford to spend foolishly.

So get ready to ride the accelerating speed of change and don't fret about climbing onto the moving sidewalk of a new business start-up, even if it feels like you're going a hundred kilometres per hour. If you already have a boss, you'll need to cut the umbilical cord. Don't worry about offending that individual by going out on your own. Says Shirley MacLaine, "The more we understand the underbelly of humanity, the better we can play our parts. Ask yourself: Why do I need her to play this part in my dream?" Make a decision, she urges. "It's not possible to make a wrong move. Every move is purposeful."

Summary:

1. Make sure you have the energy and enthusiasm required.
2. Be prepared to self-educate.
3. Spot and seize opportunities.
4. Respond to inspiration.
5. Exude optimism.

CHAPTER 2

Getting Started

*"There's more opportunity today than there
has ever been in history."*

– futurist Frank Ogden

I f ever there were a right time to start a new business, the
moment for individual action is now. Canada is under-
going a painful economic restructuring, unprecedented in
this century. Entire business sectors, such as East Coast fishing,
have disappeared. The country's resource base, the traditional
strength for exports, now accounts for less than 15 per cent of
foreign sales. Many Canadian-based resource firms are investing
in other countries, where they sense there are more welcome
business climates. Manufacturing is becoming more competitive
as firms rationalize their factories and wring productivity gains
from workers through downsizing. Foreign investors, Canada's
traditional source of risk capital, are looking to developing
countries for future expansion and expenditure.

At home, there is no longer anything called "business
as usual." Management-employee loyalty has disappeared.

High-level executives are being dumped jobless on the street.
Students are graduating with slim prospects for employment.
Families that previously had two incomes are learning to get
by on one. The very fabric of the nation is frayed, the people
almost frantic with worry. In many cities, the combination
of residents receiving unemployment, welfare, or some sort of
municipal assistance exceeds 20 per cent of the work force. "If
present trends hold, full-time work will be scarcer than ever
for the rest of the nineties," says Professor Daniel Drache.
"The income structure of society is being downgraded to fit
the new work and employment conditions." What's happening
in Canada is a profound shift from the past: there are no jobs
any more, there is only work.

Even as the Canadian economy recovers from recession, big
business will never again hire at past rates, layoffs will likely
continue, and governments – strapped by deficits – can no
longer be expected to act as society's backstops. As a result, a
critical question arises: Where will the work come from? The
answer lies in a little-celebrated subculture. Entrepreneurs,
individuals with ideas who are willing to take risks, are
Canada's last, best hope. While Canada has never been a place
where risk-takers are revered as highly or rewarded as handsomely as they are in the United States, individual Canadians
are increasingly realizing they have to fend for themselves and
are starting their own businesses.

This year, Canadians will bravely launch 135,000 new companies. Most of these firms will be small, and a majority will
go out of existence. The most sobering statistic you'll need to
keep in mind is that only one new business in five is still alive
after five years. Some, however, do hit the financial jackpot.
When Daniel Langlois, founder of Softimage Inc. of
Montreal, sold his software development firm to U.S. giant
Microsoft Corp. in 1994 for $130 million, he personally pock-
eted about $31 million.

But even if you don't hit it quite *that* big, you'll have plenty of company when your venture succeeds. There were 908,316 Canadian businesses in June 1994, according to the most recent data from Statistics Canada. Fully 97 per cent of all the businesses that now exist fit the definition "small" – fewer than fifty employees. In fact, most are even smaller. Some 88 per cent of all companies have under twenty employees, 59 per cent employ fewer than five. In recent years, this sector has created the jobs. Small and medium-sized businesses now produce two-thirds of the employment in the private sector and 60 per cent of Canada's economic output.

Ownership of these firms is changing. Men currently outnumber women three-to-one in running small businesses, but women are now launching firms at twice the rate men are, and are three times as successful as men. "Women are a little more interested in doing the homework than the average guy who thinks he knows it all," says Brien Gray, senior vice-president of policy at the Canadian Federation of Independent Business. "They'll do all the pre-planning that's required to even have a ghost of a chance of succeeding." Emmie Leung offers an additional reason for female success: "Women are blessed with this talent of vision that men struggle to find."

While the boldness required to launch a business takes a certain self-confidence, the road to success requires more than just a belief in yourself. That's a foundation on which to build, says William Jarvis, president of The Transition Group – a consulting firm in Mississauga – but you must also listen carefully to the marketplace and adapt to what you hear. "Any good organization has to look at criticism to see what's true about the comment, rather than seeing the words as an attack on yourself or your product," says Jarvis.

Here's his four-point checklist for success:

1. Know the customer.
2. Understand your product.

3. Don't lie, it'll catch up with you.

4. Take an ego-less point of view.

Even if you feel comfortable with your responses to the questions in the previous chapter, responding yes to seven out of ten, that is not the end of the thought process if you are planning to strike out on your own. Don't write out a letter of resignation for the job you now hold, and don't spend all your savings renting space in a local mall, then wonder why the world isn't coming to your door. Before making any commitments, talk to other people who have been through the process. Your local Chamber of Commerce or Board of Trade might help identify businesspeople you can consult, word of mouth will supply other names, or you may have spotted someone in your town or region whose own new business seems to be doing well in a relatively short period of time. Refer to pages 281 to 287 for more books and national organizations that you will find useful at this stage in your learning curve.

Once you have identified some possible sources of savvy, telephone them and ask for an appointment. You'll be surprised how helpful they are. This direct approach is the best way to get specific information about launching a business in your part of the country and making progress in the kind of economy that exists at that particular time. If possible, go to work for someone in the same business you want to be in, and learn what you can firsthand. Work for no pay, if you have to, in order to understand the business from the inside out. Don't, however, be sneaky about it. Be up-front about what you're doing. Decide how your idea will complement the business that already exists, so that you can show how hiring you could be to the advantage of your intended "boss" – beyond the fact that your labour is free.

Identify a specific niche you can serve with your new

product or service. "In the Canadian marketplace, it's difficult to be all things to all people," says Gerry Meinzer, a partner with PMP Associates Inc., a Toronto-based merchant bank. "People want to see value. You have to have a product that can be marketed." Do a market survey to assure yourself that what you plan to do is something that people want. Then, put something in writing about your idea. You may not need a full-blown business plan at this stage (you'll learn how to write one in Chapter Four), but some words on paper now will help you focus on your strengths and weaknesses.

Start-up tip: *Develop a well-equipped tool kit, because if all you've got is a hammer, every problem looks like a nail.*

Getting organized

The first task is to decide the legal format of your business.

Sole proprietorship is the simplest device, because that arrangement is really just an extension of you – rather than some legal entity. The good news is that you own all the assets; the bad news is that you are responsible for all the debts. When tax time comes, you just add the income from your business to other income from your day job. The downstroke is that you can't protect personal assets from creditors. In a worst-case scenario, personal assets could be seized if your business goes under. If you're going to conduct business as a sole proprietorship, using a name other than your own, you'll need to register that name with the appropriate department or ministry in your province.

All the strengths that mean you are an entrepreneur – tenacity, individualism, a headstrong nature – also mean that you'll make a terrible partner. If you launch a business with a kindred spirit who has an identical stubborn streak, you could be in for bickering, arguments, and constant disagreements about how to run the business. But if you can find someone who's willing to work as hard as you and is committed to success – and has strengths in areas where you're weak – your start-up is more likely to get off the ground.

Partnerships come in two flavours, general or limited. In a **general partnership**, you and another individual join together, come up with a business name, register it, share in all the responsibilities, asset ownership, and liability payments, and run the business together. No matter how friendly your start, be sure to have a partnership agreement to cover how profits and losses are to be shared. As with a sole proprietorship, if the business goes bust, creditors can lay claim to your personal assets in order to collect what you owe them. If your partner has nothing, you could be responsible for all debts.

A **limited partnership** has a mix of general partners who retain personal responsibility for debts, along with limited partners who invest money and therefore share in profits (or suffer losses along with you). Limited partners are usually the "silent" variety. They don't manage the business and their only monetary risk is the amount of their investment. These arrangements can get complicated, so consult a lawyer before drawing up a partnership. The "limited" portion of the partnership applies to liability. If a limited partner invests $10,000, then that's the extent of the possible losses.

Start-up tip: *In a partnership, he who has the least to lose has the most to gain.*

Everybody may get along in the start-up phase, but if the business does well and generates lots of profits (or does badly and loses money), you can bet there will be more disagreements than you could ever have predicted. If the relationships are spelled out clearly up-front, you have a better chance of surviving with your partners and being able to solve problems that erupt. If two managers always agree on everything, perhaps one of them is unnecessary. Each partner should contribute something different to the equation, but their talents should be complementary. For example, one person may have the engineering skills to design the product, the other may have the marketing savvy to sell it; one may be good at office and financial administration, the other might excel at overseeing a manufacturing operation. If both partners bring the same talents to the table, the business will suffocate as each person vies with the other to do the same role.

Deciding whether one of the two (or more) partners is going to be "in charge," or if both are to have an equal say, is a topic on which the world is divided. Some business consultants argue that only one person can be in charge and make the final decision. You might trade roles on a regular basis, but fifty-fifty deals are death, according to that theory.

Syd Kessler takes a different view on partnerships. Kessler is one of Canada's foremost jingle writers ("Me and the boys and our 50," "Thank you very much, milk") and used to run Supercorp Entertainment, a $100-million production-and-marketing empire, with partner John Labatt Ltd. In 1993, he sold his stake to Labatt and bought into F/X Corp., a Toronto firm specializing in multimedia software and hardware. Kessler and partner Eugene Foo each have 50 per cent in F/X, a firm that had $12 million in annual sales at the time. For Kessler, that fifty-fifty split is the only way to go; he doesn't agree with those who say someone has to have the upper hand.

Whichever style you adopt, you must have a partnership agreement that allows each partner to buy out the other in very specific and agreed-upon circumstances. If, for example, one partner becomes ill and cannot carry on, you'll want to have an agreement already in place that allows you to buy the partner's share of the business. You'll want the right of first refusal; the last thing you need is your partner selling to

someone you've never met and with whom you may not want
to work. The funds for such a buyout can come from cash on
deposit in the business account at the bank or by taking
on more debt, but the most effective solution is a disability
buy-sell insurance policy, into which you have been paying
premiums. That way, you don't have to take on debt or sell
assets at a time when either of those steps may be the worst
possible for your business. You want to preserve what you've
built, not dismantle the company just to keep a husk alive.

A **corporation** is much like an individual, but is a separate
entity under the law. It has most of the same legal rights as an
individual, and it, rather than you, is liable for its debts. That
doesn't mean, however, that you as an individual can escape all
responsibility for your corporation's activities when that corporation is just starting out. Banks will lend money to your
corporation, but they'll demand in return personal guarantees
from you, such as money on deposit in the bank or a mortgage
on your home. The bank doesn't want you hiding behind your
corporation; they want their money back if there's trouble.
Remember, also, that if your incorporated business becomes
insolvent, you could still be held personally responsible as a
director of your corporation for a whole host of your corporation's debts, such as taxes, wages, and GST, along with any
personal guarantees you gave the bank.

Still, there are advantages to incorporating, and most start-
up businesses move from being a sole proprietorship to incorporated status after a year or two. Advantages include being
able to bring in more investment capital by issuing shares and
the ability to take your income personally through dividends
at lower tax rates than salary would attract. Entrepreneurs with
good tax advice can also find ways of taking out management
bonuses, sheltering those payments, and charging expenses
even for luxuries like an aircraft. You'll need to file articles of
incorporation, something that many people do themselves,
using workbooks available at most bookstores.

Building a financial structure

Now's the time to assemble a good advisory team, including a lawyer and an accountant, who can help. Don't just look for a low-fee solution, try to find professionals with whom you have good chemistry. The people you tap now could turn out to be pivotal for you as time goes by, and you will need help over many hurdles. These advisers can help you with your business plan and also guide you through such items as arranging income-splitting, registering for GST, and opening the appropriate accounts with Revenue Canada for employee tax deductions and unemployment insurance. None of these requirements are onerous, but they do take time, and you don't want to run afoul of the rules.

Once you're established, probably the most important habit you can develop is to maintain accurate, up-to-date, and well-organized financial accounts. Of all the mistakes you can make, keeping sloppy books is the worst and the most common among start-ups. People pretend they're not proficient at book-keeping (or perhaps they really aren't), or they believe such drudgery is somehow beneath them, but good record-keeping is the foundation of a successful enterprise. Keeping an eye on where the money is going (and making sure there is no waste) will be the most important step you can take towards the financial freedom you seek. Initially, you'll keep the books yourself. But if you're successful, you won't want to be entering all the items. Inexpensive software programs are widely available to replace the traditional book-keeper.

You should also consider the many forms of insurance available. A life-insurance policy on yourself will mean that your estate won't get stuck with liabilities. Property insurance protects your business against fire, theft, and other losses, but you may also need liability coverage and business-interruption insurance. Premiums are an added cost during your early days, but if there is a loss, protection may make the difference between the firm's survival and its disappearance.

Developing successful habits at the launch

1. Talk the talk: Even when business life seems impossible, always talk to yourself in a positive way. You'll hear enough people point out your weaknesses; you don't need another naysayer. That doesn't mean you shouldn't be critical when it's constructive, but don't forget to pat yourself on the back too. You know when you've done well.

2. Act courageously: Don't charge into battles that can't be won, but do take risks where you know you have a chance of succeeding. There are times for caution, but there are also occasions when you simply have to bull ahead to get ahead.

3. Work first, play later: There will be days when you won't feel like advancing the cause at all. The simplest thing would be to close up shop and take off. You cannot. The discipline of doing what's essential to grow your business, hour by hour, day by day, week by week, will be what ensures your success.

4. Invent solutions: There will be times when no one seems to have the answer to the problem you're facing. It's not that they haven't faced the same hurdle, it's just not their hurdle. Don't always go by the book. Sometimes the way ahead comes from the gut.

5. Exude confidence: Even when the butterflies in your stomach seem the size of 747s, don't let the world know you're anything but on track. You don't get a second chance to make a good first impression, so pay attention to both your dress and your demeanour.

6. Don't try anything that takes too long: As George Burns says, "At my age, I don't even buy green bananas."

7. Keep overheads low: The idea is to take some money home eventually as profit, not leave it all at the office in fancy furniture.

8. Avoid court battles: There may be occasions when lawyers can win disputes on your behalf, but most of the time you'll just make them rich with fees.

9. Smile: You'll feel better – and so will everyone you meet.

10. Do the right thing: You'll feel good all day and sleep well all night.

Controlling expenses

The desire for a better lifestyle is an excellent motivation for an entrepreneur at any stage of development, but if you find yourself devoting precious cash flow in the early going to new office furnishings, or a flashy car you don't need, watch out. Those are danger signs that the role is beginning to dominate you, that you are beginning to take yourself too seriously. Rajiv Manucha, who launched Management Systems Resources Inc. of Toronto, takes pride in the fact that he drives a ten-year-old Toyota that's gone 250,000 kilometres, when he could well afford a new Mercedes-Benz.

Nor do you need to rent space in the beginning. Half of the businesses in Canada consist of one person working from home. As a homepreneur, costs are low, travel time insignificant, and you can always be available for any caller – even while doing chores. For all that most of your telephone contacts know, you could be anywhere. Over time, buy or lease pieces of equipment for your business such as a personal computer, a telephone with more than one line, a fax, and a copier. All the tools of business that were once found only in offices can now be run from home and are priced so that the individual can buy them.

The Martins of Vas-Cath ran their business from home for three years. Their first employee was their cleaning lady. They spent no money on "show" items like prestige office space. They moved out of their apartment only when they had to, and even then they went into a house in which the ground floor served as the business premises. "We started flying by the seat of our pants, but we knew we couldn't spend more than we had," says Jane Martin. They used the business address of Geoff's father as a drop for their deliveries in order to keep truck traffic on the residential street to a minimum, but even so, the neighbours eventually complained and the police visited. The Martins realized they'd better move into more conventional manufacturing premises. But by that time, in 1981, sales were $50,000 a month and they could afford to step up spending.

Geoff realizes that some firms, like retail stores, need fixtures and mood-setting surroundings, "But if you don't need to look good, you can work out of your garage," he says. Their advice: start small, keep your expenses down, use last month's income to fund this month's projects, never borrow large amounts. "Remove as much of the financial risk as you can," says Geoff. "If you're being squeezed for money [by the bank], you'll never make it."

There's one expense on which you cannot scrimp: sound professional advice from an accountant and a lawyer. "But don't let them tell you how to run your business," says Mary Black, president of Colour Technologies Inc. of Toronto, a thirty-employee firm that does colour separations for printing. "They're there to work for you." A lawyer will be helpful, for example, in drawing up a lease. But it's you who defines the space you require. Retail sales depend on traffic, so a store needs a ground-floor location, but if your business doesn't rely on passersby, don't pay higher rents for something you don't need. A second-floor location will work just as well and cost a lot less. Do you need a reception area, lunch room, change room, storage or warehouse space, shipping or receiving area, road access, parking? Work with a real-estate broker who knows the commercial market in the community. And think ahead. Make sure there's room for expansion.

Plan ahead and grow slowly

Space requirements are just one of the many things you need to plan. According to Jane Martin, 80 per cent of people don't do any planning at all. Sixteen per cent of people do plan, but they don't bother to write anything down. Even so, that smaller group earns four times more than the 80-per-cent group. Only 4 per cent of people not only formulate plans but also commit those goals to paper. The results are remarkable – they make ten times as much money as the 80 per cent who don't plan. "Plan ahead and make the plan realistic. It's important to plan and it's even more important to write it down," she says. "The sense of accomplishment is incredibly inspiring."

If and when you do become successful, like the Martins, and you move into leased or owned premises separate from your house, continue with a low-profile and common-sense attitude. Never brag about what you've achieved; let your actions speak for you. "Success comes the old-fashioned way. You grind it out every day," says Cynthia Dale, who starred in "Street Legal" for six years before the CBC-TV show was cancelled in 1994, and a woman who speaks to eager groups about how to achieve goals. "Extend yourself," she says. "Life is too short to wonder 'What if?' Do it to satisfy the one person who knows when you give it everything. Do it for yourself."

Not everything can be planned. Have an open mind when serendipity strikes. In 1989, Harold Lenett was leafing through two American trade magazines, *Impressions* and *Stitches*, that featured everything from pens to calendars to T-shirts – all bearing advertising imprints. Lenett, CEO of Pimlico Apparel Ltd. of Vancouver, suddenly realized that no one was using his firm's product, denim jackets and jeans, to carry a slogan or a brand-name logo. As a fifteen-year supplier to Levi Strauss and a long-time private-label manufacturer, Lenett knew how to make the goods, so he set out to find buyers who wanted to use denim as an ad medium. "It's more macho to sit at a bar with a denim jacket rather than a satin one," he says. Branded-product firms agreed. Pimlico's sales have since quadrupled to $15 million annually and the number of employees has risen 20 per cent annually, reaching three hundred. A typical corporate buyer like Marlboro purchases one hundred thousand jackets, then has a third party silk-screen the rugged Marlboro man on the back.

In addition to imprint products sold in Disney stores or distributed by brewers or through automotive catalogues, Pimlico produces non-imprint goods for retailers like the GAP, a firm that does on-site quality inspections every ten days at the Pimlico plant. "I've been in this stupid rag business so long," he says. "I wish I'd known about [imprints] before so I didn't have to fight with retailers all the time." Today, nearly three-quarters of Pimlico sales are in the United States where the dollar volume of the imprint market runs into the billions. "We haven't even scratched the surface yet," says Lenett, who is helped in the family business by sons Howard, the detail man who runs operations, and Gary, a lawyer who handles human resources and marketing.

As well as being a "seer" who spots trends and climbs aboard, an entrepreneur also has to be something of an amateur economist, like Gary Santini of ParkLane Ventures, a Burnaby, British Columbia, house builder with thirty years in the business. "When the market's bad, I know it'll get good," he says. "When it's good, I know it'll get bad." In recent years, a robust regional economy and a constant flow of immigration from the Pacific Rim has meant a consistent annual increase in sales of 25 to 30 per cent. ParkLane sells about 375 single-family homes each year in the $250,000 to $550,000 price range in British Columbia, Alberta, and the state of Washington. Eighty per cent are pre-sold; the rest are built on spec. In some subdivisions, particularly those closest to Vancouver, 50 per cent of the buyers are recent Chinese immigrants, most with a net worth in excess of $1 million. "A lot of them are astronauts," says Santini. "They're always in the air between Vancouver and Hong Kong."

A cautionary note

Success seems so easy. Look at all those people who have made it. The failures don't have quite the same profile. "It all sounds rosy at the start, but if I could offer one piece of advice to anyone who's thinking about starting a business, it would be, 'Don't do it,'" says Gary Curtis, a managing partner of Balmoral Partners Ltd., a Toronto-based merchant bank. "You have to be selfish, because you'll have to give up something on the home front." Curtis ran his own businesses before launching Balmoral along with six partners to help other entrepreneurs with their financing needs. "If you're married, you have to have an unbelievably supportive spouse. You just truly have to believe that it will work. You'll never have a bigger up or a bigger down. Friday at 5 P.M. you'll get the big order. Then you won't sleep all weekend, because you can't figure out how you'll finance it," says Curtis.

Today is the best time for an entrepreneur to get started, because the nineties are all about change. No one knows how things will turn out, and you are just as well equipped to chart the future as anyone else. "There are no paths, no trails, no price lists, but there's more opportunity today than there has ever been in history," says Frank Ogden, the Vancouver-based futurist who calls himself Dr. Tomorrow. Innovators will survive and prosper, because 90 per cent of the products that will be used in ten years don't even exist today, claims Ogden. In the race towards the unknown, some businesses and nations have adapted better than others. Last year, one company, Sony, introduced more new products – at the rate of five each day – than did the entire country of Canada.

Other Japanese firms are equally innovative. One makes

ceramic knives that are guaranteed forever. The main ingredient, sand, is so cheap, widely available, and adaptable to other uses that the Japanese construction company Misawa has begun to build houses with sand. The structures are so technologically advanced that prospective buyers must attend special training classes for up to four weeks in order to understand and operate their purchase, or their cheque is returned.

The key for any business starting up today is to bring added value to a product, says Ogden. Sometimes the premise can appear to be ridiculous, like the pantyhose manufacturer that added one cent worth of vitamin C to the product and was able to double the retail price to $5 because vitamin C is said to break down cellulite over time. Once that particular gimmick had run its course, the manufacturer offered pantyhose with built-in protection against the sun's ultraviolet rays.

Not everyone wants to start a business that becomes an exporter of goods employing hundreds. You may simply want to create what's known as a "lifestyle business" – one where the objective is to create a good living for the entrepreneur. The other type of company driven by growth is known as a "gazelle" and has ambitious owners who seem to live by the motto "Large business, temporarily small." This book will tell you how to tailor your effort to suit your goals, whether you seek to run a "lifestyle business" or to be a "gazelle."

While most people undertake careful research, some successful entrepreneurs claim no advance planning is necessary. "Don't even look anything up," counsels Mary Black of Colour Technologies. "The less you know, the better. It's like having a baby. It's better not to know the pain to come." Once you do get under way, says Black, always know the cause if and when difficulties arise. "On day two, buy a mirror and put it in your desk drawer. When you get into trouble and you need to know why, pull out the mirror and look into it," says Black.

Pick your moment. "Timing is everything," says F/X Corp.'s Syd Kessler. "It doesn't matter how good an idea it is, if you do it on the ebb, it ain't going to work." Yet, while you'll want to have most circumstances on your side, no one time will be precisely right. That doesn't matter because it's not the wind that takes you to your destination, anyway. It's the set of the sail, and that is something that is controlled by you. So pick your destination – a reasonable goal, but one that stretches you just the same – and get started.

Finally, a break along the way won't hurt. "You can work all your life and get nowhere if you don't have a measure of good luck," says Frank Milligan, president of Polywheels Manufacturing of Oakville. Still want to go into business for yourself? There's lots of room for you, whether you're what's known as a "lone eagle" fleeing a corporation, a homemaker looking for independence, or anyone seeking a greater sense of personal worth. If you are still interested, well, that probably means you're just a little crazy. And as any successful entrepreneur will tell you, being just a little crazy is one of the essential characteristics for success.

Summary:

1. Investigate before you invest your time and money.
2. Satisfy the only person who knows when you give your all – yourself.
3. Good luck is nothing more than hard work and preparation meeting an opportunity.
4. Decide what you want, write it down. When you achieve something on your list, strike off that goal and add a new one. Keep all your old lists. They remind you of progress made.
5. Vision is the capacity to see the invisible.

CHAPTER 3

Shaking the Money Tree

"There's no reason why entrepreneurs
can't go out and raise money."

— investment banker Gordon Sharwood

C onstruction at the new Sleeman Brewing & Malting Co. Ltd. in Guelph, Ontario, was running eight months late in August 1988. President and CEO John Sleeman had not only used up the $2 million he had borrowed from the Toronto-Dominion Bank, he had also gone through the $750,000 obtained by mortgaging his $1-million home. But after three years of effort, Sleeman was just thirty days away from shipping beer, and thought he was home free — until the bank suddenly gave up on him. Arguing that Sleeman had missed the peak summer season, the TD loan officer said, "We don't think you'll ever open, and we want out."

In fact, the banker sounded as if his confidence had always been lacking when he went on to ask, "How do you expect to be successful when your entire brewery won't cost as much as

Molson's is spending to launch its new 'dry' brand?" The bank gave Sleeman thirty days to repay everything he owed: about $3 million, including interest. Sleeman did the rounds of the other big chartered banks in Canada, but once the TD had pulled out, no one else would step in. "The rest of the banks treated me like a leper," he says.

He turned to a foreign bank and found an entirely different attitude. Not only did the National Bank of Detroit agree to back Sleeman and keep the company alive, but the bank also increased his operating line. In addition, they said, "You don't make any money in the winter, so don't pay anything back until next summer." Says Sleeman, "If Canadian banks want to know what to do to help Canadian business, they only need to look south of the border. American lenders are more prone to risk-taking."

Money and where to find it will preoccupy you all of your days. You're going to need the help of a lot of people with money, because you're unlikely to have enough yourself to launch a new business.

First, figure out how much you think you'll need for the first year, remembering that keeping overhead low is the only way you're going to make it. When you're absolutely sure you've thought of all possible contingencies, add everything up – then take your total and multiply by three. Everyone who launches a business grossly underestimates the cost to get going, that's why others who have been this way before suggest the "three times" factor. According to a study by the Ontario government, starting most companies costs $75,000, and 70 per cent of entrepreneurs put up their own money and obtain the rest from banks, friends, family, and other investors. Or you can launch a business on the cheap. The wildly successful Subway sandwich chain started with $1,000. Half of all women who start new businesses do so on less than $10,000. Maybe that careful approach is another reason why more women than men are starting businesses and why they're more likely to survive the first five years.

While women entrepreneurs have become more numerous than men in start-up ventures and successful small businesses, mid-sized firms – those larger than $5 million – tend to still be very much a male preserve. Only about 10 per cent of those mid-sized firms are run by women, usually with strong family support that may include investment capital. Often both the wife and husband are involved. Individual women who succeed are very likely to have grown up in a family that was in business and have siblings in business as well. Emmie Leung of International Paper had been familiar with the salvage business because she had worked in the family recycling firm in Hong Kong. Her brother, Johnny Wong, encouraged Leung, put up half the seed money, and continues to offer ongoing advice. "Even when we argue, we're still friends," says Leung, echoing a need others have found for honest and respectful sounding boards about their businesses. Leung has run across very few problems as a woman in business, even at meetings where everyone else is male. "I've been accepted," she says. "And if they don't accept me, I make them."

Most women do, however, face more difficulties than men in the same situation. In 1952, Wendy McDonald suddenly inherited B.C. Bearing Engineers Ltd. of Burnaby upon her first husband's death. Bankers and suppliers had trouble accepting her initially. "It took six years of hard slugging before things began to take off," says her son, Robby MacPherson, who started out sweeping floors when he was four and is now president of the family firm. Since taking over, chairman and CEO McDonald has outlived two more husbands and brought all five children into the business.

Fastforward forty years and the same chauvinist attitudes persist. The Body Shop's Margot Franssen ran into all sorts of brick walls built by men when she tried to launch her first retail outlets in the early eighties. Lawyers didn't show her any respect and had a particularly obnoxious habit at business meetings of addressing her husband, Quig Tingley, even if she had asked the question. She and Tingley finally switched to female lawyers and accountants.

Bankers were equally hopeless; they wouldn't lend any money. Franssen could only console herself with the thought "Nothing to risk means you can be creative." Even though she had secured the Body Shop franchise from the U.K. parent, the Bank of Montreal refused to finance a start-up in Canada. Nor did it make any difference that her husband – then a treasury-bill trader at McLeod, Young & Weir – promised he'd keep $30,000 on deposit at the bank. So convinced were the bankers of her eventual failure that one of the bankers lamented to Tingley, "Do you know the paperwork involved *when* she goes bankrupt?" Says Franssen, "Banks lend money to people who don't need it."

She did not, however, give up the search, and eventually got a $60,000 loan from the Royal Bank. In a later development that is rich in irony, Don Fullerton made three attempts over several years when he was chairman and CEO of the CIBC to make Franssen a director of the bank. "I just couldn't imagine being on the board of a conventional bank," she says. "We're such an unusual company." Fullerton finally convinced her to join in 1992 by saying that he needed to hear diverse points of view and wanted her knowledge on retailing in general and small business in particular, plus her input on environmental issues and social activism.

"What I thought would be intimidating wasn't intimidating at all," says Franssen. "The board is a nice blend." In addition to commenting at regular board meetings, Franssen has been asked by bank staff to advise on everything from personnel matters to child-care facilities. Even so, Franssen has repaid the Royal for its initial backing of her business by leaving her accounts there rather than moving them to the CIBC. "You just don't chuck out relationships," she says.

Few who start a business will end up with a seat on a bank board. Some will fail at the hands of those same banks. Long-term success may in the end depend on good health as much as persistence. Says septuagenarian Ben Otis, chairman of Grand National Apparel Inc. of Weston, Ontario, "I've out-lived every one of my competitors."

Success is also knowing *how* to succeed. "The object of business is not to make money," says Mary Black of Colour Technologies, "it's to make money stick. You're not going to be rich in six months. It will take three years to break even. After that, maybe 3 per cent to 5 per cent sell their businesses and make real money."

Just as Emmie Leung discovered, it's important to get family members involved. A few thousand dollars might make the difference in those first months. If friends and relatives aren't willing to back you, maybe you're not cut out for business or haven't yet got the right idea. But no matter how much money you gather, watch every penny. Let's face it, this is the most important investment of your life, and you want to scrutinize what's happening on a daily basis. Knowing where you stand financially is critical to success. Don't assume that losses in one area, or on one product, will be made up in other, more successful, lines of merchandise or service. One "loss leader," or money-losing item, might work for a while at the front of a retail outlet, if customers are drawn in by the price and then purchase other items, but losing money is no way to get ahead.

"The nineties are more like the sixties, without any money," says Margot Franssen. "Successful retailers will adapt." Competition from newly arrived U.S. retail giants will also make life difficult for the mediocre operators. "The major [retail] players that are left will end up prospering," says Jeff

Otis, president of Grand National Apparel and son of Ben. But the large firms have to become more competitive, says Otis, who served on a government-business-labour task force on cross-border shopping. "Can they come up with the marketing plans to bring consumers in? The competitive environment from U.S. superstores has eroded their business."

Start-up tip: *Volume is vanity, profit is sanity, and cash flow is reality.*

Dealing with banks

Chartered banks have a traditional and important role in financing small and medium-sized enterprises in Canada. They supply long-term debt capital so entrepreneurs can buy assets such as land, buildings, and machinery. The banks also supply working capital through credit, using inventory or receivables as security. After family, banks are the first place most Canadian businesses turn for financing; they can also prove to be the most difficult to convince.

There are two basic types of bank loans. First, an **operating loan** is a short-term way of financing the daily needs of business, such as paying bills and meeting other expenses. An operating loan smooths the ups and downs in your bank account when you've sent out invoices and are waiting for payment. In fact, the bank uses those receivables as collateral for loans of up to 75 per cent of what you're owed. Inventory can also be used as collateral to back up your needs. The second main category is a **term loan**, the type of loan used to buy land or other long-lived assets. Usually, a term loan is set for a longer period than an operating loan and depends upon your cash flow, as well as the expected life of the items you buy.

The plain fact is, however, that banks take fewer risks on

start-ups than they should. Don't believe the bank explanation about the fact that it considers small business as a bad risk because it has to protect depositors' money. Only thirteen out of every one thousand bank loans to small business go unpaid, so no one need worry about them losing some widow's mite or orphan's mitts. But, although the banks finance too few start-ups, over time you will be able to do business with them. Eighty per cent of all small businesses in Canada report that they have received a loan from one of the chartered banks. "By and large the banks have been supportive," says Frank Heaps, president of Upper Canada Brewing Co. "But the first five to six years was hell on wheels. I can't tell you how many times I drove into the lot expecting to see our bankers with locks for the doors."

Whether it's a franchise operation or new business start-up, few individuals ever have enough cash flow in the early stages. But cash flow is crucial, because while businesses can fail for countless reasons, one of the most likely causes is lack of capital. These days, bankers are less likely to be able to do what's known as asset-based lending, simply because more firms have fewer hard assets. Instead, the assets of companies are increasingly knowledge-based, and they go out the door every night (people), or the assets are "soft" (like computer programs) and are hard to evaluate accurately.

Rick Lunny, vice-president and manager of the technology banking group at the TD branch in Markham, Ontario, jokingly admits that "to most bankers, software was what you had after soaking your new jeans in the bathtub overnight." With over two hundred high-tech companies in his local area, Lunny became an expert in dealing with a sector that many bankers see as high-risk and no-reward. In 1994, after six years in Markham, Lunny became vice-president of commercial cash management, a job that means he'll be rolling out nationally the concept he developed in Markham. Yet Lunny is also the first to admit that he's not going to lend much money to start-ups. "Despite our willingness to lend to technology companies, we remain a low-risk lender with a profit margin of 1 per cent. That means that the highest-risk end of the market – start-ups – is best served by private investors and venture capitalists seeking higher returns," he says.

And TD isn't the only reluctant banker. "If we could figure out those who will succeed, we would be in the venture-capital business and making a fortune," says Gerry Lukassen, senior vice-president of commercial banking at the CIBC. "We have work to do to improve our image. But we don't make money on failing customers. The last thing we want to do is put somebody out of business."

Even though everyone likes to call the knowledge-workers of the nineties the "new economy," some traditional characteristics still apply from the old economy. When raising money, moxie remains important; the entrepreneur who shows persistence and self-confidence will do better than a shrinking violet. Marlene Conway launched Knowaste Technologies, a Toronto-based recycling and recovery firm, in 1987. For the first two and a half years, she and her half-dozen employees all lived in the same house and existed on Kraft Dinner. Her money-raising technique was to visit potential investors and sit in their reception areas until they listened to her story. "If you give me three minutes, that starts eternity," she'd say.

Appearances were important. Even when the cash flow dried up and the payroll had to be trimmed, the firm spent some of its precious money on an audited financial statement so she would have the stamp of professional approval. "The fact that you have an auditor shuts [potential investors] up," Conway says.

Start-up tip: *Small amounts of money wisely spent on big-business items can pay off.*

Experts say that banks should not always be the entrepreneur's first choice. "Canada's banking system is large and efficient, so everyone in Canada goes to the banks first and gets the equity later," says Nick Ross, an accountant with Ernst & Young who specializes in servicing entrepreneurial companies. "In the United States, it's the other way around. Business start-ups go to angels first." Ross urges start-ups to seek out an accountant who can help with financing and connections. "We call ourselves the penniless merchant bankers. We get involved in financing, we just can't professionally put any of our own money into deals." As a private investor over the years, Ross has, however, invested in some non-client entrepreneurial businesses. One success story he backed from its beginnings fourteen years ago is Enerflex Systems Ltd., a Calgary-based company founded by John Aldred, which supplies units that clean up and compress natural gas for pipelines. Ross remains an investor in the company that now employs 650 people and has annual sales of $200 million.

Firms currently trying to survive despite the difficulties that bankers can cause should take hope from the survivors of other recessions. Firms can carry on after backers disappear. "We were really hanging on by our fingernails," says Alan Grant, president of Western Water & Sewer Supplies (1978) Ltd. of Calgary. When his bank, the TD, turned its back on him, staff was cut in half, to ten employees. "The big five [banks] weren't favourable to anything going on in the West," says Grant, who was able to obtain refinancing from the Alberta Treasury Branches, the provincial government-owned banking system with a more local focus than the Eastern-based big five – the Royal, Montreal, CIBC, Scotiabank, and TD. "They saved my ass," states Grant. Today, his company is doing well again; sales are in excess of $10 million and the firm employs forty people.

Other firms have found the banks equally unhelpful – even

when their businesses are healthy. "Whenever we've wanted to acquire or expand, it didn't seem to be [the banks'] line of business," says Nelson Greenberg, president of MCI Multinet Communications Inc. of St.-Laurent, Quebec. Greenberg financed the acquisition of two firms through internally generated cash, plus a loan from a private investor that was quickly paid off. Many firms prefer not to have bank loans at all. "Use your profit to expand," says president Robert Glegg, whose firm, Glegg Water Conditioning Inc. of Guelph, has no bank financing and is debt-free. "That may have inhibited our growth, but we're extremely stable."

Frank Milligan of Polywheels hasn't had much success borrowing from the Canadian banks. Milligan has been a client of the Royal Bank since founding his firm in 1986 to make parts for the automotive aftermarket, such as replacement header panels, headlight mountings, and fenders. In 1993, when Polywheels moved from its 60,000-square-foot plant to a 340,000-square-foot facility formerly owned by Mack Truck, the banks weren't willing to get involved in his successful venture because the security for a loan would be the building, and the banks weren't doing many real-estate loans at the time. Milligan got results from a combination of three other sources: an insurance fund, a trust company, and one of the foreign banks operating in Canada. He's becoming used to Canadian bank indifference. In the early days, Polywheels had to turn to State Farm, a U.S. insurance company, after the Royal Bank and the Ontario Development Corporation had turned him down. "Without that long-term debt and an understanding lender, we wouldn't have made it. Canadian banks aren't taking enough risks," he says.

Start-up tip: *If the banks say 'no,' don't waste time complaining, keep looking.*

Milligan admits that the banks were sometimes right in their assessment of him. "I wasn't always a good boy," he says. "I'm not a financial type; I'm an engineering type. I suffered in the early days, because I didn't have a good accountant or comptroller keeping reins on the finances in here." Still, Milligan urges entrepreneurs to stay away from banks if they can. "Get a source of financing that's very understanding, so if you need to, you can go back and say, 'I can't make the payments this month.' Banks say, 'You're out.' You need somebody who's patient."

Still, a bank loan is a good sign of your likely longevity. Those businesses that do eventually manage to assure banks they are worthy of a loan seem to succeed more often than firms financed by other means. A 1994 survey by accounting firm Coopers & Lybrand confirmed that the main source of financing for start-ups is the owner's own funds or those of the owner's family. A much smaller proportion received money from banks, investors, or other partners. Later on, however, those firms that obtained bank financing had the strongest growth rates.

If you do get a bank loan, everyone agrees on one thing: be sure you communicate regularly. "Give them monthly statements – no matter what," says Jane Martin of Vas-Cath. "Keep them involved in the business and stay forthright. If we knew we were going to have a tough few months, we always told the bank. It just comes down to being honest. Don't just be there when the need is there, stay close all the time." Frank Milligan follows the same strategy even though he's had less success: "The Royal knows me – warts and all."

The banks battle back

For their part, banks claim they have begun to recognize that complaints in public about their small-business lending hurt them with other customers – as well as with members of

The buck starts here

1. **Right church, wrong pew:** When you go looking for money from a possible investor (or banker, if it's a loan), talk to the right person. Don't waste any time on people with no power, no money, and no prospect of ever having either.
2. **One shot:** Have an enthusiastic sales pitch that captures the essence of your business idea and radiates your inner drive and lack of outer limits. You've got maybe two or three minutes to create a positive impression. Don't blow your chances by being tongue-tied or self-deprecating.
3. **Wear their shoes:** Don't just talk about what your idea will do for you or the community; make sure that you emphasize the investor's self-interest, even if it's just the guarantee of profits and returns. Everyone wants to know what's in it for them, so treat your prospect like a partner. Extend an invitation to visit your business. If you're after money from an "angel," try to characterize what you plan as being fun. Investors like to enjoy the businesses they back and to be proud of their support.
4. **Research and listen:** Bone up on banker's lingo; know what types of loan possibilities there are. But don't go into this money meeting so well rehearsed and planned out that you miss hearing what the banker says. Be responsive to questions and try to listen behind the words all the way to what's really in that person's mind.
5. **Ask for the business:** Be specific. Your mere presence in a banker's office is not enough. Know how much money you want and explain what you're going to do with it. Be prepared with a detailed business plan. Outline the financial contribution you're making yourself and what you're getting from others. The bank may lend you some portion of what you need, but not all of it.
6. **Be truthful:** Hiding the real story from a banker is about as thoughtful a strategy as not declaring all your income to Revenue Canada. That approach may work for a while, but when the lie is discovered, you're toast.

Parliament who hear from constituents. The Bank of Montreal
is adding another $1 billion to a small-business portfolio that
had already grown to $5 billion, a 50-per-cent increase since
1990. The CIBC has appointed longtime banker Cliff Shirley as
ombudsman; he reports directly to Chairman Al Flood and
deals with small-business complaints. The Royal Bank has
launched a $125-million risk-capital fund for knowledge-
based enterprises and export-oriented companies. "We know
how to finance what's under our feet; we need to learn how to
finance what's between our ears," says Charles Coffey, senior
vice-president of business banking at the Royal. In this bold
new world, arrogance is *passé*. Says Coffey, "We used to say,
'We know.' Now we say, 'Let's ask.'"

Little wonder. The banks have come to realize they must be
doing something wrong in this area. They simply haven't seen
the growth in their own balance sheets that competitive institutions have enjoyed with business. Only ten years ago,
Canada's big-five banks were in the top fifty worldwide. Today,
they have skidded to the second rank. Five years ago, GE Capital, the U.S.-based mortgage insurance company, was 50 per
cent the size of the Royal Bank; today GE Capital is 50-per-
cent bigger. At the same time, loans to small business have
been shrinking. In the under-$200,000 category the big-six
banks (including National Bank) loaned $21.7 billion in 1989
and $17.9 billion in 1993. In specific sectors such as logging
and forestry, the drop was a precipitous 35 per cent.

Follow all the suggestions in the sidebar and bankers will still
be a tough sell, but at least they're changing. Some have even
taken to sitting still for verbal abuse in public. Linda Lundström
is one of many successful entrepreneurs who have no praise for
the bankers who were involved as she built her clothing business. In a 1993 speech at a small-business conference organized
by the Canadian Bankers' Association, Lundström pointed out
that entrepreneurs have long memories. Every time a banker

caused trouble along the way, she told her foes directly, Lundström switched to another institution. She said that she'd probably dealt with every bank represented in the room. "I still remember what the banks did to me fifteen, sixteen, nineteen years ago."

The politicians are also catching on to the banks. In a speech delivered in Mississauga shortly after he was named minister of finance, Paul Martin promised a different attitude towards financiers. "For far too long in North America, the productive sector of the economy has been the plaything of the financial community," he said. Referring to mergers, acquisitions, and hostile takeovers, Martin said, "The ultimate person who has suffered has been the person who has lost [his or her] job."

If small and medium-sized businesses are to grow in Canada and become major exporters, said Martin, "We cannot have a situation where the financial community indulges in periodic credit crunches, which simply mean that, three feet from the raft, 50 per cent of the Canadian business community begins to die." Banks, said Martin, must be involved in funding innovation. They have to learn how to assess not only "holes in the ground, but credit deals involving products of the mind."

The fact that bankers now allow their warts to be described in public by clients like Lundström is a hopeful sign that they are following Martin's dictum. After all, not so long ago they wouldn't have taken such a tongue-lashing. They have even agreed with demands by Ottawa to publish statistics that will detail the portion of their loan portfolio that goes to small business.

Banks are also trying to offer help with the application process. "The vast majority of new entrepreneurs who apply for a loan have no business plan," says Helen Sinclair, president of the Canadian Bankers' Association. In the past, most bank managers would have told potential customers to come back when their homework was done. Says Sinclair, "That's no longer good enough. Instead, the new breed of banker is likely to say, 'You need a business plan? Let me help you develop one.'" Only time will tell how quickly this new breed peoples every branch. Meanwhile, the Canadian Bankers' Association publishes a useful booklet, *Financing a Small Business: Working with Your Bank* (see page 282).

Bankers have also reacted to Martin's point about "products of the mind." The Royal has created community advisory boards in Saskatchewan and Ontario, and has supplied computer software to help account managers assess knowledge-based companies.

Key to the Royal's plan is a change in the institutional culture. "We won't say no without being able to offer options," says Charles Coffey. "It's a fundamental shift." Although the Royal Bank has $7 billion in outstanding loans to Canadian small business (about one in four that exist in the country with an average loan size of $62,000), the shift means that all fifteen hundred account managers will be provided with a list of alternative financing possibilities, such as venture-capital funds or local "angels," that they can provide to clients. The Royal also plans to eliminate another complaint: account managers who are transferred just when a small business is getting to know the local banker. They claim that tenure in lending positions, now averaging 2.8 years, will be stretched out to 5 years.

Such cultural change, however, comes slowly to large institutions. Increasingly, Bryan Kerdman, president of Bryker Data Systems of Thornhill, Ontario, is finding that traditional sources of debt have dried up. "Banks no longer want to be in the lending business; they want to be in the fee-for-service business," he says. As a result, his bank debt is now down below $1 million, and Kerdman has found new, creative ways to finance growth through client partnerships. Here's how it works: Bryker signs a five-year contract for, say, $500,000 a year. The last six months will cost the client $250,000 but, rather than pay the full amount at the end of the agreement, the client pays a lesser amount now – based on a "present value" of $225,000. Bryker then uses the advance to purchase equipment without incurring debt.

Venture capital

There will come a point in your development when bank loans are not enough. That doesn't mean just the amount of money available, but the expertise behind it. At that point, you'll want to turn to a venture capitalist. Seeking venture capital can be a difficult step for an entrepreneur – and one that some refuse to take. In return for much-needed risk financing, venture capitalists receive a piece of the company, often a majority position, and take an active role in management. Typically, venture capitalists buy shares in your company and expect that the value of those shares will increase over time, thus giving the investor a payback. According to Gordon Sharwood, himself a former banker and now an investment banker for entrepreneurs at Sharwood & Co., more sources of funds are springing up to complement traditional possibilities. Says Sharwood, "I see a whole effervescence out there."

Unlike bankers, who want to take few risks, venture capitalists are willing to take much higher risks. In any venture-capital portfolio of, say, ten investments, two firms will usually do very well, two will fail miserably, and the other six will be mediocre performers in which nobody makes much money. As a result, venture capitalists will want to make upwards of a 35-per-cent return on the investment made in your company.

"You give up some freedom, but you gain some support," says Amy Friend, executive vice-president of ATS Aerospace Inc. of St. Bruno, Quebec. "We still drive the bus." Venture capital for ATS has come from Investissements Desjardins,

Gestion Aérocapital, and La Société Innovatech du Grand Montréal. ATS now has $8 million in annual sales and eighty-four employees.

Frank Milligan of Polywheels takes the opposite view. He is not a fan of venture capital and advises young firms not to give up any equity in return for financing. "That can bother the entrepreneur, the spectre of giving up what you have. What's the point?"

Venture capitalists look for a good track record. If you don't have a lengthy history in the business, "You must at least convince your investor that you have thought through the management problems you're likely to face," says Denzil Doyle, one of the deans of the high-tech world. Doyle, now president of Doyletech Corp., an Ottawa consulting firm, established a sales office of Digital Equipment Corp. in Ottawa in 1963 and grew the firm to $160 million in sales with sixteen hundred employees by 1981, before he went on his own.

Be prepared to talk seriously about your product or service when you meet potential investors, advises Doyle. "Don't just 'play company.' A vague notion that you can go out and raise money and something will happen is not enough." You must have a product-migration strategy, a plan how you'll take your company to the next stage and what you'll be selling when you get there. "Nobody wants to buy a one-trick pony," says Doyle. One way of figuring that out is to ask yourself: How can I use the next generation of this product to deliver the same function at half the price? Potential investors will also want to see sales forecasts. "You shouldn't be in business if you can't forecast," says Doyle. "If you won't even try, you should be fired."

Start-up tip: *Don't let stinking pride get in the way, accept help from all sides.*

Private capital

The Association of Canadian Venture Capital Companies publishes a guide and list of members that will yield a useful starting point for your search (see page 284). These companies, however, are so well known that you will likely have to look further afield to one of the most important sources of start-up capital for business. These are the investors called "**angels**," who are just what the name implies. The term originated in New York, and was used to describe people who were willing to back Broadway plays. Such people exist in every community or region and generally loan amounts under $100,000 to local businesses in which they have faith. There's no handy registry of such angels, so the only way to find them is by networking with your accountant, lawyer, or service club. Angels can also be among your customers or your suppliers. They're out there; you'll know when you've found one. According to a study by Rein Peterson, the dean of business at the University of Windsor, and Joel Schulman, a professor at Berkeley University, 95 per cent of all the business start-ups in the approximately two dozen countries (including Canada) that make up the Paris-based Organization for Economic Cooperation and Development (OECD) were financed by angels and "love money" from family members.

A typical way for an angel to invest in your company is by holding preferred shares in the company that are convertible. That means, if the business doesn't do well, the preferred shares are converted into common shares, and those holders take over the business. If, on the other hand, the business does well, the angel can get a dividend on the preferred share and eventually have the shares redeemed. If the business does very well, and eventually goes public, then the holder of preferred shares can also convert to common shares, which have value in the open market. Preferred shares have an important benefit over common stock at the early stages of a business, because issuing common stock may require lengthy negotiations over a shareholder agreement.

The downsizing of large corporations in recent years has meant that many executives have hefty severance packages and want to invest in companies. Network International Inc. has a national data bank that might be able to match your small business with an interested investor (see page 287). The firm has eight offices across Canada and can supply names of executives looking for a chance to invest their time and up to $300,000 of their own money. Among the associates are Alex McKee, a merger-and-acquisition specialist who also does business broadcasts, and Doug Gardner, a senior banker with the CIBC for thirty-three years. The group also offers a Banking Services Equalization Program that means small businesses can become part of a larger negotiating block for more borrowing clout, reduced charges, and a better return on credit balances.

Business Centurions Centres, a firm run by Don Hillhouse and George Fells, performs similar functions. Business Centurions helps senior corporate executives with personal capital to invest (in the $100,000 to $750,000 range) to find suitable small and medium-sized business needing both capital and management advice (see page 285).

Start-up tip: *Don't leap into the unknown. You can't look at a potential partner or financial backer too often or too closely.*

Venture capital financing case study: To your good health

One endeavour that has succeeded because of backing by venture-capital firms is Columbia Health Care, run by William Brown. Like a lot of entrepreneurs, Brown spent time in larger corporations first, learning the ropes of business. "Life is like a pinball machine. You get moved around by the environment," he says. For him, the deteriorating national-health services were not just something to complain about personally, they were an opportunity professionally. "We do not think clearly when it comes to health care, because the antithesis of health is illness and death, subjects we avoid speaking about at all costs."

Brown graduated as a pharmacist from the University of Toronto in 1968, and during the seventies was a regional vice-president for Shoppers Drug Mart. "I was in a real big hurry," recalls Brown. "I stepped on more people's heads than I needed to." Shoppers altered the way chain drugstores operated in Canada by making the pharmacist an entrepreneurial owner and partner. "They changed the rules of the game from corner store to mass merchandising," says Brown.

In 1980, he became even more directly involved with entrepreneurial effort when he moved to Saskatchewan as vice-president and chief operating officer for Pinder's, a twelve-store family-owned drug chain based in Saskatoon, and helped grow the business to twenty outlets with $20 million in sales. In 1986, Brown became president and CEO of National Drug, a $600-million wholesaler that became Medis Health & Pharmaceutical Services, a health service and pharmaceutical distributor with annual revenues of $1.2 billion and thirteen hundred employees, owned by food giant Provigo Inc.

In 1989, everything changed when Provigo president and CEO Pierre Lortie left. Brown soon departed, too, with a $200,000 severance settlement. On his own for the first time and with some money supplying freedom to think about the future, Brown spent a year deciding what to do next. One thing was for certain, he would no longer work for anyone else. "I'd been president of the one of the largest companies in Canada, now I wanted to work for myself."

Columbia had originally been launched in British Columbia in 1978 by a psychiatrist, Dr. Charles Gregory, who was interested in chronic-pain rehabilitation. In 1987, he opened a second clinic in Toronto, largely at the instigation of the Workers' Compensation Board. Brown bought the firm's two clinics from Gregory in 1990 for $1 million. Since then, he has raised $10 million for growth from such venture-capital shareholders as MDS Health Ventures, Manulife Financial, the Ontario Hydro pension fund, and Prudential Insurance Co. of America. In the case of Columbia, the backing of venture capital was critical to his expansion, because he tapped into their expertise and an approach that was more patient than the banks'.

While such investors are looking for a 35-per-cent return, the individual can be more important to an investor than the company or the idea. The idea must be innovative, but venture-capital companies are going to be looking even more closely at you than at the financial numbers and the business plan you present. Says Brown, "They invest in *you*." Venture capitalists are going to investigate your background experience, listen carefully to how you describe the venture, and scrutinize what you have done to date. If you're not putting any of your own money at risk, they might not want to invest either. In the case of Columbia, management owns 14 per cent. The next step will be to take the firm public as a way of letting the investors sell out their stake to other investors and realize the increase in value of their original backing.

Start-up tip: *Investors back the jockey more often than the horse.*

Columbia has treated thousands of patients for sports and orthopaedic injury, pain management, and occupational health. In addition to investment from venture-capital backers, Columbia has also tapped new sources for its ongoing cash flow. Payment for all of Columbia's services comes not from the public-health system but from workers' compensation boards and private insurance carriers. Under the no-fault provisions of provincial insurance plans, people suffering head injuries are eligible to receive up to $1 million for private rehabilitation. In the past, such therapy was only possible at high-cost U.S. clinics, paid for by the health-care system. Now, Columbia takes the patient who has been discharged by a hospital, works to restore the patient's mobility, confidence, and dignity, teaches household skills and speech therapy, and offers vocational coaching and community reintegration.

"We'll do whatever it takes to make this person better," says Brown, claiming that every dollar spent on rehabilitation saves ten dollars on future medical costs. "We're trying to treat the untreatable, but we're not Oral Roberts. We don't raise people from the dead," says Brown. From two clinics when Brown bought Columbia, the firm has become the largest private rehabilitation organization in Canada. Within three years, annual revenues were $11 million and annual growth was 50 per cent, with 180 employees, including 150 health professionals such as physicians, psychologists, and therapists. That hiring has, in some small way, reversed a brain drain. "We've retained 150 high-quality positions that might have gone to the United States," says Brown. "We pay fisherman not to fish, farmers not to grow. But we're in the knowledge age. I don't know why we educate people in medicine, then think nothing when they go to California or drive a cab because they can't get a job. Canada has a lot of people who are underutilized. They've had to leave the public-health system. Columbia is the quintessential knowledge company. It is a company in which creativity, experiential knowledge, and innovation are core values. This is an adventure for them." An adventure that would have been impossible without venture-capital financing.

Government agencies

In an effort to encourage research and development, the federal government provides tax incentives than can also deliver another form of financing for you. For example, when ATS Aerospace was first incorporated in 1979 as Ballistech Systems, the firm received work from the Department of National Defence. There was also $30,000 seed money from the National Research Council, followed by research-and-development tax deals offered by the Quebec government. As long as there is some technological innovation and your firm's taxable income is below $200,000, government incentives cover up to 35 per cent of expenditures on:

- new product development;
- enhancement of products;
- improvements to manufacturing processes; and
- software development.

When taxable income is in the $200,000 to $400,000 range, there is a phase-out that means the company gets a tax credit rather than cash.

In addition, many provincial governments also have R&D incentives ranging from 10 per cent in Nova Scotia to 40 per cent in Quebec on certain types of expenditures, so check with your provincial government, because the total could mean that your R&D costs are reduced by almost 75 per cent after all incentives are taken into account.

Governments also have programs to cover employee training, give export assistance, and offer grants to create jobs in specific depressed regions of the country. New Brunswick has become very aggressive in wooing business; Newfoundland offers ten-year tax holidays. Some firms virtually finance themselves using government money and become quite adept at tax wrinkles to keep afloat. KPMG Peat Marwick Thorne offers a publication with a complete list of programs (see page 282 under *Government Assistance*).

But for all the effort, not a lot of firms find that government helps them grow. According to a survey conducted by accounting firm Arthur Andersen & Co., only 5 per cent of small businesses said that a government program helped them get started. Only 21 per cent said that a government program meant they increased employment, and a mere 17 per cent credited government with their expansion into new product lines.

Well-run companies don't need government help, says Derek Oland, president and CEO of Moosehead Breweries Ltd. of Saint John, New Brunswick. "Don't worry about government support programs, just go and do it. There *is* a world market. Canadian companies have got to get out there and do it. We're successful because we got out."

In fact, governments can even get in the way of sales in some sectors. Upper Canada Brewing exports beer to the United States, Sweden, Switzerland, and Germany, but, as for Canadian provinces outside Ontario, trade barriers mean that Frank Heaps can sell his brew only in British Columbia and Manitoba. "The politicians should be ashamed," says Heaps. Canada has free trade with the United States and Mexico, "but we don't have it with the rest of the provinces."

More direct financing programs that new businesses have found useful are available from the Business Development Bank (formerly the Federal Business Development Bank), Vencap Equities in Alberta, Le Fonds de solidarité des travailleurs du Québec, and Innovation Ontario. The Business Development Bank (BDB), with offices across the country, was the source of funds for no less an entrepreneur than Ted Rogers when he set out in 1961 to buy his first radio station, CHFI, at a time when only 5 per cent of homes could even receive FM signals. Rogers's philosophy, according to him, was simple: "Find a need and fill it." By 1994, his empire, Rogers

Communications Inc., had grown so large that he was able to acquire communications giant Maclean Hunter Ltd. in a $3.1-billion deal.

Until recently, BDB's role was to complement bank small-business lending by doing the higher-risk deals, with the result that its losses were about three times higher than the banks'. In 1994, the BDB financed more than $1 billion worth of small-business projects. In 1995, BDB changed not only its name but its approach, taking on financing without the pre-requisite that commercial banks reject the loan application first. In addition to debt, the BDB will also do equity loans and term-financing, and is beginning to get into so-called "patient capital" loans, in which the repayment period can be stretched longer than normal. In some cases, principal payments may not be required in the first year, and subsequent payments can be adjusted to fit your firm's projected cash flow. The maximum amortization, or payback, period is seven years. Unlike venture-capital investors, who often make their money by selling their interest to someone else, the BDB's patient approach works by taking a portion of the firm's profits. The BDB also runs a year-long program called Step-Up that helps women entrepreneurs through workshops and by matching them with business mentors. Another course, Step-In, offers guidance for start-ups.

The Export Development Corp. (EDC) insures Canadian exporters against losses on sales and offers financial assistance to buyers of Canadian goods. The EDC also insures the chartered banks, which are involved in specific deals, against non-payment of export receivables that have been used as a guarantee. The banks, however, are reluctant to get involved and prefer using the Small Business Loans Act. Still, EDC does have about $8 billion in outstanding loans, so there may be some funds available for you. Increasingly, individual banks are creating tailored plans. TD and EDC have teamed to finance up to 100 per cent of the cost of making the tools and moulds used in the automotive industry.

Other government programs include Industrial Research Assistance Programs (IRAP), scientific-research and experimental-development tax credits through Revenue Canada, and the Program for Export Market Development (PEMD), which assists firms to visit foreign markets or participate in trade shows. The focus of PEMD, which used to be on larger companies with sales of up to $50 million, is now on firms with less than $10 million in sales.

Other sources of money

Private placement: This is a securities offering that does not require a prospectus, because per-unit costs, usually more than $150,000, mean that the investor is knowledgeable and sophisticated. Still, you'll need to supply as much detailed information as if you were going public – but only to likely investors – so the information isn't as publicly available as it is in a share offering. This is a good midlife step for a company to take, because it raises funds and minimizes public scrutiny. Intermediaries, brokerage houses, and merchant banks are happy to help out, because they feel that, if the private placement is successful, they will be retained to help with the eventual public offering.

Leveraged buyouts: Champion Photochemistry of Mississauga expanded in the eighties using leveraged buyouts both in the United States and the United Kingdom, but the era is gone when cash flow in the target company paid for the deal. "Banks were climbing over each other to do aggressive deals in those days," says Champion president and CEO Peter Newton. "If the same deal came our way today, the bank wouldn't step up to the plate and neither would we. Entrepreneurism hasn't changed, but methods of financing have." Today, banking relationships are far more cautious.

Merchant bankers: Balmoral Partners Ltd. is a Toronto-based venture-capital firm launched in 1991. Balmoral sees itself as a merchant bank in the original European sense, because all seven partners are successful entrepreneurs with their own firms and have chosen to invest their own money in Balmoral rather than use funds from pension managers or other institutions. As a result, they can not only offer financing, but also give expert advice. All are CEOs or former CEOs in a broad range of businesses, including industrial fabrics, oil recycling, food processing, computer consulting, garment manufacturing, retailing, importing, equipment manufacturing and distribution, and transportation.

The average investment that Balmoral makes in a firm is $300,000 to $500,000, says managing partner Gary Curtis. The term of the loan is usually six months, and most firms are in the $1-million to $100-million sales range. Curtis has a long checklist he applies to any applicant who comes in the door, but the most important quality he is looking for is "a personality we can work with." Curtis, a Canadian who moved to the United States with his family at age twelve, then returned in 1988, is frustrated by what he sees here. "Canadians are born planning for their retirement. Americans are more aggressive, more interested in maintaining the equity in their companies and are more innovative." As a result, he looks for those American-style qualities in funding applications that reach his desk.

The criteria for how many years a business has been operating is less rigid, but, says Curtis, "applicants must have enough arrows in them that they have a dose of reality but aren't falling down yet." He likes to see three years of financial statements, but he also knows that, in the case of high-tech companies, the window of opportunity is very small and quick action may be required before the technology becomes outdated. The applicant must believe in the idea, but be realistic too. "The typical entrepreneur gets caught up in his own hype and is overly optimistic. Most times he won't admit his strengths and weaknesses, so he'll surround himself with people just like him. You've got to have a critical mass of management to succeed."

Start-up tip: *The days of the one-horse dray are gone; take a team approach.*

Balmoral will take a majority position in the company in return for the investment. But the entrepreneur can also negotiate, as part of the original financing deal, what's known as a "clawback" provision, which means the entrepreneur can regain control – if certain mutually agreed upon sales and profit targets are met. And the entrepreneur may not need to put up any money to achieve that goal. Instead, control can be regained using cash flow generated by the successful endeavour.

Penfund Management Ltd., with offices in Montreal and Toronto, is another example of a merchant bank. Over the last fifteen years, Penfund has supplied more than $1.5 billion in loans to entrepreneurs by funnelling money from pension funds to businesses. Penfund clients usually have sales in the $15- to $100-million range and receive loans with fixed interest rates over long terms like fifteen years, rather than the sliding scale based on prime that is used by banks. Penfund charges fees when the deal is completed, plus a management fee for the duration of the arrangement.

Networking can also produce funds through what investment banker Gordon Sharwood calls the "golf-club preferreds," where the placing of an issue and the raising of funds really depends on the entrepreneur's capacity to tap friends. These deals occur when an entrepreneur takes three of his richest friends out to play golf and, on the nineteenth hole, produces a share subscription and says, "Bill, you're in for

$75,000, Abe, you're in for $50,000, and Jack, you're in for $25,000. Please sign here."

"If you can't ask your friends," says Sharwood, "who can you ask?"

Suppliers: Don't be afraid to ask suppliers for help. For example, if you're opening a pool hall, and Brunswick is supplying the tables, that firm might agree to waive payments for two years. Such participation is really just an equity injection and goes on all the time.

Balmoral Partners offers two other possibilities: purchase-order financing and invoice discounting. Typical deals provide up to $300,000 for as much as six months. Here's how **purchase-order financing** works. You get an order from a blue-chip client for $100,000 worth of goods, but you haven't got the cash on hand to pay for necessary supplies, labour, or anything else required to keep the doors open while you produce the goods. Your bank isn't interested in lending you any more, so Balmoral advances the necessary money to you as needed – and takes one-third of the profit in the deal as payment.

> **Start-up tip:** *It's not how much money you receive in that loan, it's how much the amount means to you.*

Invoice discounting: This allows a company to speed up its cash flow without having to add to the existing capital. You've shipped the goods, but can't wait the thirty days for payment, so you take the invoice to Balmoral and they advance 85 per cent of the invoice's value immediately, holding back the final 15 per cent until the client pays. Eventually, you get all the money owed, less 5 per cent, which Balmoral keeps as its fee. (The fee shrinks if the invoice is paid in less than thirty days.) Balmoral also demands personal guarantees to backstop the advance. "The average business owner spends 50 to 60 per cent of his time worried about money. With money backup, the owner can go out and spend time on marketing and growing the business instead," says Curtis.

Clients can sometimes help in other ways. When president and CEO Don Taylor arrived at Engineered Air in Calgary in 1967, the heating-and-ventilation company had seven employees and $90,000 in sales. The firm, founded just a year earlier, was already struggling because of a lack of working capital. Taylor responded by winning a $150,000 equipment order, talked the client into paying one-third up-front, then convinced the bank on the strength of that purchase order to increase the firm's operating line from $15,000 to $50,000. "That got us going," says Taylor. Today, the firm has manufacturing plants in Calgary, Edmonton, Newmarket, and Desoto, Kansas.

Strategic alliances: These can mean more financial clout for a firm. CIMA Engineering Consultants president Kazimir Olechnowicz created such a deal in November 1994, when his engineering firm signed a deal with Hydro-Quebec. Rather than just act as consultants, CIMA of Laval, Quebec, put together a complete package that included financing and construction of an $8-million, 4.2-megawatt water-generating plant near Shawinigan, Quebec. Moreover, CIMA will own the project for the next forty years. "That's the new way of doing engineering. Governments have no money, so we have to find it," says Olechnowicz. "We need value-added in our projects today."

Founded in the mid-eighties when five Quebec engineering firms – each with more than thirty years' experience – merged, CIMA has ten offices in Quebec and has $32 million in annual revenue. Each office is an independent operating unit, so clients receive "local" attention from a member of the community. "The customers like to see somebody they know," Olechnowicz says. CIMA's decision to go beyond just billing for engineering time will drive growth exponentially. In the last year, the firm has added 100 new employees (for a total of 450) and made new connections with potential financial partners, including ten banks and insurance companies. "Financing's the easy part," says Olechnowicz. "When you can show a good cash flow, there's no problem."

Equipment leasing: Conservation of capital and cost depends on the risk to the lessor in such deals. Cash-flow benefits are greater than they are with purchasing, because either the lessee or lessor can use the tax benefits. This is where a firm like National Equipment Leasing Ltd. (NEL) of Winnipeg can help by actually owning equipment and leasing that equipment to companies rather than the company borrowing to buy the equipment. "Banks lend on receivables and inventory. We lend on equipment, so that business can free up the operating line for other things," says NEL president and CEO Nick Logan. "The Canadian legacy is six banks controlling all financial transactions. We can get capital back into business, where banks are not meeting the need,"

The parent company of NEL, Megill-Stephenson Co., entered equipment leasing as a sideline to vehicle leasing in 1976, created a division in 1984, and incorporated a separate company in 1987 as the market grew for lease deals on office equipment, interconnect phone systems, computer networks, and light industrial equipment such as forklift trucks or auto-repair systems. When leasing and sales-finance company IAC Ltd. became Continental Bank of Canada in 1979, says Logan, "They dropped what they were best at. We've grown into the void. Now we are in the backwash of what the banks can't do."

While NEL specializes in "small ticket" items under $100,000, it does handle deals up to $2 million. An associated firm, National Capital Leasing, looks after larger deals, and both have the backing of Great-West Life, which has held a 20-per-cent interest in NEL since 1989. Small-ticket leasing costs more than larger-ticket business, because the same sophisticated administrative procedures are required, even though profit margins are smaller. For example, NEL handles twelve thousand leases with ninety-eight hundred customers through a central computer in Winnipeg and on-line stations in branch offices in Vancouver, Edmonton, Calgary, Regina, and Toronto.

Asset-based financing: Getting this type of financing from nonbanks like Newcourt Credit Group Inc. is another possibility. Newcourt is a financial-services company that offers financing in the form of secured loans, conditional sales contracts, and leases. The chartered banks lend money for inventory, receivables, and working capital. By contrast, non-banks like Newcourt will do more innovative deals in the $25,000 to $5-million range with equipment vendors to arrange term financing on a wide variety of items like medical and high-tech equipment, construction and production machinery, as well as vehicle leasing. Corporate and institutional financings can run into the hundreds of million of dollars. Rather than put up personal collateral when you buy a truck or a fleet, the repayment is geared to your cash flow. In addition to Newcourt, other firms doing this type of business in Canada include Commcorp Financial Services, GE Capital Canada, and AT&T Capital Canada.

Credit cards: Inevitably, there will be days when you've exhausted your savings accounts and cashed the Canada Savings Bonds. Here's a tip that some swear by and others regard as extremely dangerous, because of the high cost of juggling the money that is owed. Even so, half the entrepreneurs in the first stages of start-up use credit cards to their full $3,000 to $4,000 limit. If you only have one or two cards, apply for as many as you can – submitting all of your applications at once – so that you'll receive approval of several more. While most entrepreneurs won't admit it, many have funded their start-up with more than one credit card. Yes, the cost of money is expensive at 14 per cent to 18 per cent – higher in some cases – but, if you need a fast $2,000 to pay some bills or buy supplies in order to keep the doors open, you'll be thankful for the immediate access to credit. Balmoral's Gary Curtis is now in his forties, but he still has the six credit cards he used to keep his early business afloat, just in case he needs them again, even though he knows he's well beyond that balancing-act stage.

Capital pools: Quebec has seen the strongest support for capital pools from financial institutions and the provincial government. The Caisse de dépôt, Mouvement Desjardins, Banque Nationale, and the QFL Solidarity Fund have established ten regional investment funds. The pools, consisting of money from the institutions and local sources, do deals with business in the $50,000 to $500,000 range. Private-sector capital pools include such firms as Canadian General Capital and Bedford Capital, both in Toronto. The federal government has designated $100 million over four years to create the Canada Investment Fund, which acts in a similar way to the Quebec arrangement by setting up smaller regional funds. The Ontario government has created the Ontario Lead Investment Fund, which is backed by four of the chartered banks. Labour funds, such as QFL Solidarity in Quebec and Working Ventures in Ontario, have $1.8 billion to invest.

Mezzanine financing: This form of financing has a theatrical sounding name, because such financing is on the second level, just like in a theatre, behind the better-secured lenders. This financing is available from firms like RoyNat and works like a second mortgage on your house. The first-mortgage holder gets first call on the money available or the value of the house if there is a distress sale; the second-mortgage holder gets paid a higher interest rate for taking the extra risk that results from being less likely to collect in case of a default. There are alternatives to paying a higher rate, and they include offering the lender bonus payments, guaranteed participation in your firm's cash flow, the opportunity to convert that debt into equity ownership at some point, or fees paid initially to set up the financing.

Whereas venture capitalists want to make 35 per cent per annum on their investment, mezzanine financing will likely cost less, say 25 per cent, because there isn't the same control or equity participation. While that's a high rate, you should also be able to look to such lenders for more than money. Often they will be knowledgeable about business and be able to offer advice and expertise. After all, they want you to succeed – if only to get their money back. Pension funds are a main source of such financing, and they usually offer relatively short terms, usually in the order of five years, with amounts smaller than are possible with more secure debts. That's because mezzanine financing is often based on cash flow, something that is difficult to predict. Mezzanine lenders want to be in and out quickly.

If you're taking on debt or leasing deals, increase your insurance coverage to cover losses. Basic fire and theft coverage won't be enough now that you're getting into leasing or loan agreements. In such cases, the lender will want policies to pay off financing arrangements in the case of total loss. There's also business-interruption insurance to replace revenue lost due to events beyond your control, employee fidelity bonds that protect against theft by staff, and umbrella policies for overall coverage if there is a liability suit against you or you suffer some kind of catastrophe.

While insurance coverage is prudent, and you'll need to prove you have it, the first thing any banker, venture capitalist, or angel will ask for is your business plan. If all you've got is a verbal story, no matter how lively your tapdance, no moneylender will give you five cents. Enthusiasm matters, but they also want to see, in writing, what your idea is all about, how your financial statement now stands, and what your projections are for prospects ahead. If you're going to get some of a bank's money, you'll have to prove without a shadow of a doubt that you'll be able to pay back the loan. For that, you'll need a business plan, a detailed explanation of who you and your company are, complete information on where you've been financially, and where you're going. In the young life of a new company, this is the most important document you'll ever create. The next chapter will show you how.

Summary:

1. Invest your own savings before asking others for theirs.
2. Next, look for start-up money from family and friends. If they won't back you, get a new idea.
3. Don't expect banks to fund your start-up; they'll want to see a track record of three to five years.
4. Find an angel in your community, preferably one who has savvy as well as money.
5. Suppliers and customers already have a stake in your success, they may also be prepared to help finance contracts and inventory.

CHAPTER 4

Writing a Business Plan and Getting a Bank Onside

"If people are not prepared to fight for the funds, they won't work hard in the business."

– merchant banker Louden Owen

Stock-market investors who do well have patience; the players likely to get burned are the ones who act on a hot tip and hope to double their money in a week. Entrepreneurs can be divided into two similar camps: those who grab at anything and those who are willing to work at making their own opportunities. The latter are more likely to succeed. Writing a business plan is hard work, but it forms a large part of crafting your future. At some point, you'll need to pull back from the day-to-day scramble and put a few descriptive words and detailed figures on paper if you're ever going to grow the company using other people's money.

A business plan is a written document that details the goals and objectives of your business, tells how you intend to realize those aims, and lays out how and when you'll repay the money you seek. The basic business plan is necessary whether you're approaching investors for equity (that's when someone gives you money and owns a piece of the business in return) or debt (when you have to pay the money back, but don't give up any ownership position). No application for money to finance your dream will be complete without a business plan. Approaching a bank, a venture capitalist, or a government body for seed money to get started or to grow – without such a plan – will expose you to delays at best, the discard pile at worst.

The plan should be complete, readable, and well presented. If you absolutely must, hand over a version done in your own handwriting. But with user-friendly personal computers now commonplace, you should be able to have a version that looks professional and is easier to read than a longhand submission. You should also consult your accountant or mentor for advice, because they will have had experience in preparing plans for other entrepreneurs. Once you have consulted widely and wisely, however, you must write the business plan yourself. No one knows your business like you do. Keep descriptions simple. Don't use terminology that will confuse or confound readers.

Depending on the stage of your own business development, you may not be able to deal with all the topics suggested below, but use them as a guide to develop a business plan of about fifteen pages that covers as many of the following areas as possible:

1. The company: Include a written description of the company, what the firm does or makes, the consumer needs that are met, its corporate history, the names of shareholders and major creditors, the goals you have set, the accounting firm you use, and any others who can verify your statements.

2. The market: Give a thorough summary of your market, now and for the near future. Who is your buyer or customer? How large is the potential demand? Who are your competitors, and why is what you offer different and/or better? What sets your idea apart from the dozens of other requests that the investor or banker will see that week? Give as many details as you can about the market knowledge you've developed and how you expect to price your product and distribute the goods or ensure that your service reaches a prime audience. What past evidence is there of success? What's in place that will mean continued growth? What advertising or marketing do you intend, and how do you know that effort will pay off?

3. Financial information: Include statements of your most recent three years, showing profit and loss, balance sheets, cash flow, major contracts you now have, plus your most accurate forecasts for sales, gross profit-margins, net income, cash flow, and any anticipated capital outlays. Highlight specific items in the company that have value, such as intellectual property. If there are losses on the books that will soon to give way to profits, explain why.

4. The details of the loan: The lender will specifically want to know what you intend to do with the money you want to borrow. Talk about the timing you prefer, any progress you're making with other potential lenders, how and when you intend to repay the funds. If there are risks involved, be honest about them.

5. Research and development: Describe any particular new product, technology, approach, or patented process you are using or intend to use, along with proof that it will work. If applicable, provide assurance that anything you produce will be environmentally friendly and not leave the community with toxic waste or other long-term problems.

6. Manufacturing: If you make goods, tell the prospective supplier of money how the work is done. Describe the factory, talk about production and where raw materials come from, what labour you use, and any particular edge you have over the competition, along with quality-control methods that are in place. If your product is purchased fully made or only needs final assembly by you, then give details about your relationship with that supplier firm, long-term contracts, and any other information that shows you won't be left high and dry by a fickle partner. If you supply a service, describe it fully.

7. Management and staff: Outline your background, track record, experience, and number of employees and their length of service. Describe facilities or locations, training plans in place, and responsibilities, and give brief biographical sketches of the key personnel who will be part of the ongoing team (and their compensation arrangements). If there is an advisory board or group of outside directors, mention them here. If you are currently looking for a key person or have an important vacancy, be honest and talk about that too.

8. Executive summary: Lead off your plan with an executive summary that outlines the complete story in a nutshell. It should run less than two pages, and you should write this section last. If you try to write the summary first, it will be too long. The executive summary is not just a *précis* of everything covered in the plan; this is the sizzle of the steak dinner to follow. Remember that the audience for your plan sees scores, even hundreds, of these documents in a year. They'll appreciate a readable "headline" version that touches on the main points of the opportunity you've identified, the service and market you're after, management savvy, financial strength, how much money you need, and how that money will be repaid.

9. Attachments: Be sure to include the latest complete financial statement; a sample of any selling or promotional material; surveys of product acceptance or market plans; and letters from suppliers and customers or award certificates that offer third-party endorsement of what you've done to date.

Beyond improving your loan chances, there are other advantages for you in spending the time required to prepare such a document.

• First, there is value in organizing your thoughts. If you're like most entrepreneurs, you simply want to get on with the job, but describing your business in detail will lead you to think about the business, as well as to consider prospects that you wouldn't otherwise have considered.

• Second, by thinking clearly about your story you will discover the sort of vision you need to convince your own associates that you know where you're going and how to get there.

• Third, because you have laid out a plan, you'll know if and when you're getting off track. You'll have an early-warning system that helps spot problems. Or you may simply decide that a new direction is appropriate if circumstances have changed.

• Fourth, a business plan gives your enterprise credibility. This document will say to any reader that you've been successfully able to identify an opportunity, gather a team of people around you, and devise an approach that will lead to good performance and solid profit.

Your basic aim in the business plan should be to provide lots of information and introduce yourself fully to bankers and investors – perhaps even well before you actually need their help. You will need to be prepared to back your loan request with collateral, perhaps even in the form of a mortgage on your house. You or your spouse may also be asked to sign a personal guarantee. Bankers are looking for ways to close all the possible exit doors to make certain they'll get their money back by seizing your assets. In addition to the booklet published by the Canadian Bankers' Association, you may also find useful a PC-compatible disk from the Royal Bank that gives an outline of a plan that you can follow (see page 281).

Start-up tip: *If there's one thing of which you can be sure, it's this: You can't be sure of how anything will turn out.*

The tone of the document is very important; you must sound confident, and you must maintain this impression throughout. Once the document is ready, call for an appointment at a bank branch. Presumably, you already have some kind of a relationship with your local branch; discover whether small-business loans are handled there, or if you need to be referred to a nearby commercial branch. Make sure that the bank officer you meet has the authority to act. Each officer has specific loan limits; you don't want to be asking for $150,000 if the officer's limit is $50,000.

Dress well, and when the opportunity comes to present your case orally, don't seem anxious or appear to be looking for quick action. You want to be businesslike and lay out the opportunity in a way that both arouses interest and offers reassurance. Hone a five-minute presentation that covers the highlights of your business plan. Don't hand over the written plan in advance of that initial presentation. You don't want the banker leafing through it while you are talking. Let the banker get a sense of your honest, personal enthusiasm and professional commitment to your idea and your business first.

Expect tough questions. If you can't foresee your needs well enough to plan carefully how you are going into debt, any banker will assume there are a whole lot of other things you don't see either. After the meeting, promptly carry out any undertakings you've made to supply additional information and answer any questions that were left hanging. Offer to arrange a tour of your premises, so the prospective lender can see you and your colleagues at work.

Expect to be closely investigated. Wouldn't you do the same? After all, if they aren't completely convinced, they probably won't — and shouldn't — invest in your idea.

Finally, don't take no for an answer. If the first bank you

approach turns you down, there are plenty of competitor institutions to try. So, be persistent in the face of rejection. Remember the advice of Wayne Gretzky, who said, "I know all the shots I take don't go into the net, but I know for sure all the shots I don't take don't go into the net."

Start-up tip: *Keep shooting the puck.*

Start-up case study: Homepreneur

The path towards meeting a banker who will listen attentively is a long one. There are no short cuts. Kimberley Thomas's new business, JoeJobs Inc., provides an excellent example of how someone launched a business with no money, no written business plan, and for a long time no help from any bank.

In 1988, Thomas decided the family needed extra money. Her husband was working, but she wanted to contribute (they've since split). Working outside the home was impossible for her with four children under the age of five to look after, so she took on a contract that she could do at her kitchen table. Midas Muffler was considering expanding its chain and needed someone to sift through past invoices and compile a list that showed where customers lived based on their postal codes. Thomas made $500 for her efforts.

When she told a friend what she had done, the friend brightened and said, "If you get any more work, let me know." As Thomas thought about the comment, she realized that maybe she had found a business niche that could do more than merely create work at home for herself. Other housebound men and women might also be able and willing. Because Thomas knew nothing about business, let alone how to start one, she turned to the local YMCA, where Youth Ventures Capital Loans were being offered. She was told that applicants must have graduated recently from a business course.

"If I show you I know as much as a grad," Thomas asked,

"will you help get me the money?" The YMCA agreed. Thomas did one-on-one counselling with the loan-fund staff at the Y every day for a month. She also took an enterprise program through the Y in which she worked independently on a computer. Thomas cleared the initial hurdle, received a $7,500 loan interest-free for a year, promptly put the funds in the bank as backup, and didn't touch them. Like most successful start-ups, Thomas knew she had to keep her overhead low, so she continued to work from home as she looked for "joe jobs."

Her initial approach was to send out letters, describing her service and how she could help organizations with fill-in jobs like mailing services and newsletter distribution. She was looking for the kind of work that pops up sporadically, work that full-time staff can't handle. The first big contract was a 1989 deal with the local library system, putting together a computer registry of local businesses. The work required phoning firms to get basic information, such as their product or service, number of employees, and a contact name. Thomas was paid a lump sum of $8,500. With that money she hired other part-timers like herself and kept 40 per cent as her own pay and profit.

Word of her firm spread, and soon Thomas was providing temporary fill-in services to the Chamber of Commerce and the local municipality – all joe jobs like stuffing envelopes with newsletters or tax bills, work that could be easily divided among other homeworkers. "There were more jobs than people," says Thomas. "They were looking to us for efficiency and were happy to pay a lump sum rather than hourly rates."

A friend's spouse worked at a printing company that needed piecework done, and soon JoeJobs was handling contracts that involved tens of thousands of items. A firm wanted refrigerator magnets created, someone else needed tape applied to pads, a third had information kits for assembly – all the little grungy jobs that few people want to do. Business grew whether the economy was healthy or in recession. In good times, there was lots to do; in bad, organizations liked the idea of being able to "outsource" work to people on contract rather than add to full-time payroll. Says Thomas, "It's kind of a neat business, because it'll survive both economies."

By 1991, Thomas had built a network of several dozen local residents, mostly women, who were delighted to get twenty hours of work a week that they could do at home. Thomas paid $7 an hour, twenty-five cents more than the minimum wage, and everyone was on the honour system when claiming time spent. By 1992, annual revenue had reached $200,000, and Thomas's street and driveway were bustling with the people who were under contract to her. A truckload of work would arrive, she'd alert her network, and a flotilla of vehicles filled with parents and kids would show up to collect their share of the job.

Finally, Thomas realized that she could run JoeJobs from home no longer, the chaos had become too great. The firm had begun as a sole proprietorship, but now she incorporated the company, moved into a 2,000-square-foot space in a nearby industrial mall, and hired two full-time staff to help. With expansion into the mall, her kids got the family room back and she was better able to serve blue-chip clients like Sun Life and Sprint Canada. But there was also a need for equipment, so JoeJobs spent $15,000 on a new phone system, computer, and forklift. In 1994, JoeJobs and its eight full-time employees moved again, to a 10,000-square-foot facility.

Along the way, Thomas has learned more than she ever thought she'd need to know about regulations, taxes, and people. She has permits to employ homeworkers, everyone signs a contract, and each employee receives the appropriate T-4 slip detailing income earned. "The biggest problem I have is people collecting benefits and trying to work for cash," says Thomas. "That really angers me. I'm running a legitimate business." Eighty per cent of her network is female; by working twenty hours a week each of them can earn up to $5,000 a year. All piecework is quality-checked, and one serious blunder is enough for a worker to be stricken from the list. "If they mess up or they're fraudulent, they're out. They understand how important their joe job is," she says.

Start-up tip: *Be understanding about mistakes, but not to the point where they hurt your firm's reputation.*

For the first four years, bankers would barely give Thomas the time of day. She wasn't much helped by the fact that she is a self-admitted illiterate about numbers. At one point, she had to convince her mother to co-sign a personal credit line. Finally, in 1993, she found a friend in Tom Lougheed, the manager of the local National Bank branch. Thomas had met Lougheed at a business networking group that gathers every other week, and he eventually agreed to a $40,000 line of credit, with her house as collateral. This type of loan is set up on a revolving basis, so that the loan is repaid as cash flow allows. As a result, if clients hadn't yet paid, Thomas could draw down funds from the bank loan to pay her homeworkers for their work.

The banking relationship took time to build. "She was naïve about what a bank could or couldn't help with," says Lougheed. When Thomas first approached him, she admitted that other banks said she was too small to bother with. Says Lougheed, "My reaction was, 'We'd like to deal with bigger clients too. We expect you'll become one.'" Lougheed, who is also National Bank's head of small-business loans for the region, agrees that businesspeople should not give up just because one or two bankers say no. According to Lougheed, the reason the bank has said no may have nothing to do with the merits of your loan application. Some bank managers have two hundred clients and may not be looking actively for new clients. By contrast, others may be hungry. "It's no different than obtaining a mortgage or buying a car," he says. "Shop around. Relationships are what we're talking about. You need a partner."

To a banker, partnership means that you put in at least as much money as the bank. "Most bankers are willing to match your investment. We come in for 50 per cent of the risk, but we don't take 50 per cent of the profit. We just want our interest," says Lougheed. For Thomas's loan he used a government program that's very popular with banks because the government takes the risk. Lougheed helped her finance a new computer and phone system under the federal government's Small Business Loans Act (SBLA), which means Thomas can purchase fixed assets without tying up capital. In a case where a business founders, the bank collects what it can (perhaps by seizing the assets and selling them) and the government reimburses the bank for the rest of the money lost.

Funds from the SBLA offer an advantage for the business, too, because the interest rate can be no higher (and some banks charge less) than 1.75 per cent over the prime rate, the rate that banks charge to their biggest and best corporate customers. Business-improvement loans (BILs) under this program, with a $250,000 maximum, can be used to:

- buy land to operate an enterprise;
- renovate, improve, modernize, extend, or construct premises; and/or
- acquire fixed assets.

Assets acquired this way must be used in the business, but such BILs are particularly useful for the small businesses such as Thomas's that want to acquire something like a telephone or computer system. A loan of $10,000 will go a long way towards more efficient operations, and there's a lengthy ten-year repayment permitted. In return, the bank will want to take collateral to cover the loan. A onetime fee of 2 per cent of the loan amount goes to the federal government, but that fee can be included in the financed total. The BILs can be arranged, even if you've already acquired the assets, as long as no more than six months have passed since the purchase.

The big-six chartered banks have become quite competitive in loans to small business. The Bank of Montreal has designated fifty "flagship" branches across Canada and has staffed them each with a vice-president who can give quick answers to loan applicants. The bank has also established a venture-capital fund, which was initially given $20 million to lend, and has set out to find start-up companies in knowledge-intensive industries. "This gives us a chance to learn about the new economy," says Bob McGlashan, senior vice-president of personal and commercial lending.

Dealing with the beancounters

During the start-up years, JoeJobs got by doing its own bookkeeping, but there came a point when Thomas needed help from a professional accountant, affectionately known as a beancounter, to prepare an audited statement. There are three levels of audited statement. JoeJobs started at the first level, where its statement is called a **compiled statement** or a **Notice to Reader**. In this case, an accountant prepares a profit-and-loss statement based on receipts and invoices. Such work is not acceptable to banks as proof of a sound business footing. Still, in the early stages, or if you are a sole proprietor, all you need is a Notice to Reader for internal financial management and tax filing. The statement is simply a balance sheet with a statement of income and retained earnings. Your banker will want a copy to keep on file.

The second and more detailed level, at which Thomas has now arrived, is called a **Review Engagement**. The accountant doesn't actually count the receivables or inventory, but transactions have been "eyeballed," and the business has passed certain accounting tests. The third level is a carefully audited statement, known as an **Auditor's Report**, a more expensive process, and one that most small businesses don't require.

Once your business has a Review Engagement done, people such as the bank or creditors will have more comfort about your financial position. The accountant will provide far more information, the kind that is required by the bank to go beyond a simple line of credit and, for example, let someone like Thomas do what's known as "margining against receivables." That's when the bank advances the business money based on money owed to that business by its clients.

For example, a business may have $100,000 owing from work for fifteen clients. All of that money isn't going to flow back within a week of the invoice being sent. Lots of companies wait up to ninety days to pay. Some never pay, and the bank takes those deadbeats into account, too, by assuming that $10,000 of the $100,000 will have to be written off as bad debt. The bank then lends the business a portion of the money it's owed, bearing in mind that some will come in thirty days, more in sixty days, the rest in ninety days. The rule of thumb differs among banks, but Lougheed lends up to 75 per cent on Canadian receivables or 65 per cent on American receivables (taking distance into account). On $100,000 worth of receivables, then, you might get a loan of 70 per cent of $90,000 ($100,000 minus $10,000) for $63,000 at 1.5 per cent over the bank's prime rate. Banks will also watch how the payments on receivables are flowing into the business from clients. "If too many go beyond ninety days, maybe you're not good at collecting your receivables," says Lougheed. Banks make exceptions for government invoices. Governments tend to be slow to pay, often taking more than ninety days, but bankers realize that governments are "good for it" and will eventually come through.

While Lougheed looked carefully at the numbers Thomas supplied, it was also important that he was impressed by Thomas as an individual. "She seems like a decent, hardworking person who was willing to put her name on the line – so, why not try to help her? Sometimes you go by gut reaction. Does the individual have the grit to work the seventy-five hours a week [that's] necessary?" Lougheed likes to see tenacity, persistence, and enthusiasm – even a few weaknesses. "Someone who admits to a weakness and has a plan how to handle it impresses the hell out of me," says Lougheed. For example, when a business is still small, an entrepreneur can't afford to hire a human-resources specialist to look after personnel problems. If, in such a situation, that same entrepreneur isn't good at managing people, but has registered in a course to learn how, that's a positive step, says Lougheed.

To date, Thomas has done exactly what every entrepreneur should: she's taken very little money out of the business for herself, limiting her annual salary to less than $30,000. Thomas can see the irony of working so hard for so little money. "I don't know if we're further ahead," she says with a laugh. "I sometimes wonder if we should move back to my garage." That attitude about taking the minimum money out will have long-term benefits. "The most common problem [with small businesspeople] is too-rapid growth," says Lougheed. "They don't have sufficient equity. They come in for a line of credit and I say to them, 'You didn't make a profit but you took out a salary and eroded your equity.' Increased sales can complicate things if you just take the money out."

Although Thomas is getting better with numbers, they remain a problem when talking to bankers. She has learned one important lesson, however: Keep the bank up to speed. Bankers dislike surprises, such as a sudden change in your financial position; that's when they get nervous and can call a loan. "I'm quoting on business that's four times whatever I've done [in the past]. I don't know where the money will come from. But as long as I keep [the bank] informed, they'll be fine," Thomas says.

In 1994, JoeJobs' revenues were nearly $500,000. During November, the firm's busiest month, 127 individuals did work under contract to JoeJobs, but Thomas knows she's still a long way from being successful. "I don't like to say, 'I've made it' in case the whole thing collapses around me. As recently as yesterday, I just walked out and cried. Then I said to myself, 'The boss can't cry.'"

Sometimes all that's required to turn around a despondent mood is for some new business to come through the door. Moreover, Thomas's overall lifestyle has undergone a marked change for the better. Because the office is just around the corner from the school, she sees her children during the day. There's time, too, for volunteer work in the community and various business clubs and networks. Such relationships are not only enjoyable for Thomas on a personal level, they also help professionally because others hear about JoeJobs. "I just have a lot of faith," says Thomas. "I'm helping a lot of people."

Preventative medicine: Collecting debts

When you first meet your banker, with or without business plan in hand, the loan officer will look closely at how you're managing your own financial affairs: pricing, profits, cash flow, and receivables. The banker will also want to test your muscle and see that a disciplined approach is in place. So, before you take your business plan and try to borrow money, ask yourself if you *really* need to take on debt. Maybe the money is in the business right now. Ask yourself how you're doing at collecting debts that are owed to you. You likely have a list of people who have yet to pay you for the services you supplied or the products you shipped. Such receivables are death to a young firm. That's your profit sitting out there in someone else's pocket. Keep track of how long people take to pay – thirty days, sixty days, or ninety days. The faster they pay, the better off you'll be, because your cash flow will be healthy and you won't need to borrow any money from the bank or elsewhere.

How quickly is your money going out? Just as you'd like to be paid in thirty days, so, you'll find, do most of your suppliers. Here's one trick used by A&B Sound Ltd., a music-and-electronics retailer based in Vancouver. "We're saying to suppliers, 'If you want to be paid in thirty days, send only thirty days of inventory,'" says Bob Hitchcock, directing of marketing. "The ability to have a high profit is essential." To do that, keep a running total of where you are – financially – every day. The daily self-diagnosis should include what bills are outstanding, which have been paid, what invoices can be sent. One Toronto businessman, Peter Jedlicka, who manages property and other investments for European clients, has a little rhyme he encloses when he sends someone a second invoice, just to nudge them in a humorous way. Here's what he says: "How do you do? Some people pay when due, some when overdue, some people never do. How do you do?" He then tells them whether their first notice was sent thirty, sixty, or ninety days before, then adds, "Your remittance would be appreciated." The gentle reminders seem to work more often than not.

Start-up tip: *It's more expensive to find a new customer than retain one you already have.*

Another good collection method is to contact every firm directly by phone. Don't make threats; assume, instead, that they want to pay. You want your money, to be sure, but you don't want to lose them as a customer. Send a follow-up letter. Try again after sixty days. After ninety days, offer a negotiated settlement. Throughout the process, keep notes of your efforts, in case you have to resort to small-claims court. A collection agency is another, more final, route, because the fee will run anywhere between 20 to 50 per cent (depending on the size of the outstanding amount) of any debts collected.

Keeping limits on how much credit you extend could make or break your young business. You might even want to demand cash on delivery in some cases. If a company you have been dealing with does declare bankruptcy and owes you money, be sure to file a claim quickly – don't wait for an official notice. If you have delivered goods to that firm during the previous month, you'll need to follow up aggressively with the receiver or trustee. Preventative steps are best, however, so run thorough credit checks before extending any credit. Verify the firm's standing with agencies like Dun & Bradstreet or your local Better Business Bureau.

Start-up tip: *Know your customer before you ship the goods.*

Establishing your reputation

Watch you own creditworthiness, too. You'll want to be establishing your own good credit standing in the local business community. There's no point to demanding quick payment from your creditors if you don't give them the same professional courtesy in return, even though taking the high ground can sometimes hurt. Rick Padulo goes so far as to pay all sums owed to firms that go bankrupt, even if they haven't performed as promised. "Other companies would have tried to make deals. I didn't," says Padulo. "I was on the hook, I signed for it. My integrity was on the line. I paid one hundred cents on the dollar. The people that knew me, knew that I'd be dead before they wouldn't get paid, no matter what, if I had to dig a ditch till I was ninety-five."

Start-up tip: *Try not to have too much on your plate at any given time. Remember, you're starting a small business – not a conglomerate.*

Both your knowledge base and financial standing in the community can be improved by joining trade organizations in your field like the Canadian Professional Sales Association (see page 286). They'll let you tie in with their group-insurance programs, obtain car-rental discounts, or pass along information about seminars and government programs. Such networking means that you can learn from someone else's mistakes and be among kindred spirits. Some days, those professional associations may feel like the only friends you've got!

Throughout, you'll want to keep a little of yourself in reserve. People will let you down and you don't want your irrepressible spirit to be squelched by the bad behaviour of others. Leon Lapidus at the Mibro Group in Scarborough spent twenty years as president of Fuller Brush until the father of an acquaintance took him aside one day and urged him to buy a business, saying, "You're a jerk to work for these guys. My friends and I will finance it and you'll make money for yourself rather than those guys in Chicago."

Lapidus found Mibro, a well-established firm with a good customer base. The founder, getting on in years, wanted to sell. Lapidus negotiated a purchase price of $4 million and went to his backers to organize the money – only to find the support had evaporated. The original sponsor was wintering in Arizona, some of the others were in Florida, and when the moment arrived, they had neither any interest in the firm nor the money to back him. Lapidus was near panic. "I went to the bank," he recalls. "Sometimes when I'm uncomfortable, I perspire. When I went to the bank, I was sweating." Fortunately, he was able to make his case. Lapidus put up 5 per cent of the purchase price, borrowed the rest, and bought the firm.

Finally, and *don't* mention this strategy in your business plan, pay off the loan you've arranged more quickly than you've agreed. If you take longer, a bunch of strangers will end up calling the shots. If you're early, the next time you need your bank's money, they'll be delighted to see you.

Summary:

1. Before you borrow money make sure your expenses are as low as they can be and your creditors are paying promptly.

2. Just because one banker says no doesn't mean they all will. Keep looking.

3. A well-prepared business plan will organize your thinking, build bank and investor confidence, and provide a measuring stick for progress.

4. Once you've found a source of funds, establish a relationship. Share good news and bad.

5. Keep those receivables flowing in.

All in the Family

"When we leave the office,
we have to turn it off. That's discipline."

– David Falle, Image Craft Inc.

C omedian Jerry Seinfeld captures the strength and stress of the family business situation perfectly when he says, "Parents make the best employers because, no matter how bad a job you do, they're stuck with you." And, he might have added, "and you with them." In a small business, where the family members often provide both management and workers in the start-up phase, the day-to-day problems and potential friction points are numerous. How will everyone work together? Who will be responsible for what? Who's in charge? How will one member of a family succeed another?

Family businesses represent a key component of Canadian business. They generate 45 per cent of the gross domestic product and employ half of all working Canadians, according to the Canadian Association of Family Enterprise (CAFE). Next to the difficult financial problems that face every new business, family ties and tribulations will be the next likely cause of the greatest anxiety. Families can be supportive, even essential, in providing investment funds and donated time. But family can also be counterproductive – just what a struggling young business doesn't need.

"Husband-and-wife teams usually don't work out," says Jane Martin. "It's not an easy matter to stay married, raise children, and run a business. There are too many points of possible conflict." Yet, the Martins have made the combination work. Geoff started Vas-Cath Inc. in 1977 to make catheters for medical use and, within two years, Jane, then a high-school music and physical-education teacher, announced she wanted to join him in the business. It took her nine months to convince her husband, as well the firm's accountant and close adviser, that she was right. "When I want something badly, I'll wait it out," she says. "One day I just wore them down."

Today, she is CEO of Vas-Cath, leaving Geoff more time to do research-and-development work as president of an associated firm, Med Pro Designs Inc. According to Jane, the secret of business success and a family life with three girls, the oldest a teenager, is "respect for the other person's strengths and your own weaknesses." The marriage must also be a strong one and have an existence separate from the business. "If you don't have a really good relationship, a growing business will be really hard on that relationship," says Geoff.

The Martins have carefully divided responsibilities at the office and have been equally insistent that their employees, now numbering about 140, know who is in charge of what. If employees sense there is a blurring of responsibilities, they will ask one member of the couple for approval on an item; then, if they don't like the answer, they'll go and ask the other partner, just like children who play one parent off against the other. While both members of the couple share financial aspects of the business and discuss all major decisions before they're taken, Jane specifically looks after personnel and employee motivation, while Geoff is responsible for more abstract ideas such as R&D. "Draw the line and make it clear who does what," says Geoff.

Start-up tip: *The office is where the work gets done, home is where the heart is.*

Image Craft Inc., a Cambridge, Ontario, greeting-card manufacturer launched in 1988, is 100-per-cent owned by Susan Falle, vice-president of human resources. Husband David is president of the firm that employs 125 people and exports about 20 per cent of its product to the United States. Like many families in business, the Falles agree that one of the secrets for success is to keep the worlds of business and home quite separate. Says David, "If a question happens to come up when we're at home, one of us will say, 'Let's leave that for tomorrow.'"

As president of a family business (brother John is developing U.S. sales), David knows he needs to cast a wide net and make sure he's supported by strong resources. He has never forgotten the advice given to him by his father, who was a plumber, a man who survived the Depression. "As a kid growing up my father would always tell me, 'Hire people that are better than yourself,' and that's what I've done. My staff can run circles around me. You've got to give them a job to do and let them do it, even if they don't do it the way you would, because at the end of the day it'll be done."

Getting along

In a family business, emotions and money can mix in a cocktail of trouble. The first decision you'll need to make is exactly who can participate in the firm and at what level of management. You also have to decide how much family members will be paid and who should participate in the ownership of the firm. In addition, how the family members interact with each other can pose problems in the workplace. At the simplest level, for example, what does a son call his father when other employees are around? Cam Thomson, who runs TMS Marketing Inc. in Don Mills, Ontario, with his father, Dennis, discovered that calling his father by his first name at work was a big help. "That's done a lot for me. It's distanced me from the family aspect," says Cam.

TMS, a catalogue-distribution firm, was started by Cam and Dennis after Dennis had been in a similar business, working for someone else. While at university, Cam worked in the warehouse of that firm and, when he graduated in 1982, they launched TMS together. "I was the energy, he was the brains," says Cam. He took over the reins in 1986, although his father continues to remains active. Today the firm employs eighty-five people and has $40 million in annual sales.

At one firm, the entrepreneur's mother, brother-in-law, and sister all worked together at one time. "It's really quite incestuous," says the entrepreneur, laughing. After a time, however, one family member wasn't performing at the same level as everyone else and was fired. "That can be really stressful," he admits. "You have to be honest and you have to take the honest approach." That honesty matters to the other employees, the nonfamily members too. Allowing mediocre family members to work at any firm sends the wrong signal to everyone else about what you find acceptable. Staff will become resentful if there's a layabout or a larcenous relative. The problem is called "the brother-in-law conundrum" by Loudon Owen, partner in McLean Watson Group, a merchant bank with offices in London and Toronto. "Be prepared to say no to families," Owen says.

One way to handle family hiring is to provide family members with entry-level jobs and allow those with the right talents and work ethic to rise as high as their competence allows. In the early days, however, you probably don't have room for any people about whom you have concerns. One firm found that saying no to family can sometimes be the only way to survive. The best rule, according to this sadder, but wiser, entrepreneur, is that family should join only at the firm's launch, when they can invest money or expertise or both. He hired his wife's brother and a sister-in-law, the wife of another brother. "Family expects to be treated differently. They expect privileges," says the entrepreneur. "I used to say, 'The only privilege you get is the job.'"

Family, however, doesn't always heed such dictums and assume that they can somehow abide by different rules. As time passed, the brother-in-law took to coming in to work later every day. He demanded more pay and more holidays than other employees. The sister-in-law, who served as production manager, was a clock-watcher who wouldn't work beyond 4 P.M., even if everyone else was on overtime to meet a deadline. Moreover, the two in-laws grew envious of the founders and how much money they thought the founders were making. "They think they're responsible, [that] the business isn't successful because of you," says the entrepreneur. After six stressful years, the brother-in-law left to establish a competing business. The sister-in-law quit suddenly after she concluded that the founders had sided with an employee rather than with her in a dispute.

"Family businesses can work if everybody starts on the ground floor, but it doesn't work if the business is already successful," says the entrepreneur. You have to be tough and refuse a late-arriving relative's request for a job. "The business has to survive. Family gets in the way." Don't worry that the relative will become angry with you for refusing a job, because the rift between the two of you could eventually be greater if you both work at the same firm.

Start-up tip: *Better a family member who won't speak to you than one who's ruining your business.*

From start-up through the stay-afloat stage all the way to sturdy, the family must be strong and communication must be open, whether family members are supportive at home or working in the business. If they are working with you, it's not only the other employees who need to know who is in charge; the members of the family need to work out the pecking order too. If a mother and daughter decide to start a business together, one of the first things they must do is decide who will be boss. After all, they have spent a lifetime together operating under certain rules. If that relationship is to change, and the daughter is now to be predominant, both must be in total agreement.

Sometimes the biggest problem in a family business is not having anyone to share dilemmas with – everyone is too close to the situation. You know you're reinventing the wheel, but you don't know anyone who might have been through a similar situation. The Canadian Association of Family Enterprise (see page 285) offers what it calls Personal Advisory Groups (PAGs), teams of up to twelve members from noncompeting companies, who share experiences, ideas, and information – all in confidence. PAGs meet every four to six weeks and, once or twice a year, participate in one- or two-day retreats.

At some point, however, family businesses will get to a size where they need professional management. The family itself simply may not have all the talent required to run a growing business and should be prepared to bring in key personnel who can add professional competence in specific management areas, such as human resources, financial control, or wherever else the family may be lacking. Families have to admit that they need such help and go out and hire it. In the same way, each member of the family must have clearly defined duties and not simply float around the business doing what appears necessary.

Salaries must reflect experience and responsibility – just as they do for any employee. Most important, everyone should know what the other is doing. The entrepreneurial Bitove family of Toronto – father, mother, and five children – talk each night at 11 P.M. via a telephone conference-call, just to bounce ideas around and see what's happened to each of them that day.

Some case studies: Food for thought

The Bitove Group, as the umbrella organization is called, is now a sprawling establishment that began in 1949 when John Bitove, Sr., opened the fourteen-stool Java Shoppe in Toronto. He added five restaurants to the chain and, in the sixties, opened four supper clubs in Toronto and Hamilton. From 1969 to 1979, Bitove operated forty Big Boy and Roy Rogers restaurants. In 1978, sons Nick and Tom opened the Hard Rock Café in Toronto, and now have three more such bars in Toronto, Montreal, and Calgary, with franchises planned for Edmonton and Vancouver. In 1983, the Bitoves won the food and beverage concessions at Pearson airport, added the high-end food concessions at SkyDome in 1989 and those at Pearson's Trillium Terminal Three in 1990. Son Jordan runs a catering firm called Great Moments in Catering, and daughter Vonna operates the product-licensing shop and catalogue-sales operation at Wayne Gretzky's, a popular Toronto restaurant launched in 1993 with the hockey superstar.

The firm currently employs twelve hundred people and had annual revenue of $45 million in 1989, which was the last year the Bitoves revealed financial information to the trade magazine *Foodservice and Hospitality*. Today, revenue is probably closer to $200 million, given the addition of SkyDome, Terminal Three, meals for first-class passengers on VIA Rail, and Gretzky's.

There are those who know the family who credit John's wife, Dotsa, with the strength that has held them all together and quietly moved the businesses forward. Whoever is responsible, John Bitove, Jr., is the second-generation embodiment of the modern-day entrepreneur. In 1993, he won the Toronto franchise rights for the National Basketball Association Raptors. "There's no stopping John junior," says his father, now in his sixties. "He's the most aggressive of the five [children]. Sometimes he's so aggressive he scares me. But he always does his homework. I'll ask him about something and he'll have already thought about it."

The environment in which he grew up was crucial in his development. Business was always an extension of family, but John was the most interested of the five children. Although all of them were free to attend any of the many meetings their father held at home, John sat in most often, usually peppering his father with questions later. When he was twelve, John junior regularly locked himself in his father's downstairs home office. When his brothers pestered him to reveal what he'd been working at, he showed them detailed sketches for a multisports complex.

Bitove was accepted at Indiana University before his parents knew he'd even applied. They were upset, because his older siblings had attended Canadian schools, but reluctantly they agreed he could go — if he paid the tuition fees. They were wrong if they thought that this requirement would somehow put an end to John's plans. That summer, Bitove held three jobs and earned $15,000. There were two reasons for the particular pull to Indiana. First, his mother had been raised in Fort Wayne, so he had visited relatives there often and liked the region. Second, just about every house in the basketball-crazed Hoosier state has a hoop. Recalled Bitove, "I was always the diehard sports fan."

He spent two years at Indiana (where he met his wife, Randi), then enrolled at the University of Windsor law

school, three hours away by car. He completed his Indiana
business undergrad degree during the summers, and graduated from both programs in 1984. After working in Ottawa
for deputy prime minister Don Mazankowski, he joined the
family business in 1987, doing legals, negotiating leases, and
generally acting as dealmaker. Since then, chairman and CEO
Bitove senior has ceded ownership in the family firm, split-
ting ownership equally among the five children. Because he
wanted them to spend their leisure time together, he built a
place near Craigleith, Ontario, two hours north of Toronto,
that is big enough to sleep the five kids, their spouses, and
twelve grandchildren.

"The Bitoves are very competitive with each other, but
John junior is the tiger," says Senator Trevor Eyton, who golfs
with them in Boca Raton, Florida, where both families own
property. "John junior is motivated by enormous ambition. He
wants to do great things. He'll work any number of hours and
travel anywhere to achieve that."

A similar family unity and ego-less sharing marks the management at St. Joseph Printing Ltd. of Concord, Ontario, begun
in 1956 by Gaetano Gagliano, who still serves as chairman. At
thirty-seven, Tony Gagliano is president – one of eight sons
and daughters working in diverse areas, including shift supervision, human resources, and estimating. Problems to date
have been few. "Unlike a lot of family businesses where there
is sibling rivalry, we've really grown it together," says Tony. "If
someone wants a responsibility, they let it be known, and the
board votes on it."

Age, for example, isn't the only factor that is used to establish who does what. Tony is president, even though he has
three older brothers. When he joined eleven years ago as the
eleventh employee, sales were less than $1 million. Today there

are 350 employees involved in printing and a further 100 who work at Network Studios Inc., an acquisition that does all-digital pre-press work, including creative-concept development, electronic page makeup, film preparation, printing, and distribution. "Although my father started the firm, we're really still a first-generation business. The real challenge will be the next generation," he says. "We'll have some of the difficulties then making them understand how the company grew. We made it grow together, and we know where it came from and what the values are."

Making those appropriate judgements about the next generation requires thoughtful insight into the qualities of family members and enough diplomacy to see the plans through. Frank Milligan of Polywheels has three children, but only one is employed at his firm. "I think if all three were here, it might not work," he says. "They get along as siblings, but I don't know about the business." His daughter, for example, was at Polywheels for a while, but she was bothered by the anxiety levels caused by financial crises, such as the realization on a Wednesday that they needed $100,000 by that Friday. "My youngest son, Sean, is more my personality in saying, 'The money will be there,' and it always was." Sean joined the firm after taking a marketing course at a local community college and didn't start anywhere near the top. His first jobs included mucking out the pits, sweeping floors, and operating the presses. Today, as Frank approaches age sixty, he's grooming Sean to take over. "I can see that the company can survive me," he says. "That's important."

Spousal support can be crucial. When Mike Buckley started Expographiq in Hull, Quebec, in 1978, there wasn't enough money in the visual-communications company both to keep the firm alive and draw a salary as well, so he and his partner went without incomes. In both households, the spouses were working and kept food on the table. "Pride didn't allow me to go on UI," says Buckley. "I was living off my wife. Finally I got enough gumption to go down to the UI office to see what was available." As Buckley recounts the scene, the conversation went something like this:

"What are you doing?"

"I'm trying to get a company going."

"Sorry, you don't qualify."

Says Buckley, "Our system is unjust. There are a lot of people who could use help from the social system and don't get it."

After a year, the two partners had built the business to the point where they could each take out $100 a week. Today, Expographiq is successful, employing more than fifty people. Even so, the feeling of struggle never quite leaves; they always feel on edge. "You never *make* it. It's a constant risk cycle. You're always striving to be successful," says Buckley.

Succeeding at succession

The potential for family infighting exists even after a company has grown large enough that you'd think there were enough roles and profits for everybody. Some of the most bitter corporate fights in Canada have occurred among family businesses that have started small, grown impressively through the first generation, then had the behind-the-scenes bickering turn to bitter public battles as succession loomed. Look at the Birkses in jewellery, the Steinberg food chain, the Billes family at Canadian Tire, and the most recent, explosive example, the McCains. In 1954, the four McCain brothers – Harrison, Wallace, Robert, and Andrew – launched their french-fry business in Florenceville, New Brunswick. Their initial investment of $100,000 was buttressed by a $400,000 loan, and in 1956, they built the first plant to process locally grown potatoes.

Forty years later, McCain Foods Inc. had become a $3-billion family empire with more than sixty plants in Canada, the United States, and Europe.

For years, Wallace and Harrison had both been CEOs, but when they reached their sixties, and the time arrived for succession planning, they found that they were able to agree on almost nothing. Each began jockeying to place family from his particular branch in the best roles. In 1990, Wallace put his son, Michael, in charge of U.S. operations without Harrison's approval. In retaliation, Harrison appointed a favourite nephew, Allison, to run the U.K. operations without Wallace's consent. As the situation deteriorated, frosty memos replaced previous face-to-face consultation, until finally a judge was retained to arbitrate. When that didn't work, Wallace tried to buy out other members of the family, who reacted by trying to get rid of him. Finally, the dispute went into open court for the world to see their differences, and Wallace was ousted in 1994, all of it modern-day proof of the gospel of St. Mark, which says, "A house divided against itself cannot stand." Peace finally descended in 1995 after Wallace bought Maple Leaf Foods Inc. and called off the fight with Harrison.

The McCains are far from alone. Seventy per cent of all family businesses don't survive into the second generation of the family; 90 per cent of family start-ups never get to the third. The reasons are as simple as they are predictable. If two separate branches of a family both decide that they have next-generation leaders who should take over, the debate can become quite rancorous.

Start-up tip: *Hiring outsiders may be the only way to run the family business, help decide who will be in charge, or plan succession.*

In 1940, Françoise Miville-Deschênes started the Montreal-based plumbing and heating company that later became

Groupe Deschênes & Fils. His sons – Jacques, Gilles, and Pierre – joined the firm in the early fifties and took over from their father in 1959. At the time, the business was in rough shape, and the three brothers worked hard together to build it up. "As long as we were struggling like hell there was no problem," says Jacques. "We made sacrifices for many years, working night and day." Come the better times, however, not every member of the family wanted to continue working full tilt. "When we started to be in better shape, the problems started. When you've got a few bucks in the business, some people want to enjoy life a little more," he says. First one brother wanted out, then a second, so Jacques bought out both of them.

While succession is something that no one wants to consider ("I'm irreplaceable. I'm not ready to be put out to pasture"), you should begin to plan earlier rather than later. There will always be too many things to do, but planning how the firm will continue isn't something that can be taken lightly or that can be carried out by anyone other than you. Succession will certainly cause rifts if the founder won't cede control or rivalries develop. "I did a lot of reading, and I could see that the figures regarding succession were pretty tough," says Herbert Hough, age sixty-six, chairman and CEO of MBS Bearing Service Inc. of Lachine, Quebec. "The best way is to hire professional management for the next twenty years." In 1991, Hough brought in Dublin-born chartered accountant Vivian Doyle-Kelly as president until either Hough's twenty-nine-year-old daughter Susan, advertising and marketing manager, or twenty-five-year-old son Eric, now in inside sales, is ready for the role.

Your succession plan should be a written document that details everyone's responsibility and role, shareholder agreements, and financial security for you as the founder. Pick a successor, designate that person publicly to others who might think they have a chance, and make your heir rampant the majority owner, so there can be no dispute about who's going to be in charge. Make sure your successor is surrounded by talented managers (some of whom should be nonfamily) and help the successor's transition process by involving everybody in planning decisions. The toughest step of all? Extricating yourself. The last thing your successor needs is you second-guessing. Be prepared to offer advice when asked, but don't hang around.

Leonard Lee, president of Lee Valley Tools Ltd., is in his mid-fifties and offers an excellent example of planning ahead for succession. He is currently grooming his purchasing-manager son, Robin, age thirty-two, to take over. For the last few years, Lee has been careful to have Robin report to an executive vice-president in the organization, arguing the importance of keeping some family distance for professional development. Leonard and his wife, Lorraine, own 80 per cent of the company and have established an estate freeze by transferring the firm's assets to a family trust. Capital-gains taxes were paid at the time, and life-insurance coverage was purchased to offset the additional capital-gains taxes that will have accrued and be owing when the parents die. With those funds available, the company can remain intact and won't need to be broken up or sold off.

Sometimes the best way to train the next generation for succession is to make sure that they have a chance to learn how to fly on their own. Bob Goodman, son of the founder of Manpower Services (Toronto) Ltd., has been involved in the business eighteen years. Goodman went to Calgary and Edmonton in 1976 for eighteen months to learn the staff-placement business in another of the franchise operations, away from his father Marvin's scrutiny and protection. There Bob did everything – accounts and service and building a division. Next he went to the U.S. headquarters in Milwaukee, Wisconsin, and worked in various departments, including marketing, corporate sales, and operations. "For me it was a trial by fire, but my father had the right balance of knowing when to give someone an opportunity and when to back off," says Goodman. When he returned to home base in 1979, he was no longer just the boss's son. Instead, he had proved himself elsewhere, had earned credibility and developed expertise that could be applied to many areas of the family business. Goodman became president four years ago, and in 1993, he bought out his father. "It could almost be a study in successful family succession," says Goodman.

Former Bank of Montreal CEO Bill Mulholland once captured the need to be both astute and cold-blooded in assessing the capacity of the next generation when he said, "The question is, can you mass produce? Do you want to achieve a self-perpetuating process, one that goes on after you walk out? The ultimate accolade is when they say, 'Mulholland, we don't need you anymore.' Like man's earliest effort, you have created a tool that can be used over and over again. In fact, there's no way of knowing how you did until after you've left."

Summary:

1. Family members must be involved from the beginning; no latecomers are allowed unless they're prepared to start in learning roles.

2. Duties must be carefully delegated and everyone must know who's responsible for what. If possible, family should report to nonfamily.

3. Keep communications open and honest; keep home life separate.

4. Don't let emotions interfere with the business.

5. Plan succession in sufficient time to make the generational transition as seamless as possible – both for the family and the financials.

CHAPTER 6

Franchising: For Yourself, but Not by Yourself

"There is no magical, perfect franchisee.
The most important thing is an open mind."

– Dennis Klein

T he relentless expansion of new restaurants in Canada seems to know no bounds. The pattern of growth amazes even Jim Treliving, president of Boston Pizza International Inc., a restaurant-franchise operation based in Richmond, British Columbia. "When I grew up, eating out was an occasion," he says. "Now, kids eat out 90 per cent of the time, and when they do eat at home, they want to eat what they eat out." According to Treliving, who owns Boston Pizza with longtime partner and vice-president George Melville, a new restaurant franchise needs a community of ten thousand people, combined with a surrounding trading area that adds another ten thousand mouths. "I don't think there's a ceiling on the food industry," he says. "Canadians treat restaurants as a second arm of their home."

Boston Pizza was launched in 1963 in Edmonton and, by

the end of 1994, had forty-eight hundred employees working in ninety-two outlets with twelve more under construction and plans for a further twenty. Sales had reached $95 million a year or 13-per-cent growth every year since 1983, when Treliving and Melville – who were then franchisees themselves – bought the firm from previous owner Ron Coyle of Edmonton. The two men paid $3 million, an amount they raised from private lenders. The chain is currently expanding east from its longtime beachhead in Thunder Bay, Ontario, and south into Washington.

Franchising is now a $90-billion-a-year business in Canada. About 40 per cent of every retail dollar spent in Canada goes to a franchise operation. The main benefit of franchising is that, while you're in business for yourself, you're not all by yourself. Rather than having to go out and reinvent the wheel, you've got the backing of an already-existing organization that can help you negotiate leases, arrange bank financing, train you and your staff, and supply everything from inventory to computer systems.

Treliving, age fifty, a former drum major in the RCMP band, opened his chain's first franchise outlet in Penticton, British Columbia, in 1965. That's where he met Melville, a chartered accountant who did his books. By the time they bought the firm, the two men owned sixteen of the thirty-six existing outlets, but sold all sixteen to new franchisees. "We felt we had to concentrate on the franchising and become a management-consulting firm," says Treliving, who now has a head office staff of forty. "We didn't want to compete against people we were trying to recruit. Our purpose was not to look after *our* stores – we look after other peoples' stores. There's no favouritism."

At Boston Pizza the typical franchisee tends to be a man (only seven are women) who has seen a lifelong career snuffed out by a large firm because of downsizing. They've received

golden handshakes or a similar payout that flows over a one-
or two-year period, so have money to invest in a new venture.
"Most of them are in the mid-forties, and they got whacked
by the company. They say to themselves, 'I don't want to start
with another firm and have the same thing happen ten years
from now; I don't want to work for anybody ever again,'" says
Treliving.

But a franchise like Boston Pizza doesn't come cheap. Each
new investor needs $200,000 in unencumbered capital (which
means you can't go out and borrow that part of the required
payment), an agreement whereby the landlord pays for
$200,000 worth of leasehold improvements to the property,
and a $200,000 bank loan. Boston Pizza helps line up the bank
loan, but strong first-year pretax profits — which usually run to
$150,000 — mean that a franchisee can begin to pay back the
start-up loan in that first year.

"They make an investment based on a three-year payoff,"
says Treliving, who notes that the spouse and offspring often
join in with the franchise holder to create an instant family
business. "Probably their best partner is their wife. She's
usually well educated and ready to get involved, because the
family's grown up." There's two months' training and two
meetings each year attended by all franchisees, but, even with
all that coaching, not every new franchise-holder succeeds.
"We don't blow them out the door, but there's about eight or
ten we're working with to try and find a buyer so they can get
their money back." The outlets themselves aren't usually the
problem, it's the people running them. And that can't be predicted until the franchise holder is in place. Says Treliving, "It
isn't until they're under pressure that you know how people
are going to react."

Start-up tip: *No amount of pre-testing can identify the
potential failures.*

Franchisees have to be prepared to run a full-service restaurant. As with most fast-food outlets, Boston Pizza serves more than just what its name implies. Outlets average 5,500 square feet and items include other pasta dishes as well as soups, salads, sandwiches, ribs, snacks, and desserts. All the outlets also have bars that produce about 30 per cent of the total $1.1 million in annual sales, a per-unit average that the firm claims is the highest in the franchise industry and 10-per-cent higher than second-place Pizza Hut.

Franchisees also need to be able to identify, hire, and train a constant stream of new employees, because at Boston Pizza the slogan is "Service with the works." Again, head office offers plenty of backup support once the local franchise has picked the right people. Each new employee receives a handbook supplied by head office that opens with the message "Nobody leaves unhappy. Whether you work here or eat here as a customer." In order to find out how customers are reacting, clients are constantly measured, using what the company calls the Guest Enjoyment Meter, which combines phone surveys, comment cards, silent shoppers, focus groups, and full-time quality-control personnel. Top-ranking outlets get prizes that run to $400 in cash per employee at the winning franchise. Every employee's performance is reviewed annually, and each receives direct feedback from the franchise holder. The individual findings are all personally reviewed by Treliving and Melville.

As Treliving says, new franchise outlets don't very often fail, although some of the people owning and operating those outlets do come up short. For the entrepreneur then, the odds for success are better working with a franchise operation than simply launching a business on your own. According to government statistics, 90 per cent of all franchises are still going concerns after ten years – about five times the success rate of independent businesses. By the year 2000, franchised businesses will likely account for more than half of all Canadian retail sales with sales in restaurants like Boston Pizza creating the most dynamic of the franchise sectors.

Not only does a franchise mean built-in friends at head office, firms in the system can actually get along without having to rely on banks. The eighty-six outlets of Fountain Tire Ltd., based in Edmonton, use what's called a "concentration account," where cash is gathered daily from all the stores and pays interest at prime, a rate that's always several points higher than the interest that is paid depositors. If one of the stores needs money for renovation, for example, the store draws those funds from that pool and again pays prime rate on the debt.

A similar cooperative approach at Fountain helps managers buy a share of the outlet they run, once they've proved their capacity, usually after a year or more in the role. "There's no point in someone becoming a shareholder if they haven't demonstrated the ability to earn a profit," says Fountain president Brian Hesje. Fountain guarantees the necessary $500,000 bank loan taken out by the owner-manager, who also contributes a relatively modest $10,000 of his own money. "We're looking for expertise, not capital," says Hesje. "If there's no investment, people take things for granted." After tax, an owner-manager can make in excess of $100,000 annually.

Like Boston Pizza, new franchise owners at Fountain tend to be former middle managers in their forties who have been fired from large companies. The compensation package they get goes a long way towards buying into a business that will mean they don't ever have to worry about being fired again. Support they receive from the franchiser makes them feel as comfortable as they did in a large corporation, where help was usually handy and decisions were made by groups – or someone else higher up.

Benefits of becoming a franchisee:
• less risk because you're involved with a proven business;
• economies of scale; you buy what you need based on prices that have been negotiated on the huge volumes of the entire chain;
• others are developing and test-marketing new products for you;
• no special skills or knowledge in the particular product or service area are required;
• financing packages are available; some of the banks even have franchising experts who are already familiar with the particular program;
• site-selection help; and
• backup teams provide ongoing assistance and problem-solving.

Drawbacks:
• even after you're up and running and feel you could be okay on your own, you'll still be paying royalties to the franchiser;
• decisions may be made with which you disagree, but you'll have to buckle under anyway;
• the system may feel too rigid to you and snuff out the very entrepreneurial flair you had;
• rules about selling the business will be very strict; you may not be able to get out when you want; and
• fellow franchise-holders could cause trouble for you if they don't maintain business standards as high as yours.

There are always unscrupulous franchisers looking for a chance to take money from the unwary, either in the form of up-front fees or ongoing royalties; these scammers deliver little or nothing in return. The Canadian Franchise Association has a kit called "Investigate Before Investing" that anyone considering a franchise purchase will find useful (see page 286). Still, franchise deals can become more than just a business for you or your family: they can become international empires, as this next case study shows.

Case study: Body language

In 1979, when Margot Franssen was a twenty-seven-year-old philosophy student in her graduating year at York University, someone gave her a gift basket of cosmetics from The Body Shop in the United Kingdom. Franssen's first thought – to copy the idea – was soon replaced by a plan to investigate the concept thoroughly. Her husband-to-be, Quig Tingley, a T-bill trader with stockbroker McLeod, Young & Weir, bought her a ticket to England, where Franssen visited all seven stores then in The Body Shop empire. Once she saw the shops, she knew she had to know more. "There was a song in the air," she recalls. "I knew the tune, but I didn't know the words."

To learn the lyrics, she visited Body Shop founders Anita and Gordon Roddick at their home in Little Hampton, West Sussex, for dinner. After dinner and numerous brandies, Gordon finally asked Franssen at 2:30 A.M. what exactly she wanted. "I don't want just one store," said the appropriately fortified Franssen, "I want all of Canada or nothing." Came the swift reply, "You've got it."

Franssen returned to Canada and contacted her younger sister, Betty-Ann, who at nineteen had just finished high school in Edmonton. The two sisters opened the first store on a shoestring nine months later, after doing all the painting and preparation work themselves. Tingley joined in the third year of the business, and today The Body Shop has 106 stores in Canada and 27 in the northeastern United States, where Franssen's operations expanded after completing another deal with the Roddicks which covered that area. Total sales amount to more than $120 million a year.

Franssen paid no money for the North American franchise

– the U.K. partners prosper by supplying their products for resale – but new franchises are expensive. The cost of opening a Body Shop outlet is now $300,000, and includes nine weeks of staff training. Stores then buy cosmetics, haircare items, soaps, and creams from a central source. They are all made without animal testing, a key marketing tool. Franssen has relied on gut instinct for business decisions and, since they do no advertising, word of mouth to attract customers.

To be as successful as Franssen, you need chutzpah and toughmindedness to face real-estate developers. "When we were young and nothing, they wanted us to take rotten locations," she says. "When we were rich and famous, they wanted us to take poor locations to spice up a traffic area."

Get professional advice

Buying into a franchise or an existing firm can produce a ready-made package for you, but, as noted, either approach has drawbacks. If someone has a business for sale, you'd better understand why. If the company is successful, why is the owner bailing out? Professional advice is essential. At the very least, you'll want to pay for an independent audit of the books.

You can hardly overdo the basic research in order to find out what sort of standing the business has in the community. Buying a business is no different than buying a used car; you may simply be acquiring someone else's headache. The current owner's banker (or other investment backer, if there is one) is an essential reference point. Don't let the banker beg off on the basis of confidentiality; with the current owner's permission, the banker should be free to share all financial information with you.

Franchise laws in many provinces are loose. Don't count on much government support if you get into a dispute. Alberta has the toughest disclosure requirements. The Canadian Franchise Association has begun work towards more self-regulation in the industry by preparing disclosure documents, an ethics code, and guidelines for members (see page 286).

For the most part, however, you're on your own when it comes to investigating the franchise in which you're interested. Remember, disputes between franchisers and their franchisees are commonplace. For example, there are often concerns about how money collected from all the franchise holders is being spent on national advertising. Because you have a central source of supply, there can be questions about pricing. And what happens if another outlet of the same franchise is granted permission to open in a location that's very near to yours?

So investigate carefully before you invest. Other franchise holders are excellent sources of information about the particular company you're considering, but here are some other ideas on where to turn when you're checking into your potential investment, whether it's a few thousand dollars in a going concern local business or $500,000 for a nationally known fast-food outlet.

Information sources:

- current employees, customers, and suppliers;
- local trade associations;
- Better Business Bureau;
- credit-rating agencies such as Dun & Bradstreet;
- business neighbours; and
- newspaper files.

Here's what you want to discover:

- the reputation of the business and the expertise of current management;
- rent arrangements, equipment leases, and other similarly ongoing commitments;

• past problems, either public or private;
• labour or other personnel difficulties;
• transferability of sales contracts and supplier agreements;
• location of outlets and prospects for growth in the business in the next year, and in the next five years; and
• level of competition in that field, and the government regulations you'll have to follow – including tax risks.

As a prospective franchisee, here are some questions that you should also ask yourself:

• can I fit into a system where everything is tightly regimented?
• can I train staff to fit into that same system?
• how well do I know the franchise and the current franchise holders? and
• is the contract I sign for life, or are there escape hatches along the way that allow me to realize a capital gain on my initial investment?

Case study: Dollar daze

The launch couldn't have been less auspicious. There was Dennis Klein in 1987, a twenty-seven-year-old accounting dropout, running a dollar store in the decidedly downscale Dixie Value Mall in Mississauga. With his stock on the main floor and a cramped office upstairs, Klein worked long hours each week, bringing in close-out merchandise (end-of-line goods, manufacturers' over-runs, and other one-off items) for resale in the $1 to $2 price range. But despite the modest beginnings, first-year sales amounted to $400,000, healthy enough that Klein not only survived and made a living but, in subsequent years, has also been able to franchise the idea to others. In 1994, he opened the hundredth store (in Quesnel,

British Columbia) in his national retail chain known as A Buck or Two! with its head office in Concord. "We're the Birks of dollar stores," says Klein, who is chairman, president, and CEO of what he sees as the class act of dollar stores. "It's a shopping release without spending much money."

Klein worked first for his father at Magnasonic Canada, an electronics wholesaler; then, in 1985, he founded Denninghouse Ltd., a company that purchased close-out merchandise in the United States for resale to Canadian retailers. While he was attending a close-out convention in Chicago, Klein concluded that there was a trend towards close-out stores and decided to jump aboard. In 1987, he borrowed $25,000 from his father for the first store, got a $100,000 line of credit at the bank co-signed by his father, founded A Buck or Two! and has tried to stay out of debt since. "I absolutely abhor debt," says Klein. By 1989, he owned stores at four locations. At the same time he was moving away from close-out goods to regularly available items, all with prices under $5, most at $1 or $2, a concept Klein calls "value retailing."

Individuals were asking how to join his system, so Klein sold his first franchise that year. By 1992, there were thirty-three franchises; in 1993, he added forty more, thereby proving that he had a new idea that successfully belittled the recession. "I have to admit, when I first met him I had doubts about dollar stores," says Howard Bloomberg, president of Encore Sales of Concord, one of two hundred firms supplying goods to the chain. "But he's a very determined young man, and he's achieved his goals. Offering new items is the key. They are impulse stores, not destination stores." That's why A Buck or Two! locates in malls with traffic-building anchors like K mart Canada Ltd. or Zellers Inc., focuses on small and medium-sized cities with value-conscious citizens, and keeps operating costs modest. Sales in 1993 were $33 million; in 1994, they were $51 million.

Typical stock includes greeting cards, gift wrap, party items (plastic cutlery, napkins, balloons), toys, candy, crafts, housewares, and toiletries, as well as seasonal items for holidays such as Easter and Christmas. China is the source of 40 per cent of all items; a further 40 per cent is imported from Indonesia, India, Malaysia, and Mexico, with 10 per cent each from Canada and the United States. "There will always be a market for this type of store," says Jack Caplan, vice-president of sales for Tye-Sil Corp. of Montreal. "Dollar stores feasting on closeouts will have a difficult time once the economy gets better. His secret is constantly putting new product in the stores."

In November 1993, Klein took A Buck or Two! public at $5.875 per share. The initial public offering raised almost $10 million and, because Klein had no debt at the time, all the money was available to develop a new computerized ordering system for the stores, to study new retailing concepts, and to finance possible acquisitions. Share price rose to $6.375 before the January 1994 announcement that Wal-Mart Inc. had purchased 122 Woolco stores and was coming to Canada. After that, stock value spent a year in the $3.00 range, but executives of the franchise argue that Wal-Mart will help, not hurt, the stores. "They don't concentrate on dollar merchandise," says Bob Poirier, vice-president of operations of A Buck or Two! "I'd like to be next door to every one of their stores. We survive on traffic." A Buck or Two! has stores in 25 per cent of the malls where Wal-Mart is located. (The corporate name under which the stock is listed was changed in 1995 to Denninghouse; the store names remain the same.)

The retailing venture has paid off for Klein personally. He holds three million of the company's shares, receives an annual salary of $250,000, and takes hefty annual bonuses: $300,000 in 1993; $800,000 in 1992. Says Keith Pope, president of Keefco Sales, a Mississauga greeting-card supplier, "He's been one of the pioneers in the dollar stores, and he's the leader now."

For franchisees, the $150,000 investment can also be very lucrative. Stores average $560,000 in annual sales; six of them do over $1 million. Many owner-operators earn $80,000 annually from profit and salary. "It definitely has exceeded our expectations," says Kerri Cannon of Victoria, who employs six people in her Tillicum Mall store.

Buying into the concept also means freedom. "I like the idea of being able to go home early every once in a while and have a lemonade," says Wayne Cuttress, a former purchasing agent whose store in Windsor's Tecumseh Mall opened in 1991. It has twenty-two employees and tops all the outlets in the seven-province chain with $1.3 million in annual sales.

But the freedom of being your own boss is accompanied by demands. During start-ups and busy seasons, seventy-hour weeks are common. "Make sure this is what you want to do. This isn't like a clothing store, where you get your inventory and sit back and wait," Cuttress says. "You get stock in every day. Everything needs to be priced and merchandised. It never stops."

Competition comes from local independents and regional chains in the twenty- to forty-store range like Everything for a Dollar and Dollar Bill's. "There are a lot of these dollar stores, but A Buck or Two! seems to have found a niche, competing in smaller urban centres," says Art Anderson, manager of national franchising at the CIBC. The bank has established a special program for potential franchisees, so that individual branches aren't reinventing the wheel every time a new prospect approaches them for start-up debt in a chain they already know. When a franchisee visits a branch, the CIBC sends that local manager the applicable lending guidelines, so the manager is familiar with the particular concept and knows that head office is comfortable with the company.

Individuals must still meet stiff criteria when approaching banks. "We're very selective on franchisees we do business with," says Anderson. Typically, a franchisee needs $150,000 for inventory, leasehold arrangements, and working capital. (At $300,000 each, Tim Horton Donuts franchises cost twice as much. Midas Muffler shops go for $225,000. A McDonald's opening will cost $700,000, including the franchise fee.) Whatever franchise you're interested in, any bank will insist that you have one-third down in unencumbered equity, with some money left over. "We don't like to see a franchisee putting every nickel into a venture," says Anderson. Some of the financing (for store fixtures, for example) can come under government small-business loans, but the bank will usually demand collateral, such as a mortgage on the home. Funds in Registered Retirement Savings Plans cannot be used as collateral.

Klein says that he prefers new franchise holders with no previous retail experience. "It's sometimes easier to train people than to break bad habits," he says. A Buck or Two! offers new franchisees five weeks' training, including two of those weeks in one of the stores in the chain. There is also layout and merchandising help, regular visits from a field consultant, two buying conventions a year – plus the most important element, four binders containing thousands of items available for their store. Each store then places its individual orders with the suppliers based on pre-negotiated prices. Although two hundred suppliers are represented in the binders, forty suppliers tend to be the most popular. Most stores stock about four thousand SKUs (stock-keeping units). "It's a lot more sophisticated business than it appears," says Klein. In 1994, Klein launched Complements . . . Your Accessory Store, a bed, bath, and body boutique for women, with products under $10. "You've got to believe in yourself, but you've got to listen to what's happening," Klein says. "Roar ahead, but be flexible. You have to have an angle and you can't be scared to take chances. If you're ever bored, you're probably not developing the [franchising] concept properly."

Case study: Painting the town

Greig Clark launched College Pro Painters in 1971 in Thunder Bay as a summer job while he was at university. He knocked on doors to get business, and when he finally did find someone who was interested in having her house painted, she asked for a quote. He suddenly realized that he had no idea how to draw up an estimate. Recalled Clark, "So you learn what all entrepreneurs do – to wing it." The figure $390 popped into his mind, and that became the number he used for estimates on several of those first jobs that he was able to land based on the force of his personality and presentation, not because he could demonstrate talent. "You need commitment and competence," Clark says. "Build number two before you run out of number one."

That first summer he made $3,000, the next summer, $7,000, the third summer, $13,000. After graduation he worked at General Foods and built College Pro on the side until 1977, when he had success by picking other university students to run painting businesses in six Ontario test markets. Then he quit his day job, and within a year Clark had twenty franchise arrangements. Students used a manual he had written, but they were all entrepreneurs and ran their own businesses just as he had. By 1989, when sales had reached nearly $40 million, with five thousand students in six hundred franchises across North America, Clark decided it was time to move on. At thirty-seven, he needed a change from helping students get rolling. "All night beer-ups with twenty-two-year-olds left a different taste in my mouth," he says. Moreover, his wife finally asked him, "Where's the twinkle in your eye? I married a man with fire in his eyes, and I want him back."

Clark sold out his interest to management. "I'm starting all over again," he says, "right back at the beginning." He took a year off, lived in France, and now regards that period as a necessary, if fallow, time. "It was not immediately apparent that it was the right thing to do. Life doesn't always perk up right away." Clark felt he was riding a J-curve that has to go down before it eventually comes back up again. In the end, Clark decided to help other entrepreneurs get started by supplying venture capital – usually less than $1 million – through a Toronto-based firm called Horatio Enterprise Fund. His advice to fellow start-ups:

- trust yourself and your instincts;
- do what you love and success will follow; and
- surround yourself with a few key people who love you and can tell you the truth.

Clark says that football coach Vince Lombardi called those key people his "Armageddon Squadron" – the group he wanted by his side when he marched off to meet his maker. "This group will be different for all of us. For me, it was my wife, my mother, and a few trusted friends. The concrete platform on which all else is built is that you trust them to truly have your best interests at heart."

Summary:

1. Franchising isn't like going on your own; you have to follow someone else's regimented system.
2. Research the franchise carefully to make sure that particular operation is right for you.
3. Don't invest every last penny; keep some cash in reserve.
4. Be prepared to work seventy-hour weeks; family members may have to work equally hard.
5. Be flexible; don't be afraid to take chances.

CHAPTER 7

Contact Sport:
Getting Close to the Customer

"You don't have to spend megabucks, you just
have to be single-minded and listen to the customer."

– Amy Friend, ATS Aerospace

In the 1985 film *Back to the Future*, Michael J. Fox's character returns to a place and time more than two decades earlier. As he lurches about the central square of the small town, unable to comprehend exactly where or when he is, one vignette immediately makes it clear that it sure can't be the present day. In the background, a car pulls up to a gas pump and a flurry of uniformed attendants who had been standing at attention come charging towards the vehicle. They swarm about the car and, within seconds, the hood's up, the windshield's being washed, tires are checked, and the gas is merrily flowing. When the film first played in theatres, the scene looked so antiquated that some members of the audiences guffawed at the fond recollection. After all, that's why those places got their names: service stations. Today, everything's self-serve – as if that's the way consumers want all business to be.

Yet, according to just about every survey conducted, what Canadians really want is good service.

If that's the case, succeeding in business should be surprisingly simple. All you have to do is convince people to part with their money and feel so good about doing so that they tell others what a terrific experience it was to deal with you and your firm. When that happens, over and over again, your business will grow. "Stay really close to the customer," says Boyd Stevens, president of Calgary-based Cyba Stevens Mandate Inc., a food and drug broker. "We had a tendency in the early days to go get caught up in our shorts by trying to please the manufacturer – the companies we represented. We learned to spend more time with customers and play back what we were hearing from them to the companies, rather than the other way."

Whether the economic times are good or bad, everyone worries about creating jobs in Canada. Politicians looking for tax revenue, businesspeople looking for growth, people looking for work – everyone is interested in jobs. While entrepreneurs like to think of themselves as the source of jobs, in fact, *customers create jobs*. Without customers, there would be no need for the products or services your young firm is providing. Jobs are created when you, as an entrepreneur, hire people to meet demand in the marketplace.

The successful business owner talks to lots of people every day. The more people you talk to, the more likely you are to find someone who will buy from you. The store with the most traffic does the most volume. Often *you* have to generate that traffic. Once you've captured their attention, it's important to your customers that you be cheerful. Don't tell the world your troubles. If the weather's bad, don't complain about it to everyone you see. Be positive and people will respond in a similarly positive manner. After all, without customers, your expertise is worthless. "The customer will tell you what's missing in the market," says Amy Friend of ATS Aerospace.

What's missing in the market may be right in your own kitchen. For years, Renée Unger had made salad dressings as gifts. Friends and relatives began pressing her for more jars of her creations, so, in 1985, she decided to turn her hobby into Intercorp Foods Inc. of Toronto. "My first love turned out to be my last love," Unger says. Her blue cheese, Russian, and four other types of dressings quickly caught the wave of public interest in healthy, preservative-free food. Consumer surveys, in-store tastings, and careful monitoring of what sold offered guidance. "I never lost sight of the consumer. I believe in the intelligence of the consumer," she says. "Too many people believe in the marketability of a product."

Start-up tip: *Believe in the customer more than you believe in yourself.*

Unger began by selling to local food retailers north of Toronto, but, as Loblaws and other large chains signed on, the business grew. By 1988, Intercorp had moved to a 35,000-square-foot manufacturing facility capable of producing twenty thousand bottles of dressing a day. As Intercorp added sauces, sales grew, and the firm moved again in 1993, this time into an 80,000-square-foot building. Along the way, Unger's learning curve grew ever steeper. With a growing number of products on the shelves, she realized that customer tastes were more adventuresome than she had imagined. Unger also learned how to profit from blunders. "I never think I've made a mistake; I regard it as a learning experience," Unger says. "You learn how to deal with adversity. Now I look at situations and say, 'I can deal with that.' Fifteen years ago, I would've wanted to go back to bed."

A first lesson for young firms is that customers want quick responses, especially on products or services being offered by telephone. Callers should not have to wait through many rings, track their way through a long voice-response system, then get tossed from one customer-service representative to another. At Toronto's Rider Travel, no phone is allowed to ring more than three times before that incoming call is answered by a counsellor. Once the firm is dealing with a customer, they try to ensure that there are no mistakes. The firm has achieved an error ratio (defined as a wrong quote or a routing mistake) of 1 per cent. To get to that level, Rider sends a quality-control card along with every ticket mailed out, asking for the client's views on the service received.

Customers need to feel that they are an important part of the process. Your best asset is a happy customer, so regularly ask customers these three questions: What did you like? What didn't you like? What would you like? Service is the only way one travel firm can set itself apart from another, argues president Mark Rider. "The market has become more competitive and aggressive," he says. "Everybody has access to the technology." Listening carefully to the customer is one of the ways Rider responds. Twice a year, Rider senior management meets with an advisory council consisting of ten corporate clients for a morning feedback session. As well, internal reports that measure changes in service levels are carried out every quarter, and each client receives a formal annual satisfaction review.

Start-up tip: *Fulfil customers' dreams and exceed their expectations.*

Rider also hires personnel carefully. A typical travel firm hires young staff, sends them on familiarization trips so they see some of the destinations they book, and hopes for the best. Instead, Rider's seventy top managers all have government or corporate backgrounds that are similar to the clients with whom they deal. "As a result, the contact is more empathetic," says Rider, who calls the technique "adaptive listening. . . .We can interpret what the clients say."

Competitive pricing is another way the company tries to make customers happy. Corporate and government clients get price breaks through service contracts with Rider – up to 24 per cent off the lowest economy airfares. Hotel-room rates can be 25-per-cent to 40-per-cent lower than "rack," or regular, rates. For government employees, room reductions can reach 50 per cent.

For Rider, the whole package he's creating at his firm makes him feel ready for any and all competitors. "A travel agency is seen as a mom-and-pop industry. It's an industry that's been traditional for too long. There's more to it than answering the phone, supplying a ticket, and knowing something about Hawaii. We'll reinvent the travel business," he says. "We're not afraid of the future."

But all the good service in the world won't work if potential customers don't know that your firm exists, so remind them regularly through advertising, promotion, and sales calls. Don't expect people to remember your firm, even if they have been patrons in the past. "Business is a contact sport. You have to tell your customer over and over again how good your product is," says Mary Black of Colour Technologies. "And the product your factory must produce is long-term customers."

One of the ways of doing that is to hire a public-relations firm to offer advice about raising awareness in your firm. "You no longer need to explain to CEOs the contribution that PR can make," says Luc Beauregard, president of National Public Relations. "But clients expect more for the same money. We do as well as we used to, but we have to work twice as hard," adds Beauregard, who founded the Montreal-based firm in 1976. Annual billings are now in excess of $15 million from clients such as Molson Companies, Provigo Distribution, BioChem Pharma, National Bank, Laidlaw Inc., and Ro-na Disnat Group, the Quebec-based hardware chain.

Presentation costs have been driven sky high by the combination of stiffer competition from other PR firms and the fact that many companies assess several communications consultants before signing a contract. In 1993, National won a four-year, $10-million contract from Hydro-Quebec for an energy-saving program. National's preparation work for the bid ran to $150,000, an expense that would not have been recouped if the firm had lost out in the competition. "Business comes to us with bigger problems but they want a lot for their money," says Beauregard.

The result is that firms no longer hire National on a flat-fee basis then blithely mail off a monthly retainer – even if little or no work has been done. Instead, clients are more likely to want project-oriented work and insist that the team include specific professionals with recognized expertise. That means no more bait-and-switch, where the top people pitch the business and juniors do the dog work. As a result, PR firms and professional consultants of all sorts need to have more expertise in particular sectors, such as financial services or health care. "The old PR generalist doesn't sell these days," says Beauregard.

But you can't totally turn over your image to others. Dealing with prospective clients or current customers also demands all your personal skills of persuasion. Rejection can be depressing, but you can also turn that to your advantage. "Don't resist resistance," says Peter Lowe, a Miami-based Canadian who tours North America, giving pep talks to salespeople and others looking for ways to improve their lives. "Embrace it, dance with it, and feed it back. Use phrases like 'I appreciate,' 'I respect,' 'I agree' that deflect the resistance. Never say, 'I understand.' They won't believe you. Turn the circumstance that's a stumbling block into a stepping stone."

But how do you to create those stepping stones to success? "You have to be focused," says Emmie Leung of International

Paper. Leung says that reaching customers requires unlimited persistence and patience. "Whatever happens, you keep going, rain or shine. You make a commitment to yourself and to the project. There are no secrets, you just keep plugging away." That kind of leadership also motivates staff to act in the same way, to follow your vision. "Once you've established the direction, and have your staff at the same mental level, you're on your way," says Leung.

In their book *Raving Fans: A Revolutionary Approach to Customer Service*, co-authors Ken Blanchard (*The One-Minute Manager*) and Sheldon Bowles (a Winnipeg entrepreneur) describe the usual problem people find with companies: "Service stinks. Nobody gives a hoot. Rude is in. Smiling's a sin. Nowhere is it worse than at your company." Their argument is that satisfied customers aren't enough. "Today you need Raving Fans. You have to create Raving Fans to be successful." Instead, consumers have actually come to expect poor-quality goods and indifferent service. Blanchard and Bowles offer three pieces of advice.

1. Discover what the customer wants.
2. Create a vision of perfection centred on the customer.
3. Deliver plus one, meaning 1 per cent. A 1-per-cent improvement in customer service every week means a 50-per-cent improvement in a year.

Happy is as happy does

The best route to happy customers is a happy staff in your own business. If your own people are happy, they'll be delivering quality products and service. Proper employee training builds bridges to customers, says Boyd Stevens of Cyba Stevens Mandate. "One of the things we did badly was not to train our people. For three years we just had an informal training program. Now there's a full in-house program that includes information about our company, geared to people we're trying to hire. We'll tell them – warts and all – what we're trying to match them with. If it doesn't work for both of us, we won't proceed."

Measuring employee satisfaction is not easy, but some temperature-taking should be an ongoing part of your management technique, so that you can spot problems early and move to correct them. There's lots more to employee relations, enough to fill the next chapter, but meanwhile, here's a six-point questionnaire you should administer to every employee every month. You might even try this one on yourself.

1. Do you have a meaningful job, one that satisfies you and makes you feel part of a whole?
2. Do you know what's expected of you? Are the measuring sticks that are applied to that expectation fair?
3. Is appropriate training available to deal with the work or service that you're supposed to be delivering?
4. Is your career path going in the direction you want?
5. Have you received either positive or negative feedback from your boss in the last thirty days? If the news was negative, were you told specific, constructive steps you could take to change the situation?
6. Are there any personal barriers – such as age, race, disability, or gender – that prevent you from doing your job?

Unhappy staff, poor morale, and indifferent service can hurt any firm, but the problems are particularly obvious in Canadian retailing. "There's been a cultural malaise in the Canadian retail environment. We haven't treated staff as professionals," says Jeff Otis, president of Grand National Apparel. As far as he's concerned the trouble with Canadian retailing is, well, Canadian retailing. That failure in turn has meant poor service for customers. Free trade with the United States and increased cross-border shopping has meant that many Canadians have seen firsthand what service can be like in the more competitive American environment. With the arrival of aggressive U.S. retailers, such as Wal-Mart and Price Club, Canadian firms are realizing that they have to become better merchandisers. "There's a big lesson to be learned," Otis says. "Customers want to be treated well."

Know your product

One of the benefits of starting a business based on a hobby is that you, as a user, know much more about what your customers might want. Because both Leonard and Robin Lee of Lee Valley Tools are hobbyists who work with the tools themselves, they know what's needed and what works. "We're users, not just pushers," says Leonard. He is cool towards using television home-shopping networks for his products, arguing that Lee Valley's audience is not the type who will watch much TV. "People buy from us to get away from today's technology. Our catalogues are literate to a fault," he says, adding with a laugh, "I know. I write most of the copy. People want to know if we tolerate an item or recommend it. They read the catalogue and know our degree of enthusiasm."

Start-up tip: *Test-market products and services on yourself before you inflict them on customers.*

You should treat staff as professionals, ensure proper training is available, and let them participate in ownership and benefit from increasing profits so that their joy in the job is readily apparent to customers. For example, Lee Valley tries to be different from other retailers by offering employee training for product knowledge. His more than two hundred employees are told to "treat the customer like a friend" and to solve a customer's problem in the most economical way possible – even if that means pointing out a competitor's line. "If he already has his mind made up, let him buy what he wants, but if he asks for a recommendation, give him an honest one – don't overload him with product," warns Lee in the employee hand-book. "If he wants to overload himself, that's his business. Maybe he is a tool collector." Just like Leonard Lee.

The technological edge

Customers have also come to expect the best in technology; you'd better have the most up-to-date systems if you want to survive. Grand National Apparel, supplier of menswear lines such as Haggar, Arnold Palmer, and London Fog to Sears, Eaton's, and The Bay, has bet the future on technology. Rather than simply deal with an individual who's a store buyer, Grand National has established strategic-partnership committees in broad areas such as marketing, accounting, and technology. Electronic links mean, for example, that Eaton's can do what's called "automatic replenishment" by transmitting orders elec-tronically to Grand National every Friday. Grand National ships to all ninety Eaton's stores across the country the follow-ing Wednesday.

The technology means more choice for retail customers and sales increases for Grand National in the 25-per-cent range annually – all with no additional office staff. Total employment is about one hundred, with sales of $15 million. The firm's long-standing partnership with the U.S.-based Haggar has allowed Grand National to ride trends early. "The major, suc-cessful U.S. retailers, like Wal-Mart, have been technology-driven. Canadians are coming to the same *modus operandi*. If you don't have the technology, you don't do business with them," Otis says.

The true ring of customer service

Whoever your ultimate client is, best practices start with each individual employee. "You need the right attitude to look after the client," says CEO Roger Jarvis of Jarvis Travel. His people are constantly in touch with clients, making sure they are satisfied. "If you don't hear from your customer, you'd better call," he says. That doesn't mean you hound people, but you want to make sure that no news is good news. "We're interested in long-term relationships," he says.

At some firms, a sale is celebrated by ringing a bell to let the other members of staff know that someone has been successful. At Jarvis, a compliment from a client sets off the ringing of a bell, known as "the true ring of customer service." Here are just a few of the specific techniques Jarvis Travel uses to keep tabs on clients and their attitudes:

- Jarvis staff, bearing coffee and donuts, call on clients to see them in their environment, let them know they matter, and discover how service could be improved;
- the firm has created partner plans, a program that brings in office secretaries (the people who often book all travel) to see Jarvis offices, meet staffers, understand the systems;
- a quality-control card, asking key questions about service, is sent with every ticket for return by the client;
- quality-advisory councils, consisting of clients, meet regularly with Jarvis staff and management to offer advice, complaints, ideas, and suggestions for new services; and
- exit interviews are conducted if a client goes elsewhere.

Of course, staff aren't the only people who should be acting as envoys for the firm. The boss has to be leading the way. "CEOs can get sidetracked," says Hector Jacques, CEO of the Jacques Whitford Group of Dartmouth, Nova Scotia. "You can be busy and going home late – but what have you achieved if all that you've done is internal? You have to be out serving clients too."

Here's the credo developed by the environmental-engineering firm: "Clients are the most important visitors on our premises. They are not dependent on us, we are dependent on them. They are not an interruption of our work, they are the purpose of it. A client is not an outsider in our business, but the reason for it. We are not doing our clients a favour by serving them, they are doing us a favour by giving us an opportunity to do so."

Case study: Customs-built

Getting new customers is the only way for any firm to expand. You know what you're going after; you know you can stretch and do the job. If you're working smart, maybe you'll have heard about an opportunity before your competition and have some of the necessary work done before others are as far along. But you also have to decide the following:

- can you make a profit on the job?
- do you have the personnel and necessary raw materials? and
- who is the competition; what are *they* going to be offering?

The problem is that specific contracts, if each is different from the last, can hurt your firm. Here's how one firm learned to work smart for customers and build on what it knew rather than reinvent the wheel every time.

When Rajiv Manucha graduated from the University of Toronto in 1976 with an engineering degree and a master's in business administration, he followed the same path that many ambitious young people took at the time: he joined a large organization. In Manucha's case, he signed on with IBM. As he worked his way through various divisions, including finance, systems, and sales, Manucha could see that the firm known as "Big Blue" was not positioning itself for the future. IBM was a leader in computer hardware, particularly mainframes, the giant behemoths guarded by programmers, but he realized that the future was going to be dominated by personal computers with their own software.

Once Manucha felt sufficiently established to make suggestions, he urged senior executives to steer IBM into software development, so they would have something to put together with the hardware. "There's so much more money on the table," he'd say. His vision of the future found no fans. The reply was always, "We're in the hardware business." So Manucha left IBM in 1982 and launched his own company, Management Systems Resources Inc. (MSR), to develop custom-designed software. During the first five months, operating from the second floor of his Toronto home, he added four staffers, mostly programmers.

Clients in those early days included soft-drink giant Pepsi-Cola and brokerage firm Merrill Lynch. Revenue was flowing into MSR, but there was a root problem. Each job involved custom work; the products didn't have much value to other buyers. In addition, time was required to understand the client well enough to develop the packages they needed. Recalls Manucha, "You had to keep learning a new business." Manucha was also falling into another trap that snares so many entrepreneurs: He was restricting his company's growth by trying to scrimp on employee salaries. Manucha would hire rookie programmers and pay low salaries to keep down costs. Inevitably, once they'd received all their training at MSR, they'd get a better offer for more money elsewhere and leave.

Cash flow always seemed to be a scramble as well. As initial payments from each new contract came in, the money seemed barely able to cover costs for the job just done. MSR would finish work for a client that was worth, say, $40,000, but rather than go on to a larger job worth $50,000, the firm would take the next likely client, even if the contract was worth only $25,000 – just in case nothing else came along. "You keep needing the next job to pay for the last one. As long as you're a typical Canadian firm, you can't get out of this vortex," says Manucha, who claims that a firm can last only three to five years operating like that.

Start-up tip: *Live hand-to-mouth and you'll always be hungry.*

Chasing new customers meant that Manucha had to keep his costs way down. In turn, that meant he wasn't pricing his employees properly. As in most computer consulting businesses, MSR billed the customers more than he paid his staff; that difference supplies the firm's profit. In this case, he was paying $30,000 to an individual in salary then marking that salary up to $50,000 for purposes of billing that employee's time to a client. But that $20,000 gap was not enough to cover all the other costs associated with business. "We were wondering why we weren't making any money," says Maria Sheppard, an anthropology graduate who worked as a programmer and analyst before joining MSR in 1983 to oversee marketing and other internal functions. One rule of thumb says that sales per employee should be $200,000 per person, so MSR's twelve employees in the early start-up period should have been generating annual sales of $2.4 million. Instead, sales were only $500,000.

Profits were certainly not being pinched by Manucha's personal take from the firm. After four years at MSR, he had just begun paying himself the same $30,000 salary he had been receiving at IBM when he quit. He also felt he had structured the firm properly as a sole proprietorship, rather than have a partner. In Manucha's view, partners can sometimes have different and incompatible needs. For example, one partner might have a family, children, and a mortgage; the other might be single, with fewer expenses. If the married partner takes a $50,000 salary out of the firm each year because he needs the income, the single partner might be tempted to draw the same amount. The total would be a drain on available cash. Manucha was clearly the boss and made all the strategic decisions. "It's very difficult to steer if there's two helmsmen," says Sheppard.

Overheads were also in line. Employees worked in Manucha's home before moving to a modest 2,000-square-foot office in downtown Toronto in the fall of 1983. Everything seemed to be going by the book, but profits were slow to come, because MSR staff were spending inordinate amounts of time with each customer to make every software package unique.

In 1986, MSR at last got the break it required to change direction. A Swiss customs broker asked MSR to develop a software package so that the broker could handle imports on behalf of its client firms. Another company heard about the system and bought it too. Even then, with a second sale on what started out to be a custom-made product, Manucha was not convinced he had identified a niche. "Because of machismo, we'd try to do that one-of-a-kind work," says Manucha. "And we'd lose the money we were making on the package." Revenue stalled.

A change in the regulatory environment provided the final piece of the puzzle. Canadian customs regulations were altered in 1986, so any importer could calculate duties and taxes, document them, and pay what was owing, using an electronic system called Customs Automated Data Exchange (CADEX). The change created a business opportunity for MSR because, suddenly, firms no longer needed to use a customs broker. They could look after imports, classification, payment, and paperwork themselves, because CADEX allowed for the computerized transmission and validation of what's known as the B3 form, the heart of the clearance-documentation process. Previously the B3 had to be prepared manually and presented in person where the goods entered Canada. Since the introduction of CADEX, over two-thirds of commercial shipments crossing the border have moved to the new system.

Prior to CADEX, the import-export business was so complex that there were five hundred firms acting as customs brokers, because every company needed brokerage services to negotiate the regulatory minefields. With an alternative now possible to the old system, Manucha realized that he should focus on the customs "package" they had developed, which could be sold to many companies, without incurring new development costs each time. What MSR had was a proprietary item – one that had no competitors, and one that could readily be adapted to any end-user's needs. Over the next half-dozen years, MSR focused on individual end-users and now has $25 million in annual sales, thirty-nine employees, six hundred clients (such as Sony, GE, Firestone, and Alcan) for the firm's rules-based software. "We're not selling software, we're selling a business solution," says Sheppard.

Once Manucha had identified his customer niche, however, there were a few more hurdles to clear. He realized he needed a sales force and assumed he could simply convert some of his programmers into reps and send them out knocking on doors. The switch in roles failed, because the skills of the two jobs are so different. Programmers knew the system, but they had trouble communicating with potential clients. "We paid the salaries and didn't get anywhere," says Manucha.

Finally, MSR hired people with a background in sales and taught them enough about computers so they could successfully interest new clients. At the same time, Manucha realized that the firm needed to supply technical support to clients and upgrade the system regularly to reflect changes in duties and other rules in the tightly regulated world of international trade. That meant new skills had to be hired – but, with care, that worked too. "We discovered we needed a different kind of person, who is happy because he likes solving problems," says Manucha. Combining programmers, marketers, and techies meant that MSR was becoming a radically different company. "The infrastructure changed," he says. "It had to. Without good infrastructure, your product is not well supported and your sales staff is out doing a technical call."

Start-up tip: *Don't 'make do' with staff. Make it work.*

A typical MSR client, Honda Canada Manufacturing, imports twelve hundred to fifteen hundred items monthly from the United States or Japan for its plant in Alliston, Ontario, where Civics have been assembled since 1986. Because Honda is not an auto-pact company, duty must be paid, and so the firm needed a customs broker to figure out tariff categories on items, to assess duties, and to supply paperwork. Brokerage fees ran to $1 million annually. "As we gained experience, we realized there was some potential for savings," says Jim Zwygers, Honda's manager of production control. Since MSR's software was installed in 1993, Honda now has electronic data interchange (EDI) with its U.S. operations and annual brokerage fees are only $200,000, an 80-per-cent drop.

"It's not only the huge savings, it's the control we have over the function," says Zwygers. "Nobody knows the products better than the manufacturer, so we know the right classification for parts." Honda paid about $75,000 for the software, hired one new employee to run the setup, and pays $7,500 annually for MSR's regular upgrades and technical support. That ongoing relationship is another key to MSR's success, because those annual fees also supply about 25 per cent of MSR's revenue.

Getting governments as customers

Successful entrepreneurs, like Mark Rider at Rider Travel, who have landed large government accounts advise against hiring expensive lobbyists to do a sales pitch. Instead, Rider says, you're better off working directly with the bureaucrats who are involved. "If you win it at that level, there's no reason to politick. Bid effectively and you'll be in good shape," he says. "In Ottawa, we took the high road and got to know the politicians later." As a bonus, winning the federal government travel contract meant that Rider developed proprietary software that he's also selling to his travel-industry competitors and corporate customers. Rider has created thirty software engineering jobs and an "automated agent" package that allows reservations without human contact, plus an "automated administrator" package that looks after all the administrative elements of travel, such as budgeting and approvals.

Anyone can bid for federal government business, because every firm in the country is on an even footing. Government business can lead to other work, because potential clients assume that, if you can meet government standards, you must be able to meet theirs. The best method to discover what contracts Ottawa wants to sign is by using the electronic bulletin board called Open Bidding Service (see page 287). This service, updated daily, lists everything the government wants to buy. You can order the necessary documents directly and electronically with a PC and a modem.

If you don't yet have the necessary computer equipment, a publication entitled "Government Business Opportunities" is available by annual subscription. While sales to governments or contracts for work with governments are always welcome, landing them can take time. Decisions are painfully slow, and even if you do win a contract, payment for services you render or goods delivered can be even slower. Invoices to government are often paid only after ninety days.

The process begins when a government department or agency issues a Request for Proposal (RFP). At that point, you should already have done at least some preliminary thinking. Establishing a rapport is important; so is making sure that you understand what they want. If the prospective purchaser will give more details than are in the RFP, try and get them. Appoint a proposal manager (even yourself) to spearhead the effort, and plan everything from what will be in the RFP to how the final presentation will actually look. Remember, you are creating a sales tool, not a technical document.

You should include, in clear, well-written language, the answers to all the questions in the RFP. Watch spelling and grammar. Follow the format of the RFP, because that means you'll address each concern in turn and be speaking to the prospective client in understood rhythms. Include a short company profile, brief biographies of key personnel who will be involved, and some information about other projects you have done that are similar in nature to this one. And make your submission look good. You don't need to trick up the presentation with foolish graphics, but software packages that allow some readable design and different typefaces can yield a professional polish.

Case study: It's in the book

Sometimes you can share customers with a powerful ally. You don't even need a direct relationship. In that way, you piggyback on the loyalties another firm has built with a national customer base and help them build further ties by cross-selling other products or services. TMS Marketing handles merchandise catalogue sales for large department stores, financial institutions, and airlines, so TMS has to keep two groups happy: corporate clients and the buying public. "They want to be in the business with as few hassles as possible," says TMS president Cam Thomson. "If we leave their customers with a good feeling, there's no reason for the client firm to switch to our competitor."

In the past, oil companies would use several direct-marketing firms to offer a variety of products to their credit-card customers. TMS has consolidated all aspects of the direct-response merchandising business. "We've created an infrastructure that's hard to duplicate," says Thomson, whose firm selects merchandise, designs and produces catalogues, finds the target audiences, and fulfils phone and mail orders for a wide range of corporate clients such as Air Canada, American Express, Imperial Oil, and the Hudson's Bay Co. All of the customers of those companies have a value that can be tapped because of the trusting relationship that has been built up. Just as a movie star will endorse a product and give that item stature it wouldn't otherwise have had, people will buy items being offered by an airline because some of the value of the customer's relationship with the airline rubs off onto the sale item. As a result, a catalogue of consumer items backed by a well-known institution will have a lustre not possible if they were offered by a local merchant.

Because TMS does everything, including inventorying the items, the high-profile client has no costs, and 5 to 20 per cent of the purchase price (depending on the promotion) flows right to the client's bottom line. Best-selling items include camcorders, TVs, stereos, and silver-plate flatware. "Old-style luxury items like jewellery and executive toys are no longer successful. Brand-name value is," he says. TMS tries to ship orders within forty-eight hours of receiving them. "We're trying to move the industry," he says. "We don't want to continue the four-to-six-week shipment that's common. We're dealing with a spur-of-the-moment decision. If [customers] get the product in three days, they're happy." For TMS, such buyer pleasure translates into lower return rates on what's shipped.

Cocooning, the nineties phenomenon that means people stay home rather than go out to shop, has been a boon for TMS. "The economic problems we've had have been a shock to the psyche. People haven't been looking far afield for pleasure," says Thomson. "Rather than travel, or buy a vacation property, people are sprucing up their homes," he says. TMS also pays particular attention to another constituency as well – suppliers. Unlike some firms in the same field, TMS does not import cheap products from Pacific Rim nations for resale. Competitors did, and the results were catastrophic. "Inventory killed those companies. They had too much of the wrong product," says Thomson. Competitors who order from far-off have all their money tied up in container-loads of goods moving slowly across the ocean. TMS has chosen instead to work with local suppliers, keep control over inventory, and ensure shipment times are short. The result is a recession-proof business. "Even in the worst times, if you've got a winning product, it sells."

Start-up tip: *Like politics, all business is local.*

Customer attitudes can define your firm's unique selling proposition. "The client is the most important aspect in setting the need," says Stuart Lazier, president of Enterprise Property Management, a Toronto firm that manages real-estate holdings for blue-chip clients like the Royal Bank and Standard Life in Alberta and Ontario. Enterprise is the second-biggest such management company in Canada, and part of the reason growth has been so quick since the 1984 launch is because the firm embraced the "green revolution." Enterprise concluded that clients were becoming more conscious of their impact on the environment. While people were recycling at home and at the office, the surroundings had yet to reflect this popular trend. A pilot project "green office" building in Toronto uses recycled clear, plastic soft-drink bottles for carpets, recycled vinyl from car seats for rigid floor material, has reduced normal office lighting by two-thirds, and offers built-in light and motion detectors so that, five minutes after someone leaves a room, the lights go out. Says Lazier, "It's a marketing edge."

Finally, if one of your client firms gets into financial trouble, try to help that firm do a workout. Such assistance will be less expensive for you than finding a replacement for that customer's business, says Bernard Wilson, senior partner at accounting firm Price Waterhouse. "Many businesses spend more time, money, and effort trying to acquire new customers than holding on to the ones they have," he says. "On the other hand, a business that has ceased to be economically viable should be taken out of its misery as quickly and efficiently as possible." Unless, of course, that business just happens to be your own.

Summary:

1. Stay close to the customer, or you'll be far from success.
2. Remember that customers create jobs, growth, and profits.
3. Exceed customers' expectations.
4. Make sure your staff is happy and well-trained. A happy staff means contented customers.
5. Give excellent service. It's not an act, it's a habit.

CHAPTER 8

Empowered Employees: Hire Well, Higher Rewards

"Employees take a lot of time and energy, but if you treat them well, they'll be the reason for your success."

– Mary Black, Colour Technologies

Ask any small-business owner what makes his or her firm smarter, more innovative, or more responsive than the competition and the answer is always as pointed as it is predictable: the employees. But the answer must also be based on specifics, not just lip service. And it's not only the level of pay that sends the right signal to employees. While compensation needs to be adequate, most surveys indicate that an employee is more likely to leave a job because there was a lack of recognition and praise rather than because of money matters alone.

So, how do you find the right people, the employees who are going to be loyal and bring the right skills and attitudes to the job? The responsibility for putting square pegs in square holes rests with you. While you have a long list of things to do in the early days of your business, the time you spend on careful hiring will pay off more handsomely than just about any other pursuit. Once someone is on the payroll, getting them off staff can take an inordinate amount of effort, so try to make the right decision the first time. "You don't hire employees, you extend your family," says Mary Black of Colour Technologies. "You become all things to all people."

One of your biggest problems in the first five years of a growing organization will be to find and keep the team together that you need to go forward. That's because many of the people who join you to work in this entrepreneurial environment you are creating are also entrepreneurs. Just as you wanted to be your own boss, some of them may want to be the same. "Our strength is our weakness. When people develop, they're like teenagers. You give them the skills, and they want to go on their own," says Bill Watchorn of ENSIS Corp., a Winnipeg manufacturer. "I don't want to tamper with that. If you wait too long, you squash them."

So, is there an adequate reward system in place to keep the right people? Can you create the enthusiasm and momentum for change? Can you transmit the sense of urgency that something needs to be done? Are you listening carefully to the ultimate purpose of your company and what you're trying to accomplish?

"In most service organizations, the front-line people who meet the customers are the lowest paid. We decided that was fundamentally wrong," says Quentin Wahl, owner of Cadet Uniform Services of Toronto. As a result, he made the forty-five service representatives who deliver the uniforms into the caring core of his business. Each driver is a mini-entrepreneur, with 80 per cent of compensation based on job performance. A sophisticated tracking system measures over thirty-two hundred items that relate to customer service and satisfaction in a process that's reviewed by forty people. "This acts as our 'distant early warning' system and drives our strategic plans, marketing plans, and customer-service initiatives," says Wahl.

In an industry where most drivers are unionized and make $28,000 a year, Cadet's nonunion reps average $46,000, and can make as much as $65,000 annually. Ninety per cent of the reps have university degrees, each handles about 125 clients, and some haven't lost a single customer in three years. The incentive to keep customers happy means that Cadet has become the fastest-growing uniform-supply company in Canada with sales up 22 per cent each year for ten years. Today, one hundred thousand Canadians wear seven million Cadet-supplied uniforms in a year.

Finding the best people

Before you go looking for a new employee, first draw up a job description, so that you know exactly the qualities you're seeking, then cast the widest net possible by advertising jobs in the local media and the trade press. Go fishing in any other employment pool that you can find. The best approach is to keep a list of potential employees you've met or heard about – even when you're not actually hiring – so that when you *are* ready to expand your team, you have someone with good credentials in mind. Scrutinize written applications yourself and check all references carefully. "Hire honest people," says Hazel de Burgh, principal of Lindquist Avey Macdonald Baskerville Inc., a forensic-accounting firm based in Toronto. "Screen all hiring carefully, including checking of references. You'd be surprised to know how many people falsify information on their biographies." If a previous employer will only confirm employment dates and won't say much more about the individual, assume the worst. You don't want to hire someone else's headaches.

Start-up tip: *Employees know best who will fit in with the current workforce.*

In some of the best-performing firms, personnel departments are becoming *passé*, as peer assessments replace formal interviews in the quest for employee competence. New hires at Cadet Uniform Supply, for example, must pass intense scrutiny in a minimum of five meetings with current staff and need unanimous approval by the employees. "We also have them come in and get paid to work for a day to see if they're suitable," says Wahl. As a result, annual turnover at Cadet is 8 per cent, compared to an industry average of many times higher.

Cross-training is available at Cadet, and anyone can switch jobs with another employee as long as the change isn't just ordered from the top. At Cadet, both workers must come up with the idea themselves and agree to the swap. "People like the variety, but job rotation that's top down doesn't work," says Wahl.

Start-up tip: *Role-switching among staffers not only avoids boredom but also give employees a better understanding of someone else's problems.*

Wahl has also devised a three-point business philosophy with which new employees must agree. Each signs a document that states they promise to:

- treat others they work with as they would want to be treated;
- do it right the first time, every time; and
- do it now.

Hiring help from a temporary staff agency is a not only a good way to fill a short-term need, but the process also allows you a close look at someone in your business environment.

More than 40 per cent of temporary staff goes on to work for a firm after they've served there for several weeks. That's a trial process that works for both sides, because each can get an accurate look at the other.

At more senior levels, you should consider dealing with an executive search firm, known colloquially as a "headhunter." They'll find the right person, but the cost is steep. You'll pay a fee that's equal to one-third of the person's first-year salary to such search firms as Heidrick & Struggles, Caldwell Partners, or Egon Zehnder.

At any level, after you've hired the winner, set up a specific probationary period of, say, three months. Establish clear written goals and make sure the new hires know that their performances will be reviewed; if found wanting, they're gone. Never extend the probationary period. If three months leaves you feeling shaky, three more months won't likely make much difference.

Among the most complete and analytical processes to find those "best" people is the one used by Manpower Services (Toronto) Ltd. to find temporary workers, who are in turn employed by other firms. More than half the new employees are referred by existing staff. If a new employee completes forty hours with Manpower, the referring staffer earns a bonus of up to $100. Each applicant for a Manpower role is tested to find their individual skill level, then they're trained using Skillware, Manpower's proprietary computer-delivered training system. The courses cover more than 350 programs in such areas as word processing, communications, databases, spreadsheets, desktop publishing, and graphics applications. All new employees undergo a three-week self-study course. Top employees who have worked for at least four hundred hours and received excellent evaluations from clients are given the Tiffany Award, a Manpower logo on a sterling silver tie-tack, pin, or necklace, designed by Tiffany of New York.

"Finding and keeping the best people is key," says Gavin Semple, president of Brandt Industries Ltd. of Regina, Saskatchewan. "It's not an exact science. Once you've found them, people have to be able to achieve their own goals. That requires an upper-management approach that allows people to try their own ideas, even to the point of rewarding honest, unintentional mistakes."

"Get the best people you can with the best interpersonal skills," urges Tim Moore of AMJ Campbell Van Lines, who resigned as president and mistakenly installed a vice-president to replace him. The company lost $2 million in five months before Moore stepped back into day-to-day control. Moore now resides in Chester, Nova Scotia, and runs his national business from there. "I'll never resign again. It hurt a lot of people." Moore says his mistake was in promoting someone whom, he realized later, he hardly knew. "He was the vice-president of the eight [VPs] I never got close to. . . . You have to remember that the perks go with the office, not with you."

Two-way communication

Employees need to know what you have in mind for the firm and how they can work with you towards that goal. This isn't just a wish list, you need a clear vision for the future and you must share that vision with your colleagues. Communicating through haphazard conversations is not enough, you need a regular forum. While most companies have some sort of newsletter with names of new staff, births, and other announcements, the best way to share your vision with employees is through regular staff meetings. Successful retailers like Wal-Mart hold meetings with all staff in each store every day. The meetings might only last fifteen minutes, but that time gives managers a chance to bring everyone up-to-date, hear people's concerns, share problems, and involve them in the solutions. The capacity and the opportunity to transmit your enthusiasm for the future and your expectations of them as members of a team in that future cannot be overestimated.

In addition, management must be perceived to be readily accessible to everyone and actually embrace such two-way flow of information. Give feedback when appropriate and celebrate success whenever you see good performance. Be very clear about what you're saying, so that you reduce the likelihood of misinterpretation; control anger and other negative reactions. What to you might just be a light remark or an off-the-cuff comment could seem like an order to an employee or may get repeated and embellished around the organization until the words have been altered far beyond their original intent.

Bend every effort to make employees feel that they have some control over their own lives, some say in what goes on in the workplace, and a relationship with you and others in management that is one of credibility and trust. All of those elements take time to build; nothing can be an overnight success. "You never get anybody totally up-front with you right away," says Boyd Stevens, president of Cyba Stevens Mandate. "But, over time, people learn they're not going to be judged if they're honest with you."

A key management practice that Ron Besse, chairman and president of Canada Publishing Corp. of Agincourt, Ontario, learned as a member of the Young Presidents' Organization is "roundtabling." That's the term for a regular discussion group that can be requested by any employee and is made up of employees from various levels in the organization. "There's no head of the table," says Besse. "Problems are put on the table and everybody offers solutions." Among the suggestions to come from such fora is a bonus system that sets out specific performance criteria, that, if met, can add 20 per cent to editorial salaries by making each individual responsible for costs and profits on specific book titles. "If you publish more books at less cost, you get an incentive bonus. They might work to nine o'clock, but they also get out to talk to buyers about trends," says Besse. "Instead of being in their little closet with a manuscript, they're seeing the full gamut of publishing."

The roundtable method is also used for regular corporate-planning sessions away from the office. A typical four-day event might include fifteen people. Although the specific topic could be something as grand as the shape of the business in the year 2005, there is no set agenda. As a result, participants feel free to raise any issue or idea. "You don't necessarily take the top brass away," says Besse. "Reach down in the company. They come up with the freshest ideas." Besse urges discussion at these meetings about personal goals, too, and the wrap-up session includes a five-minute period for each attendee to reveal their personal hopes and aspirations.

Seeing and being seen are important parts of communicating your vision and send a strong signal that you are involved with the employees in moving the company forward. If you're going to be an owner and leader, you have to give direction; to do that you have to both be seen and heard by your staff. In the eighties, one of the hot ideas was called "management by walking around." That was all about visibility, solving problems immediately, and hearing about aspects of the company that you wouldn't have heard if you stayed in your office all day.

While such a technique is no longer urged by management gurus (these ideas tend to run their course, only to be replaced by some new organizational buzzword), some positive aspects of the idea should remain part of your management style. Management by walking around is all about remembering how you used to be, and actually carrying out some of the roles you used to do: calling on customers, packing shipments, preparing the payroll, or simply helping out from time to time in an area that needs an extra pair of hands. Some managers confidently position their desks in the middle of the shop

> ## Seven best habits of a successful boss
>
> 1. Develop your people; ensure appropriate training programs are available.
> 2. Every person is different; manage each of them differently.
> 3. Communicate openly; expect no less in return.
> 4. Establish standards and stick to them; have no truck nor trade with incompetence.
> 5. Focus on what people are doing, not just on the results you want.
> 6. When things go wrong, don't go looking for a scapegoat; accept responsibility yourself.
> 7. Top performers need recognition, but don't forget to stroke a few honourable mentions as well.

floor, where people can easily see them and openly talk in a wall-free environment.

At ParkLane Ventures, Gary Santini shares his vision by encouraging employees to see the real customer in each successive step of the construction process. "The customer isn't just the end user," he says. "It's also the next person in line on the project." Santini's philosophy towards employees is simple. "Hire the best, then get the hell out of the way," he says. "People can accomplish incredible heights of achievement if they're given the chance. My people don't work for me, they work for themselves. The worst thing people can do is work somewhere they don't like."

Another mistake too many start-up business bosses make is to hire people who are just like they are. You want the chemistry to be excellent, but if you constantly replicate yourself, everyone ends up having the same weaknesses.

Start-up tip: *Look for strengths in staff that you don't possess, so that your firm grows not just in size but also in categories of knowledge.*

At ParkLane, suppliers and tradespeople are so deeply involved with the business that the firm drafted a mission statement using a process that involved outsiders as well as employees and their spouses. Spouses, says Santini, are every bit as important as employees. Twice a year, the firm sponsors events that include spouses. "If I can get the partner at home on my side, that helps me too."

One of ParkLane's most successful events, now going on for a decade, is the annual weekend retreat. ParkLane invites not just employees and their spouses, but the extended family as well – the firm's lawyers, accountants, sub-trades, consultants – all the people they work with on a regular basis. In all, about 350 people gather on Thursday night for a "meet and mix," followed by a jam-packed program, ending with a brunch on Sunday. The 1994 meeting at Harrison Hot Springs Hotel, two hours from Vancouver, featured a number of speakers, covering a broad range of topics, including personal investment, leadership advice, and dealing with stress. Among the high-octane speakers was Major-General Lewis MacKenzie, recently returned from Sarajevo.

In other sessions, management presents complete corporate and financial information. Employees get to grill the boss in a bear-pit session called "Ask the President." Evening programs are given over to fun. They include such things as skits, line-dancing lessons, and a masquerade ball. CFO Jim Brambley, who organizes the events, is among the most active skit participants. One year he wore a ballerina's tutu; another year he dressed as a Jamaican reggae star.

That same family spirit can be nurtured in ways that revitalize a failing company. Margaret Armour runs Aerobics First, a sporting-goods store in Halifax. She was an investor in the store when it opened in 1980 and, during that decade, put in $150,000, while a succession of poor managers almost drove the store out of business. When the bank threatened to fore-close in 1989, Armour, a former teacher who had been working in the store, took over the business and united the staff in a survive-and-prosper mode.

Armour convinced suppliers to wait for payment, built a new customer-loyalty program, and moulded the staff into a united group. "I'm the coach of the team. As a [former] teacher, you think about what people need to know. Empowerment is a buzzword, but it's about bringing people along, allowing them to make mistakes." At weekly staff meet-ings, everyone is encouraged to bare their souls. There, people have to talk about difficulties they're having with other members of the team and try to find solutions, with Armour as facilitator. "I don't have any business skills, but I have people skills," she says. "I learned not to let things go unsaid."

As a result of her leadership, the 3,000-square-foot store is now profitable, has twenty-three employees (including seven full time), and does $1.3 million in annual sales. The turn-around is so complete that, in 1994, Armour opened a separate shop to sell snowboards in the same mall on Quinpool Road. Staff helped her design the store to appeal to the snowboard crowd. Even the name, A1 Snowboards, was their choice. But there's a practical reason for the free-standing location. "If it fails, it won't take down the [other] store," she says.

Outsourcing

Top employees don't need to work under your roof all the time. At Progestic Inc., an Ottawa-based consulting firm, 70 per cent of the 125 employees are full time and the rest are called contract associates. "You need to extend your services, using people with particular expertise. You need a number of experts on your team," says president Jean LaBelle. "That will be the trend in the consulting business." In fact, LaBelle finds some of the most talented personnel he comes across are doing work for a number of businesses, because they like the variety and freedom. "For people who are very good, the tendency is to freelance," Labelle says.

With the high cost of group-insurance plans, training, and turnover, more firms are turning to contract workers. Such "off-staff" employees come with many advantages, including particular expertise, a built-in desire to do a job well (so they will be hired again), and an interest in completing the assigned task within a specific time period. After all, they have a fixed-term contract with you for an agreed-upon amount of money and performance. Metro Canada Logistics Inc., a Montreal-based warehouse-service company, handles personnel hiring through this increasingly popular method known as "out-sourcing." Rather than have a large personnel department, Metro contracts a human-resources consulting firm to find, screen, and test all prospective employees, who then must work on the job site before final approval. Up to thirty applicants are considered for every job at the firm that employs four hundred in Ontario and Quebec.

Reward performance

While people feel good when they're involved in the inner workings of the business, they like tangible rewards as well. Polywheels gives out jackets and T-shirts for jobs well done and, after five years of employment, a gold ring. According to the Promotional Products Association of Canada, incentives are popular across the country and could be worth about $800 million annually when items for employees and customers are included. Most popular choices are wearables with corporate logos or other messages, followed by writing instruments, then glassware and ceramics.

But giveaways only go so far. More meaningful programs are required. Polywheels had added a gainsharing program. Such ownership possibilities for staff mean that they can join the growing number of companies willing to empower their people by letting them buy into the corporation or participate in profit-sharing. Some provinces make available grants that can be used to set up employee share-ownership plans (ESOP). In Ontario, for example, individuals can invest in labour-sponsored investment funds, and employee groups can buy their employer's company. The funds allow individuals to invest up to $5,000 annually in small business and receive a $2,000 tax credit. Under the employee-ownership program, an employee can contribute up $15,000 annually and qualify for $4,150 in tax credits (see page 287).

Ownership of a firm is now more commonly being shared even at professional-service firms that have often in the past been tightly held by the founder or a few senior partners. Among the 350 people at Beak International Inc., an environmental-engineering firm based in Brampton, 160 are shareholders. That includes 35 principals and associates as well as 125 other employees, including such nonprofessional staffers as senior secretaries, lab supervisors, and technicians. "We don't have a classical hierarchical structure," says president Dr. Karl Schiefer. "Our share-acquisition plan has created an entrepreneurial group of people."

Participation in the plan requires top performance. "We see the opportunity as a right, not a privilege," he says. By the time an employee who is doing well becomes an associate, after five years with Beak, that person has invested about $70,000 for thirty-five hundred shares, or a 1-per-cent interest, in the firm. By the ten-year mark, when principal status can be conferred, the employees could own another ten thousand shares for a total investment of $200,000. Annual compensation can be increased by up to 20 per cent through profit sharing.

Moreover, the value of those shares has increased tenfold in the last fifteen years. The combination results in low turnover and high levels of loyalty. "When we get together, it's not just as employees, it's as fellow investors," says Schiefer.

Such employee-ownership programs, including those run by the company, can prove to be a loyal source of funding. When Upper Canada Brewing Co. went looking for growth capital in 1986, two years after the firm's founding, employees chipped in $1 million, then followed that with a similar amount, injected a year later to hold a total of about 20 per cent of the firm. "I was surprised to see the number of employees, even on the production line making $25,000 to $30,000 a year, who bought shares," says president Frank Heaps. Heaps remains the majority shareholder, but among his sixty-seven employees, one-third are shareholders. Some employees who have left have kept their shares, while others sold them to current employees.

Heaps holds four regular meetings a year, at which he shares financial information with staff, including, if they wish, what he refers to as "all the gory details." The firm also has a reward program that includes incentives for reaching designated performance targets that are mutually agreed to by management and employees. At Upper Canada, strong increases in sales and volumes mean that 10 per cent of an employee's annual compensation can come from bonuses, a meaningful increase, given the fact that regular pay levels are about 15 per cent below those in a union shop.

Heaps sets specific goals, saying, "If we get to this level, I'll be earning more and I'll pay you more." Heaps first encountered the reward concept as a student working in a Bancroft, Ontario, uranium mine in the fifties, and he knows such a system is more likely to keep people happy and less likely to seek out a third party, like a union, to act on their behalf. "Unions don't like production bonuses," Heaps says. When employees hit the designated targets, they also collect a prize from the company store that stocks various items decorated with the Upper Canada logo.

As with other successful entrepreneurs, Heaps also makes sure that there is adequate employee training. Employees need to know clearly what's expected of them, be given a respectful audience for ideas or complaints, and receive regular feedback beyond a few fine phrases in some speech delivered at a holiday party. "Most people are happy here," says Heaps. "There's always a push and a pull to these things, but I don't think there's much push."

At Calgary's Jarvis Travel there's a profit-sharing plan that sees 20 per cent of annual profits paid out to employees. Roger Jarvis doesn't fool around on bonus day. His banker, accompanied by security guards, arrives carrying a box of cash, up to $200,000 – in twenty-, one-hundred-, even one-thousand-dollar bills – for distribution to staff.

Benchmarking

While it's important to set goals, the difficulty is to set appropriate levels that offer an incentive to workers that's realistic and attainable, drives people forward, and rewards them adequately for top performance. One key, as Frank Heaps pointed out, is to ensure that management and employees agree in advance what those goals are. Another useful device is to compare productivity in your operation with output by competitors in the same field through a process called benchmarking.

Benchmarking is a way of improving customer-service levels or production quality by giving employees something to shoot for in what's usually a difficult area to measure. Enterprise Property Management has a client-ranking system in place for office buildings under management. Enterprise won't let any ranking fall below four on a five-point scale. All such systems give companies a base from which to measure themselves and forcefeed new growth.

B.C. Bearings Engineers conducted a customer survey to measure three things: service levels, the quality of problem-solving by its employees, and the firm's contribution to client profitability. On a scale of one to five, the company consistently scored well – in the middle fours – and the results gave management and employees not only a place to start from but a goal-oriented approach to improvement called "raising the bar."

International Wallcoverings pays bonuses to employees and supervisors quarterly for doing better than others in the industry. Typical product returns to wallpaper makers are 1 per cent, but International Wallcoverings has reduced returns to one-quarter of 1 per cent by taking particular care in setting up the printing presses, installing automatic scanners to spot problems, and employing two people to do nothing but check random samples for quality.

Surprisingly, these tight controls have not caused higher wastage in the production process. Compared with industry scrap rates of 10 to 11 per cent, International Wallcoverings enjoys rates in the 7 to 8 per cent range, according to president Colin Beasley. The benchmarking program has also pleased customers. That's important because unhappy users of wallpaper who discover a pattern problem partway through a job will demand their money back, plus compensation for lost time on a construction site or during home decorating. "It can be even more expensive when it comes to your reputation," says Beasley.

Benchmarking can also be an in-house device used to compare production rates with promised delivery schedules. At furniture manufacturer Keilhauer Industries Ltd. of Scarborough, profit-sharing is tied to quality and on-time delivery. The firm makes executive and conference chairs, lounge seating, and side chairs for business and institutional use. Production schedules are determined weekly, and, if staff reaches 90 per cent or greater of the established targets, their share of the bonus doubles, using a commission-based formula. Keilhauer has more than one hundred employees and sales that are closing in on $20 million annually. "We customize every order we manufacture," says CEO Mike Keilhauer. As a result, each order must be treated very differently, so the firm has created penalties that can reduce the employee share. If an item is returned by a customer due to a manufacturing problem, eight times the original commission meant for employees is taken out of the shared pot.

The results of the program have been spectacular: 98 per cent on-time delivery and minimal returns. (One production day late, for example, knocks two percentage points off, even if the one day is made up elsewhere and the customer receives the order on time.) Previously, management had to monitor employees; now they need so little direct supervision that a plan to name a plant foreman was scrapped. Employees not only see the gain from doing top-quality work, they benefit directly, and all of them have a vested interest not only in what they do but also in what their co-workers do.

Start-up tip: *Early detection by employees is the key to quality control.*

Other considerations

While size won't be a problem for you in the early going, keeping the number of employees at your facility manageable will become crucial at some point. Although Magna International is now a $3.5-billion auto-parts giant that has factories as large as several hundred workers each, for the first few years no plant was allowed to grow larger than fifty employees. When the complement bumped up against that ceiling, founder Frank Stronach established another facility, always making sure that he promoted a new manager from within the organization to run the new factory. Stronach's corporate philosophy ensured that the new manager and the assistant each received a percentage share of the plant's profit as an incentive to do well. "If you've got too many people in a building, you lose the family feeling," agrees Adam Okhai, who has built a multimillion-dollar retail empire catering to kids' educational needs through stores named Moyer's and Kids Are Worth It!

Sabbaticals and other time-off arrangements mean individual freedom for employees and can cause increased creativity. Bryker Data Systems offers employees special deals, like a nine-month maternity program that pays half a mother-to-be's salary up-front. For a new father, there's eight weeks of paid paternity leave. In addition, staff change roles regularly to reduce boredom, are reimbursed for any accredited course they take successfully, and can disappear on a two- to three-month sabbatical after five years. "Our best ambassadors are people who have left Bryker and come back," says president Bryan Kerdman. "They tell the others, 'You don't know what it's like out there.'"

Creating appropriate working environments will also make for a happy staff, who in turn will mean contented customers. The headquarters of The Body Shop, in Toronto's north end, was planned with employees in mind – not just business functions. There's a day-care centre and an indoor garden-cum-greenhouse where water is recycled. The environmentally friendly tone, with recycled carpets and nontoxic paint, reflects the philosophy behind the cosmetic products the franchises sell. As with many successful entrepreneurs, they view business as fun. Some words from the lobby capture that spirit: "Relish adventure. Expect the best. Walk the dog."

Appropriate working environments also mean having the best tools. You need to have the most up-to-date technology available for your organization, not just because technology will keep your business competitive, but because the new technology has an empowering aspect, one that will help you find leaders within your organization. As everyone has been moving away from mainframes to personal computers, that shift has put real power into the hands of ordinary people. By the end of the decade, 99 per cent of all the available raw computing power will be sitting on desktops. All the knowledge you have, they have. The only limit is the one that the individual places on himself or herself. As managers, you have a responsibility to create the sort of environment that allows people to find and unleash the leader within themselves. Decision-making needs to be done more quickly and further down in the organization, way down where titles don't matter.

Of course, there's a downside here too. You may not like what you hear bubbling up from beneath. You can't expect your employees to have the same level of loyalty you have, and you may actually have to act on some of their ideas. Doing so may even make you feel like you're losing control of the enterprise.

With more employees becoming knowledge workers who have access to massive amounts of information through computers, society is going through wrenching change. There will be much more mobility among employees. "We will never again have a single employer," says Lesley Southwick-Trask, president of The Proactive Group of Companies of Halifax. "We'll have three or four at the same time. And CEOs will be just as temporary as clerks." Employees no longer trust the boss, because so many firms have shed longtime staff like snowy galoshes at the door. That lack of corporate loyalty is mirrored in the attitudes of employees who say, "You've got my peak performance only as long as what I'm doing is interesting."

Southwick-Trask argues that the voyage anyone takes in life is influenced by the maps one uses. Her theory is that too many CEOs are vainly following the old trading routes as they try to retain control. "The banter about who's going to control the information superhighway is the same as the banter in the feudal era when serfs became free," she says. Southwick-Trask urges companies to look beyond their own ranks for answers. For example, she recently told a financial-services client to include some outsiders at a corporate-strategy planning retreat. They balked at showing their warts to people with no previous relationship with the financial institution. "When you're in the midst of chaos," she told them, "that's when you invite outsiders in." The firm relented and, after the three-day meeting, agreed that the most useful ideas came from the outsiders. For their part, the outsiders became fans, committed to the ongoing health of the company.

In the midst of chaos, there's one human need that hasn't changed, says Southwick-Trask. People want some structure in their working lives; they don't want to live totally "on the edge." They also want benchmarks, so they know when they're doing well, and they need rewards – both backpats and bucks – to show appreciation. Loyalty begets loyalty. Remember the first rule of being an entrepreneur is enjoying what you do – so don't forget to apply that formula to your employees.

Still, whatever loyalty-building plans are in place and no matter how good an employer you are, staff will always cause some headaches. If you are close to your people – as you should be – you'll hear about their problems, both personal and professional. But that close relationship should help you recognize what's wrong too. "Management can't always see the problems associates can," says Roger Jarvis of Jarvis Travel. In return, the employees receive more than just your ear. "I don't believe in a vision, I believe in management and coaching," he says.

Start-up tip: *Sometimes customers come second. Employees are first.*

Phoenix International Life Sciences Inc. of St.-Laurent, Quebec, sets such high standards for employees that, even after careful hiring procedures and quality coaching by a full-time three-member department, half cannot make the grade. "Finding people is our most difficult problem. It's not just a science, it's an art too," says Dr. John Hooper, president and scientific director. The balance between creating loyalty and empowering employees so that they all feel that they're part of the decision-making process is a delicate one: they might up and leave. "The top thirty or forty people here are all mini-entrepreneurs," says Hector Jacques of Jacques Whitford Group. "Any of them could set up their own firm tomorrow." While that is a great compliment to you, the result is that you're losing good people and maybe acquiring a tough, new competitor in your market at the same time.

How to fire someone

Most employees are just like you, they work best when there are goals set that extend their reach. In the best companies, such goals are established with the participation of everyone, so there's a consensus about where the firm is going and what sort of effort will be required by everyone. If targets aren't hit, you have to be ruthless. If someone in sales has a bad month, that's okay. Two bad months . . . well. Three bad months, you'll have to set specific goals together or they're out. Sales must be the wrong career for this unhappy, unsuccessful soul who's doing your firm no good.

If you are looking beyond an individual salesperson to a head of a division, three months may be too long to wait before beginning the process of firing someone. By then, you may be so far behind that the future of the whole enterprise is in doubt. Take a page from the gambling casinos. They know what a particular game, say blackjack, should produce. If five tables produce a certain level every day or every month, and one is doing much worse – you know you've got a problem.

> **Start-up tip:** *According to the Japanese proverb, the nail that sticks out gets hit. Have a hammer at the ready.*

If you do have to let someone go, make absolutely sure you have given them the opportunity to measure up before you show them the door. Keep careful and complete notes of how they've let you down, as well as the discussions that you've had with them about the need to improve their performance. Send memos to the employee, detailing improvements you want, how these steps will be measured, training that will be carried out, and the time allowed to meet these standards. Do a follow-up memo citing what's still required. Working with below-par employees requires a lot of time. Firing someone is tough on both of you. Good hiring practices will keep such misfits to a minimum.

Finally, if the employee continues to fall short after several months of everyone's best efforts, firing is the only answer. Documentation will assist you if the employee sues for wrongful dismissal. Be sure to change computer passwords and collect all keys, passcards, manuals, or other information that might be useful to competitors.

Poor performance isn't the only cause for firing. No matter how careful your hiring process and how closely you work with employees, there is always the chance that someone on staff is acting fraudulently. They could be carrying out minor pilferage or hurting your firm in some more serious way, like selling secrets to the competition. Every business is susceptible, but a young start-up business can be severely crippled by employee fraud. Even a well-established firm can be dealt a hurtful blow if an employee fiddles the books. Once staff has been hired, Hazel de Burgh of Lindquist Avey Macdonald Baskerville urges that they be kept honest. Here's how:

- treat them fairly;
- pay them equitably;
- listen to them;
- watch for behaviour changes (like expensive cars or clothes); and
- recognize and reinforce good work.

In one case, three engineers who had responsibility for supervising and tendering company contracts suddenly were each driving new red Jeep Cherokees – all from the same automotive dealer. It turned out that, behind the largesse, was a complex kickback scheme. "The first type of deterrent is psychological," says de Burgh. If your firm is lax about sleazy activities or turns a blind eye to downright illegality, employees will feel they can get away with a scam, because you have provided the environment for them to carry it off. On the other hand, if there are consequences for inappropriate actions, other employees will know there are rules that must be followed. "Crimes are committed when the rewards outweigh the risks of punishment," says de Burgh. "Effective fraud prevention relates to increasing the risk of punishment."

Making it clear you will act is a prevention strategy that works against all allegations of fraud, says de Burgh. "You can't just do nothing. Whether it be dismissing the employee, taking the complaint to the police, or following through with a lawsuit, the key is to actually follow through." In addition, useful preventative steps include employee education, random or surprise audits, and establishing a code of ethics or fraud policy that details who is responsible for detection and investigation – and sets out the consequences, such as dismissal, complaint to the police, and lawsuits.

The problem of fraud and corruption is also rampant in foreign markets. Exporters must be careful not to run afoul of foreign laws. In many countries, kickbacks are expected when contracts are signed. The most straightforward approach for employees and their companies is not to pay. "Bribery and corruption are a way of life in many emerging nations. Don't start feeding the bear; get out of the park," warns Rod Stamler, a thirty-three-year RCMP veteran and now a principal with Lindquist Avey Macdonald Baskerville.

Managing others

As difficult as it is to fire someone, the entrepreneur's toughest role, once the firm is well and truly launched, is to be able to manage people on an ongoing basis. That's not an easy task, given the fact that many entrepreneurs can't even manage themselves. "I thought good management grew on trees and making money was the rare thing," says Leon Lapidus of The Mibro Group. "Now that I have some money, I know that the reverse is true."

Managing others sometimes means allowing their ideas to hold sway. In 1991, when Expographiq was facing layoffs to offset lost sales, the employees suggested instead that everybody, including top management, take a 10-per-cent salary cut. The drastic step saved jobs both immediately and over the longer term by keeping the firm alive. Compensation was frozen for eighteen months and didn't return to previous levels until 1992. Once conditions had improved in 1993, management paid back all the withheld pay – even though that generosity wasn't part of the original rollback agreement. In addition, everyone got a 4-per-cent raise. "We're trying to find nontraditional ways of operating," says Expographiq president Mike Buckley. "We've taken a beating."

Getting those good ideas requires a program or a way of thinking that might best be described as lifelong learning, or lifting managers and employees to a constant level of awareness that spurs ideas, ideas that are essential to going forward. After all, good ideas are the building blocks for any business.

Sometimes the best way to manage is to minimize negative

reactions to new ideas. Here are seven negative reactions you don't want to catch yourself having. And if a colleague or employee happens to respond with one of these lines when a new idea is proposed, you know you've got real trouble:

1. We've never done it that way before.
2. We tried that once.
3. We're already market leaders. Why fix what ain't broke?
4. It costs too much. It's not in the budget.
5. It's not our responsibility.
6. It won't work.
7. Yah . . . but.

Those kind of reactions can kill a company, unless the phrase is uttered by a person who then continues to talk constructively about a way to get around a situation. The best philosophy to follow is this: If it ain't broke, keep looking.

What works best for happy employees comes from the key values that only you, as boss, can create. In other words, the environment in which people operate yields the results. If the tone of the place is authoritarian, everyone will be too cowed to come forward with a fresh thought. If, on the other hand, there is a sense that good ideas are welcome, those good ideas will follow. "Some of the best innovations come from freedom, no mandates," says Rob Burgess, CEO of Alias Research Inc. of Toronto. The question becomes: What is it about your company that will let employees have the right value system? One aspect is that decision-making must be quick, something that Burgess says works best when people don't have job titles. "It's leadership that matters," he says. Leadership must nurture talent, harness knowledge, and make policy in conjunction with people who know the subject and feel both motivated and involved. And if everyone can be convinced to buy into company-wide improvement programs like total quality management (TQM), spirit and output can soar.

"Employees at all levels feel like they're participating in the business – because they are," says Doug Loughran, CEO of Reliable Parts Ltd. of Coquitlam, British Columbia.

The mix of people in your firm is also important. While most people should fit into the particular culture you are trying to create, take a few chances with some of your employees too. Vancouver-based futurist Frank Ogden urges that businesses pay less attention to schooling and experience of applicants, trusting instead to instinct and gut assessment of the candidate. "Hire on attitude alone," says Ogden. "Hire some people who are off the wall – or they'll go out and become your competition."

Summary:

1. Hire carefully, train thoroughly.
2. Don't just try to manufacture loyalty. Empower employees so that they feel they have a measure of control over their own lives.
3. Communicate your vision clearly and let employees participate in planning, so that the future is formed by consensus, not fiat.
4. Establish clear goals for each employee, help each individual achieve those levels, and give rewards in pay and praise when they get there.
5. Honour what people have to offer.

CHAPTER 9

Growth Rings

"You're either innovative – or you're deceased."

– Peter Egan, NUTAT Technologies

I f a company were an apple tree, it would need the sun-light of bright ideas, fresh water supplied by employee effort, nutrients in the form of financing, and the good earth of an appreciative market. And just as a tree needs pruning to take on the right shape over the years, a company needs the discipline that can only come from strategic plan-ning, establishing budgets, and setting goals. Along the way, every entrepreneur needs to recognize the various stages of development, his or her own and the company's. "After start-up, as you grow towards ten employees, you realize you can't do all the things yourself," says Peter Egan, president of NUTAT Technologies of Ottawa. The first hurdle comes when the company hits the symbolic $1-million mark in annual sales. "You have to pull away a bit as an entrepreneur and apply management skills. You're not billing your time anymore; you're relying on others."

That realization is one that some entrepreneurs never come to. Letting go some of the controls in a growing company is the most difficult step any entrepreneur can take. The next barrier, at which the company changes again, and the entrepreneur should back off some more, comes at $3 million. "Now, you're a real company," says Egan. At that point, and again at the $6-million to $7-million sales level, you have to let go of the reins even more, perhaps by bringing in outside investors or additional managers. "You have to decide when it's the right time to add infrastructure." The economy will always play a part in how you act, but more so as the firm increases in size. Breaking through the $10-million sales barrier, for example, is difficult when the economy is slow, says Egan.

Egan founded the firm in 1985, working from his den. Today NUTAT offers document-management services for law firms, document storage and retrieval, library research, desktop publishing, and catalogue automation. Typical projects have included a records-management system for the Privy Council in Ottawa, a mail-order entry system for MCI Telecommunications in Washington, and a reporting-and-analysis system for Stentor Canadian Network Management. The firm is also working with a Leesburg, Virginia, hospital to develop an electronic guarding product that uses a bracelet on each newborn to transmit a radio frequency. Monitoring the whereabouts of infants wearing such a device could stop the 650 abductions that occur annually from American hospitals.

Entrepreneurs will face stress points through every growing season. After all, the idea for the company sprang from within and, as new managers are added, control becomes shared. "Sometimes it's difficult when you see the results and you think, 'I could have done it ten times better,'" says Emmie Leung of International Paper. That's when ego can get in the way, but you've got to let go of that feeling because you simply cannot do everything yourself. You need management help to grow your business.

Peter Egan literally awoke in the middle of the night once, and realized that the firm had outgrown him. He further realized that he needed help to separate the wonderful ideas from the wild ones. "I realized that I had a problem, and the problem was me," says Egan. "That's a depressing thought for an entrepreneur. Every time you grow the company, you're running something you've never run before. If you have an idea and you articulate it, a whole bunch of people implement the idea because you're the boss," he says. "But we entrepreneurs are not always right," he says. "So I hired a boss."

For Egan, the "boss" was a board of directors consisting of three senior executives from outside the firm, who were hired by Egan to meet with him for one day each month. They review the strategy that is in place at the software firm and tell him when his notions are nuts. Total annual cost to NUTAT for their consulting fees is $35,000. "I realize my weaknesses, and I try to use others to fill those weaknesses," he says.

The talent pool for such part-time assistance is large: retirees from business, local bankers, other small-business owners, or community leaders. You may be able to find advisers who are willing to serve for modest payments, even for free, if the sessions are stimulating and they get something out of the process as well. At some point, however, you'll want to offer compensation in order to keep things on a professional level. Moreover, payment of a fair retainer will mean you'll be able to tap into higher-quality help. Such a group should help you with current problems, point out business opportunities, suggest new customers, and serve as a sounding board for ideas. Make sure that each adviser is trustworthy; you'll be sharing confidential information. For their part, they may want a letter from you indemnifying them if lawsuits are brought against you or your firm.

The six stages of growth

A publication from accounting firm Arthur Young (now out of print, regrettably) lists the six phases of high-tech start-ups. Here they are, as described in the pamphlet "Helping High Technology Companies Grow" by author G. Steven Burrill.

Phase 1: The start-up:
- preparation and evaluation of business plans;
- analysis and advice on form of ownership;
- acquisition of patents, licences, and technology;
- establishment of professional and supplier relationships;
- assistance in obtaining financing;
- analysis and projection of business data; and
- determination of impact of venture on personal tax situation of founder.

"Too often, some basic business matters are neglected at this stage due to time pressures and limited internal resources," says Burrill.

Phase 2: The demand for creativity:
- choose appropriate computer programs and equipment;
- develop marketing and manufacturing expertise; and
- design financial-reporting system.

At this stage, there can be "a crisis of leadership – the owner or the entrepreneur has very broad responsibilities and functions as manager, marketer, salesman, financier, and much more."

Phase 3: The need for management and control:
Symptoms of the problem include:
- inadequate sales forecasts;
- deficient planning and scheduling of manufacturing;
- poor communication;

- rapidly escalating costs;
- obsolete inventories;
- collection problems; and
- ineffective second-generation product development and introduction.

"During the early stages of high-technology businesses, anticipated results are generally high and market demand is strong. This kind of success can mask serious organizational and administrative flaws, which can hinder further growth. At some point, prices are forced down, more capital is needed to support expanded research and development, costs to maintain the company's market share soar, and the company gets too big to work with its original concepts and procedures."

Phase 4: When delegation becomes an issue:
- management begins diversifying and acquiring other companies; and
- cumbersome, centralized hierarchy can begin to restrict growth.

"The company that remains growth-oriented responds by reorganizing itself again. It decentralizes operations, delegates authority, and encourages managers to take initiative and seize profit opportunities."

Phase 5: Coordination
- decentralization continues to the point where the sense of unity is weakened and management wants closer control again.

"Success in moving into the next phase will depend on designing new systems to fit the new approach; finding new people for newly created staff positions; evaluating and adapting hardware, software, and manual systems; and training people to work in teams."

Phase 6: Collaboration:

Problems at this stage include:

- supervision of overseas divisions and subsidiaries;
- increased need for internal controls;
- need for more complex financial reports;
- inventory control and delivery problems;
- resistance to innovation and new product development;
- lack of effective productivity incentives; and
- increased competition for market share.

"Red tape now hinders effective management, as the company's earlier growth problems are replaced by a crisis of how to deal with a cumbersome organizational bureaucracy. Interpersonal collaboration and management flexibility are essential for continued success."

Growth by looking within

Peter Egan's board of directors is just one approach to achieving that kind of continued success in managing growth. You may also have spotted employees within the organization who are capable of professional growth themselves and are ready to take on new responsibilities that you once kept to yourself. Putting the right people in new and more demanding roles is a good way to create the growth rings of your company. You'll still want to know, however, what's going on. Through regular reports or budget meetings you should monitor exactly where your firm stands – without getting in the way of the people you've picked. The worst thing you can do to a person is promote them, then hover anxiously. If you have to hover, you've got the wrong person in the role.

Throughout the various stages of growth and consolidation, an entrepreneur must convince associates and employees to share the vision, to become excited by the prospect of working to achieve that vision and their own goals too. The most difficult management job for any business leader is gaining acceptance for decisions, says Jane Martin of Vas-Cath. "I can't involve everybody in all the decisions I make, but I need everyone to understand and support those decisions," she says. "Once I realized that I needed more than me and four or five senior managers, that's when we got into leadership training."

Martin went beyond seeing her staff as employees who needed to be managed, she began to see them as fellow managers who could help her grow the company. To help create the kind of entrepreneurial thinking *within* the organization that such sharing requires, she hired Ruth Matheson, of the Mississauga-based Leadership Skills, to teach selected Vas-Cath employees about personal strategic planning. Each Friday, eighteen Vas-Cath staffers gather with Martin at Matheson's nearby office for five-hour sessions in a twelve-part series that uses readings, audio tapes, and worksheets geared to prod participants into setting personal goals. "If I don't like what I do, I won't do a good job at it," says Martin. "So I want employees to feel challenged and like what they do. That's a big learning curve for people."

Sometimes, as an entrepreneur, you'll simply pick the wrong person to help you manage the growth at your company. Just when you think you've found a promising colleague within the organization and promoted that person to help you reach the next plateau in the business, you can come a cropper. Lorraine Lush began Newfoundland Career Academy in St. John's in 1979 as the first private college in the province. The institution offered a range of courses from dental assistant through business administration to electronics servicing. In 1983, she tried to expand to Nova Scotia and hired an ex-nun to run a similar school there. Everything seemed to be going well, until one day Lush arrived unannounced and found that her principal had taken the curriculum and the entire student body and moved down the street.

Lush kicked herself that she hadn't seen this coming and refocused her efforts at home. The first secretarial programs were finally going after two years in Newfoundland, then, after three more months, Lush suddenly found herself as a single parent running a school that wasn't producing enough profit to pay herself or her teachers. She was able to convince staff to work without pay, while she found new investors to keep the school going.

Her advice to entrepreneurs trying to grow their companies is "Take advice." Lush does not agree that women are more likely than men to listen to good ideas. "I've called in all kinds of experts and taken their advice," she says. "Lots of people won't." Today, her programs hold 40 per cent of the private-school market share in Newfoundland. In 1993-94, she opened five new schools and has adopted a new slogan: "Be an Academy graduate so you don't have to compete against one." Crucial to success and continued growth is an annual convention for employees called "Staying at the Top," where everyone participates in planning future strategy.

Just as particular sales levels can be designated points for growth action, a firm's budget can be a focal point to help manage just about everything a firm hopes to accomplish in growth and profit. Goals – both spending levels and sales targets – should be established with employee input and consent. That way everyone agrees with the direction and knows when progress is being made.

The budget is the contract between management and the board of directors, according to Denzil Doyle, an Ottawa high-tech consultant. That budget must be established at the beginning of each fiscal year, then followed religiously. "Take a look at the numbers every week, or you may face panic at the end of the quarter when you ship out garbage just to make budget," says Doyle. "Unless you run these meetings with a financial song sheet, you can inadvertently get snowed."

The right organizational structure is also relevant for growth. Too many start-up firms have a loose structure, says Doyle. They typically begin with three main players, all of whom put themselves in the box marked "president," then never quite get around to sorting out their respective duties. Such dallying about determining duties and who's in charge of what can lead to squabbling or warfare among founding shareholders, as we shall see in Chapter Eleven.

Start-up tip: *Only one person can be in charge.*

Doyle takes a contrarian position on some accepted management practices. For instance, he tells entrepreneurs *not* to spend time walking around the operation, pretending the very act is a management tool. According to him, such unstructured forays can only mean trouble. For example, an employee might tell the boss about a half-baked idea that evokes a positive response because the entrepreneur, who hears a dozen such suggestions in a day, is a born enthusiast and takes the view "Let a thousand flowers bloom." The employee assumes that the enthusiasm means approval and charges ahead developing the idea. Weeks later, the entrepreneur discovers a well-advanced project that should never have been begun. Money and time may have been wasted; morale drops when the undertaking is cancelled. The boss is seen as a scatty soul with a short attention span.

Growth doesn't always bring recognition – and that can be a realization that takes some getting used to. "My biggest frustration is that we've got a General Motors mentality but we haven't been discovered yet," says Mike Buckley of Expographiq. Begun in 1978 with five people doing screen printing and woodworking, the firm now does a full range of visual-communications services, including exhibit design and manufacture, desktop publishing and typesetting, screen printing, custom signage, and graphic design using Macintosh computers and Corel workstations. One recent project was to design and build a "healthy house" for Central Mortgage and Housing Corporation. The $125,000 travelling exhibit visited fifteen locations across Canada, promoting ergonomic design, minimal energy use, nontoxic products, and new materials. Expographiq also does museum work, plus custom furniture and signage for Canada Post franchise outlets, but the firm is still looking for the sort of breakthrough project that can mean the kind of profile Buckley seeks.

While the need for public recognition and professional acceptance is natural and drives any firm and its entrepreneur president to greater heights, periods of consolidation are just as important. Mitec Electronics Ltd. of Pointe Claire, Quebec, used the recent recession to take a rest from growth and get costs in line. "We needed this time to consolidate and to improve our bottom line," says Mitec president Myer Bentob. While Mitec sales have stayed flat for three years, profits are up 40 per cent. "We got our costs under control and streamlined operations," Bentob says. "You can't grow at too fast a pace. You'll lose something, profitability or something else."

Growing and grooming the market

In addition to growing your firm by using employees or workers on contract, another way to expand your company can be by calling on volunteers to help out with specific "fun" occasions. When the ten-day Montreal International Jazz Festival started in the summer of 1976, it had neither sponsors nor government backing. Now it has both, and more. "It has a life of its own; it's a social phenomenon. One hundred thousand people gather for concerts in the streets every night," says Alain Simard, president of L'Equipe Spectra Inc. of Montreal, an entertainment and communications company that helps mount the festival. While few firms will

> ### Seven ways to grow your company, distilled from General Lewis MacKenzie's management seminar
>
> 1. Be yourself. As you become more successful, remember that you are still working with your original smarts. You don't get a new brain.
> 2. Follow the Leadership by Wandering Around approach so you can get out and see what your employees are doing.
> 3. Learn to listen to people and discover their passion. Everybody's boring until you scratch that passion.
> 4. Bend the rules a bit. Don't be so regimented you can't find a new way to solve a problem.
> 5. Exhibit a bit of bravado. Show people every so often that you're prepared to do what you're asking them to do.
> 6. Have a buddy system, someone you can turn to for advice and counsel.
> 7. On bad days, be an actor. Even if you don't feel like a leader, your followers are looking for consistency from you.

ever draw such crowds, the technique of appealing to the community through volunteers can be adapted to other profile-raising pursuits.

"Entertainment is more and more consumed at home," said Simard. "When people go out, they want a big event." Spectra now has seven entertainment divisions and has produced three hundred television titles, organized concerts by Wynton Marsalis, recorded Celine Dion in the digital studio in the Laurentians, and produced Rush concerts at the Spectrum.

The festival means $150 million to the local economy, but only 25 per cent of the 1.5 million who attend live outside Montreal. The next step in Spectra's growth is to attract a more international audience to the festival, by positioning it along with the carnival in Rio de Janeiro or the film festival in Cannes. To begin that growth process. Simard is setting out to raise the profile of the event. He's making available, on a worldwide basis, a one-hour TV special about the festival and designing a travel package with Air Canada.

In addition, he is ensuring that, as distribution of music and entertainment changes, Spectra is ready. "We are strategically well positioned for the information highway," says Simard. "We have a critical mass of content, of intellectual property." The firm's catalogue includes fifteen video laser discs that have been distributed for sale in Japan, plus 150 hours of festival concerts. Although the concerts date back fifteen years, all the work was done on high-quality forty-eight-track equipment, so the reproduction continues to be excellent, even though broadcast technology has changed drastically throughout the period.

Simard believes that advertising can change consumer perceptions about products or services. The theory applies across the board and offers another approach to growing your business. Upper Canada Brewing Co. saw steadily increasing sales from its launch in 1984 until 1992, when suddenly the sales figures went as flat as the proverbial bottle of beer left open for a few hours. The firm had not been advertising, so Frank Heaps hired Toronto ad agency Richards & Co. to redesign product packaging and prepare a media campaign. The combination worked; sales headed up again. Agency fees to create the campaign were $400,000, and Upper Canada now spends $400,000 annually, primarily in newspapers and on radio, with Heaps acting as spokesman for his own product. Among his messages is a description of the 4 natural ingredients he uses, compared with the 106 – including preservatives and other chemicals allowed by government regulations – used by his better-known competitors.

Advertising costs money, but there are also ways of getting your story out for free. A well-placed feature on your firm in the local newspaper doesn't cost anything and may have a greater impact than paid advertising. After all, if your muffin shop is cited by the local media as serving the best coffee in the community, that third-party endorsement is worth far more than any amount of paid advertising in the same paper. Don't wait for the media to contact you, figure out who the local business journalists are and write to them. Introduce yourself and lay out your areas of expertise that might be helpful to them in researching a story. Journalists are always looking for new sources of information, fresh names to quote, and such a letter can serve as a useful initial contact. Follow up by phone and invite the journalist to see your place, but remember that, if the journalist does decide to do a story on you, you have no control over what appears. All you can do is be positive, supply names of happy clients, and try to steer the end result as best you can.

Start-up tip: *Remember that during an interview with the media, there are no indiscreet questions, just indiscreet answers.*

Case study: From tiny to titan

In 1985, Adam Okhai bought The Teachers' Store, successor of a store originally founded more than a century earlier, from Molson Companies Ltd. He closed ten stores in the chain and sold off the furniture and film-strip divisions, leaving him with only the two stores that traditionally sold educational products to teachers. The slimmed-down firm had twenty-two employees and annual sales of $3 million. Today, Okhai-Moyer Inc. of Weston, Ontario, operates more than 125 stores across Canada, the United States, and Europe under a variety of names, including Moyer's, Kids Are Worth It!, and The Teachers' Stores in Canada; Latta's, For the Love of Kids!, and Morgan's Educational in the United States; and Kids are Worth It! in Europe. Retail and catalogue sales are now in the $500-million range, through some seven thousand employees offering educational toys and videos, games, puzzles, arts-and-crafts supplies, music, maps, chalkboards, teaching aids, and computer software.

The first year, however, was a disaster. "I got everything wrong and nearly destroyed the company," Okhai says. "I was in too much of a hurry." In the second year, he opened what he thought was a manageable number of new stores – six – but still ran into cash-flow problems. The bank cut his operating line, sending the firm into a survival mode. Throughout that period, however, Okhai persisted in his efforts and kept refining his store designs, learning how to appeal to anyone with children under their care, including parents, teachers, day-care operators, and hospitals.

By 1991, he had experimented sufficiently that he had defined the market and figured out what store layouts worked best. With the arrival of the recession, he was still able to expand, using inexpensive retail space. Moyer's stores are 2,000 square feet in shopping centres; Kids Are Worth It! shops are three times that size and usually in larger regional malls. Employees are stationed near the door as greeters, signage is colourful, and the maze-like layouts mean customers wander in separate selection areas for different departments like science or music. A monthly catalogue goes to school boards; another catalogue aimed at parents appears every other month.

But, behind the scenes, teething problems continued. Okhai decided that, rather than have employees handpick items from the firm's distribution centres for shipment to the individual stores, he would have a computer-driven carousel bring the items to an employee. The idea flopped. The $500,000 investment was inoperative throughout its first year. "Not only did it not help," says Okhai, "it actually got in the way."

He finally did what he realized he should have done in the first place – have experts in place rather than muddle through on his own. So, he hired Richter & Associates, a Toronto-based management-consulting firm, to advise on logistics and computers. Once the experts were involved, the bugs disappeared. Today, Moyer's has warehouses in Moncton, Toronto, Winnipeg, and Vancouver. Of the four, only Toronto has the carousel technology, but it works, and the automation means the firm can do twice as much with half the space, 65,000 square feet versus 120,000 square feet in Moncton.

Strategic alliances

Rather than try to fly solo, like Okhai mistakenly did for a time, companies can grow by forming strategic alliances that build on a partner's strengths. Such a combination means you are able to face competition with more resources, better access to technology, and more expertise than you otherwise would have. What you're looking for in a strategic alliance is the same kind of combination of skills you crafted when the business was still small. If your strength was marketing, you wanted a partner who knew engineering or finance to complement, not replicate, your knowledge.

So, too, with a strategic alliance. You want business partners who can add to your firm's talents in different fields. An alliance is a difficult leap for an entrepreneur, because you are ceding more control and responsibility, not just internally, but to a whole new, outside organization, so you're going to have to make sure your corporate cultures can mesh. If you're a risk-taker, and you hook up with a conservative outfit, you may find that decisions are too slow in coming or that attitudes are too different for a good fit.

Strategic alliances should offer the perfect fit, but the arrangements don't need to be exclusive. "You have to have the right relationship with the vendors," says Derek Johannson, president of Carlyle Computer Products Ltd. of Winnipeg, but he points out that sole-distribution rights are not always possible. Other firms may have snapped up those rights in their geographic area. But, if there is no partner for a large company in your region, you may be able to gain an advantage in your local market. "Strategic alliances mean they can tip the wagon your way," says Johannson.

Another increasingly common alliance is an electronic tie-in known as electronic data interchange (EDI). This technology has been one of the main causes of Wal-Mart's success, because Wal-Mart suppliers know what items are moving on the retailer's shelves and can ship more inventory, even before Wal-Mart places an order. You may not be able to afford such sophistication, but sharing information is another way of forming alliances that will work for both parties – if there is benefit for both. At Mibro Group, the firm's six hundred customers can place orders directly through its data system. Once connected, those customers become committed and are less likely to shop around for a new relationship. Says Mibro president Leon Lapidus, "They only remember to do a review if we screw up – and we don't screw up."

Start-up tip: *Choosing a strategic partner is like picking friends, sometimes they can let you down.*

Case studies: Strategic partnering

The numbers are frightening. Every year, ten million people arrive at hospital emergency departments or physicians' offices in North America with one worrisome symptom: chest pain. Despite all the medical advances made to date, until recently there has been no quick and certain way to decide whether or not the patient is suffering from an evolving myocardial infarction (heart attack) or has indigestion from eating too much pizza. Of the ten million, half are examined then sent home. Of those five million, 5 to 10 per cent die within a day.

The other five million are swept into the medical system

and spend, on average, three to four days in hospital. Of those, three million have no cardiac problem, thereby wasting expensive resources. Among the remaining two million who do have cardiac problems, there are two possibilities: myocardial infarction (MI) or unstable angina. MI treatment can kill a person who is suffering unstable angina. All told, each year $25 billion is wasted on unnecessary hospitalization and one million people needlessly die.

Dr. George Jackowski, director of research at Spectral Diagnostics Inc. in Mississauga, invented a cardiac panel that allows emergency-room staff to use a few drops of the patient's blood and thereby decide within eight minutes whether the patient is having a heart attack or can be sent home with some medicine to settle an unhappy stomach. Inventing the panel and obtaining the money was hard enough (see Chapter Thirteen), getting a strategic partner was even more critical. Spectral established strategic partnership links with Princeton BioMedica Inc. of Princeton, New Jersey, to handle manufacturing and Baxter International, North America's largest marketer of cardiac diagnostics, for research and marketing. Baxter is huge and offers 120,000 products to health-care providers in more than one hundred countries, so Spectral has instant access to that network.

Such alliances mean that Spectral wastes no time getting the product manufactured and into the market. "We want to take advantage of an opportunity that might not be there that long," says CEO Douglas Ball, who has watched other medical developments fall behind the competition because that firm fiddled with production methods or built a sales force from scratch. Clinical trials are currently being conducted in seven American and Canadian hospitals for the necessary U.S. Federal Drug Administration approval. Initial approvals were granted in 1995. Meanwhile, Spectral's growth is providing a home for the knowledge-intensive jobs so crucial in the new economy. The firm employs forty research scientists, up from four in 1991.

Just as Spectral's Jackowski sees himself as a potential Nobel Prize winner, you need to have a larger-than-life view of yourself. How you see yourself as your firm grows can matter as much as how others view you. If you don't have a larger vision of your company than its current size, you may be stuck at low levels of growth for longer than you want. The simple approach is: Think Big.

In 1991, Rider Travel won the $1-billion competitive contract for federal government travel, the largest single travel contract in the country. Even the tough-nosed auditor general signed on to use Rider; the firm handles ninety-five thousand government frequent flyers. In order to bid on such a piece of business, Rider had to think of the firm differently and "visualize" the firm growing to the next level – staying well ahead of the competition.

When the CIBC launched a travel service in 1993 as a way of building loyalty with the chartered bank's credit-card holders, Rider was the selected operator. Because the firm had worked with Canadian Tire on a similar, if smaller, travel-club program, the firm was able to visualize what was required and anticipate demand. As a result, Rider established a strategic alliance with the CIBC by setting up a separate division with fifty people to help bank-card members use the travel service in return for a 5-per-cent discount. Says Rider, "We're a fulfilment centre."

Growth into the United States

If your company is to grow into the United States, you're going to have to think big. Teknion Furniture Systems Inc. of Downsview, Ontario, had success that paralleled the leap in growth made by Rider. Teknion sales to specific clients are usually in the $100,000 to $250,000 range, but in 1992, the firm landed a massive $20-million deal to build seventy-three hundred work stations for Boeing Corp.'s office towers in Washington, where the company designed and developed its new 777 aircraft. "It was," says Teknion chairman Monty Brown, "a real bonanza." The competition to win the contract was against giant U.S. firms Steelcase and Haworth and took two and a half years. Since the order was completed, Teknion has matched all that Boeing business with new sales to other U.S. firms, much of the business as a direct result of winning that job. "Furniture systems are recession-proof," says Brown. "When businesses are expanding, they need us. When times are tough, they have to maximize space. We can help them reduce their need for rented space."

Teknion, founded in 1982, grew quickly for the first few years, often at rates as high as 50 per cent, but now that sales have gone over the $100-million mark, annual growth has slowed to about 20 per cent. That kind of slowdown is normal, because the firm is now growing from a much larger base. In fact, any faster rate of growth might be difficult to accommodate from a financial and production standpoint. After all, if sales are $20 million, and growth is 50 per cent, that's $10 million in new sales. If sales are $100 million and growth is 20 per cent, that's still a healthy $20 million in new orders.

Teknion is now looking for growth in a different geographic area – Europe – with a new line called "Transit," produced at Teknion's plant in Israel. But such a step requires more than a cookie-cutter mentality. Teknion has been careful not to simply export successful North American designs, preferring instead to study the European market and tailor systems for use there. European offices demand interconnecting desking systems with a smaller footprint than the panel systems popular in larger North American surroundings.

Start-up tip: *Growth is more than just doing the same thing better.*

That same thinking applies to any firm trying to grow through its first exports in the United States. Canadians are the first to point out that we are different from Americans, so why should a product that's doing well in Canada automatically sell in the United States? In fact, the corporate landscape in the United States is littered with big Canadian companies that went south and were eaten alive. Canadian Tire, Peoples Jewellers, Robert Campeau, and others all saw their American forays fail in that sharp-elbowed market.

Free trade with the United States has also meant that American competitors are invading Canada. Keilhauer Industries was among those firms hurt by free trade after the pact was launched in 1989. For the next couple of years, sales were flat in Canada, and all but stalled in the U.S. markets. CEO Mike Keilhauer knew he couldn't succeed against the Americans by imitating them. "Companies get into trouble when they copy something from the south, then get killed when that firm comes here with its lower costs," says Keilhauer. As for exports, "You need to be tenacious in a new market."

In response to U.S. interlopers, Keilhauer set out aggressively to reposition the company with major clients: interior decorators and architects. In 1992, he hired San Francisco designer Michael Vanderbyl to create a new marketing program. "We wanted to appeal to Americans, so we thought, 'Let's go to the source,'" says Keilhauer. For his $500,000 fee, Vanderbyl changed everything at Keilhauer, from business cards through catalogues to the look of the showrooms in Chicago, Toronto, and New York. The hefty expenditure paid off; sales shot up 50 per cent the next year, with two-thirds of all sales consisting of exports to the United States.

One of the temptations for many firms with a high percentage of their customers in the United States is to pull up stakes and move there. Most states are so happy to have the new corporate residents that they offer financial lures in the form of tax breaks, training assistance, and cheap money. Fripp Fiber Tennessee Inc., makers of polystyrene takeout food trays and egg cartons, doubled the workforce in Memphis, Tennessee, to 110 after mothballing Winnipeg operations in 1992. Noma Outdoor Products Inc., a Canadian company, supplies all of the United States and parts of Canada with lawnmowers, edgers, trimmers, and snow blowers from its plant in Jackson, Tennessee, that employs 1,000. The firm invested U.S.$20 million to triple the size of the Jackson plant and build another one in nearby McKenzie, Tennessee. Two-thirds of those funds came from a program that offers out-of-state firms (including foreign companies) state revenue bonds at two to three percentage points below going interest rates.

Tennessee offers other incentives: no personal income tax, a five-year business-tax freeze, state-paid rail and road links, and labour and housing costs that are half those found in Toronto. Union membership represents only 8 per cent of the workforce, about one-third of Canadian levels. With the reduction of duties under the Canada–U.S. free-trade agreement, firms can consolidate production wherever they like. For Noma, that may mean shutting down facilities in Brampton. "Production costs are better here," says Noma president Jerry Smith of the Tennessee plant. "I'd run six lines instead of three."

Canadians who have moved to the United States find an attitudinal difference too. Fripp couldn't convince Canadian customers to buy; Americans do. "The buyer in the United States has a more open mind. Many of the markets in Canada are controlled by too few groups," says president Brian Fripp.

Not every Canadian entrepreneur has been convinced by the siren call, however. Frank Milligan of Polywheels looked closely at Kentucky and Illinois, two U.S. states that would have brought his auto-parts facility (which exports 95 per cent of production) closer to his major customers. Serviced land at U.S.$100 an acre would have cost ten to twenty times more in

Canada, but, in the end, he decided not to relocate. "My gut didn't feel right about it," Milligan says. "Productivity isn't as good there. Despite our problems, this is a pretty nice place to live. We're going to stay here and fight it out. I'm just a Canadian." And there's nothing wrong with home-grown.

Growing the larger company

Once a firm gets to about $35 million to $50 million in sales and employs several hundred people, the organization must develop increasingly efficient methods. In 1993, Glegg Water Conditioning Inc. reached $41 million in sales after being in business since 1977. President Robert Glegg knew that the focus had to change; the firm couldn't just keep growing without a new vision of itself and a new mission.

The firm supplies water-purification systems to such industrial sectors as petrochemicals, pulp and paper, pharmaceuticals, nuclear-power plants, and semi-conductor manufacturers. More than 95 per cent of Glegg's sales are outside Canada (it has captured more than 20 per cent of the U.S. market), simply because most of Glegg's installations are in new plants costing $200 million to $1 billion, and there are few such megaprojects under way in Canada. "Canada does not have the infrastructure construction that's going on in the rest of the world," says Glegg, who has set a tough new target. "We want to move from being a U.S. market leader to being a global market leader."

Glegg is a mechanical engineer with his MBA from McGill, who first worked at Pratt & Whitney doing jet-engine design. He learned about water-treatment systems as a salesman for Gaco-Sternson Ltd. in Brantford and founded his own firm in 1977, using $10,000 he had saved from his commissions. Initially, Glegg took established chemical processes and built them to be more cost-efficient, using no patented methods. On-time delivery and lower prices built credibility in the

United States, and the firm acquired various patents and licences along the way, including one for Amberpack, a European process that reduces waste water produced by Glegg's systems.

Until 1989, every system was custom-built, usually from specs running to as many as five hundred pages. "We realized we had to do something different," he says. "Everything started as a prototype." So Glegg's engineers spent two years designing standardized modules, using a trademarked computer software called Glegg Reference Design. Now, clients order from Glegg's specs. "Engineering that used to take six weeks now takes six minutes," he says. Drawings can be issued and work begun the same day that an order is received.

The next Glegg growth ring flows from a 1994 strategy session at which he set an ambitious five-year sales target of $410 million. (Sales in 1994 hit $63 million; 1995 could reach $80 million.) The strategy includes a revolutionary approach to manufacturing. Glegg's two hundred employees have been doing engineering and design at the Guelph facility, but contract out all manufacturing. The firm even buys raw materials from suppliers who then send finished parts to Glegg in Guelph, where everything is assembled, checked, dismantled, shipped to the eventual site, then reassembled. The average system that is now produced costs $1 million and requires a flotilla of eight forty-foot tractor trailers to transport the steel, valves, pipes, and other parts that are then assembled on site under the supervision of Glegg service engineers. The largest order ever delivered took fifty full truckloads. The future may well involve asking suppliers to deliver parts directly to the final site for assembly there, thus eliminating a costly and time-consuming middle step and allowing faster growth.

Just as Michael Douglas was able to don a helmet and peruse files electronically through virtual reality in the film *Disclosure*, Glegg Manufacturing is growing towards something equally as futuristic — virtual manufacturing — where there are no production facilities except those that belong to someone else. Just as virtual reality appears to be real, virtual manufacturing encompasses all the aspects of manufacturing — inventory, production, and quality control — without having the expense of your own premises.

In the new economy, firms of every size will have to adopt this kind of innovative thinking. Whether your firm is a high-tech entity or not — and the particular problems of those firms will be explored in the next chapter — you'll need to use every possible scrap of modern management technique and employ the most up-to-date information technology in order to achieve not only productive growth, but growth with profitability. After all, if your green-thumb efforts in the apple orchard produce sturdy branches and healthy leaves — but no fruit — your efforts have been to no avail.

Summary:

1. Hire excellent managerial help; you can't do everything yourself.
2. Set financial and sales targets in conjunction with employees; make sure an independent board keeps you on track.
3. Don't be afraid to experiment; treat every disaster as a learning experiences.
4. Strike strategic alliances that complement your strengths.
5. Be prepared to reinvent both yourself and the company every year.

CHAPTER 10

High Tech:
Out on the Bleeding Edge

"Entrepreneurialism is the art of creating
something out of nothing."

– Sam Gur, DynaTek Automation

For its relative size, Canada has many high-tech success stories. During the last thirty years Canada has produced such winners as Northern Telecom and Soft-image. A particular area of expertise has been in software, developing the internal programs that solve business problems or produce entertainment. Although high-tech businesses can exist anywhere, they seem to do best when they are located near other similar companies. The synergy of ideas and the ready availability of talented people has created several centres of excellence. In Ottawa, the presence of Bell-Northern Research and the National Research Council has meant a focus of science, around which industry congregated. The University of Waterloo's computer-science and engineering departments have spawned more than a hundred companies in their immediate orbit. High-tech firms have also sprung up in the York Region north of Toronto, in Longueuil, Quebec, and Vancouver, and in these areas each firm feeds off the other. Sheridan College in Toronto has produced the software animation graduates who join such successful firms as Softimage and Digital Domain, which are popular as producers of Hollywood special effects.

As a result, high-tech start-ups deserve special study in this book, because they seem to offer more chance for international success and recognition than any other sector. Software companies such as Corel Corp. and Delrina Corp. have very quickly taken their places in the global marketplace from their Canadian bases. Perhaps one of the key reasons is the educational system. Places like Sheridan and the University of Waterloo are top-ranked in the world. While many graduates are snapped up by U.S.-based companies like Microsoft, others are looking for opportunities at home.

Moreover, another positive aspect about launching a successful high-tech company is that only a small number of people are required to run them. "You can create great technology with few people," says Rob Burgess, CEO of Alias Research. "If the technology is right, everything else will fall into place. The right product is absolutely critical." Equally important is maintaining leadership, or what's called a sustainable competitive advantage. "Technology is the market, technology defines the market," says Burgess. Your firm's technology must be the best in a world where the next version or generation of a product always seems to be only hours away. "Everything is changing so quickly that it creates the opportunity to be lucky," he says.

In addition to luck, entrepreneurial success in high-tech business requires a successful coming together of your mystic vision and the marketplace vagaries. A study of twenty-nine small technology-based companies, done over twenty years by York University and published in 1992, found that during that time nine disappeared, ten had been bought out, and, of the ten still existing, many were struggling.

Start-up tip: *The good news is that your firm has the technology; the bad news is that your leadership will not likely last long.*

"In the high-tech business, you have to look forward, but you can't afford to be too much of a visionary," says Karl Brackhaus, CEO of Dynapro Systems Inc. of New Westminster, British Columbia. "You can dream, but you can only go so far off into the future. We focus on trying to create saleable products as quickly as possible."

Brackhaus grew up in British Columbia and in 1975 completed his PH.D. in engineering physics at the University of British Columbia. After nine years of university, he could have stayed on to teach and do research, but "I got a little tired of being a student," Brackhaus says. "I thought the world was much more exciting than that."

Although he had no particular role models in business (his parents had been farmers in the Fraser Valley after emigrating from Germany), Brackhaus decided that he wanted to go into the private sector. He joined Columbia Engineering International, working on industrial-control projects, before starting Dynapro as what he calls "a bootstrap operation" in 1976 when microprocessor technology was in its infancy. "We partook of the wave," he says. Dynapro's forté is colour-graphics display systems with touch screens for industrial use. The firm now has 340 employees and sales in the $40-million range. Brackhaus claims that Dynapro's success hasn't gone to his head. If ever it does, he reminds himself that, just as he began with nothing, "It can all be taken away quickly."

High-tech success poses some particular problems. Unlike other business sectors, ironically, staying ahead of the competition can be hazardous to corporate health – as Brackhaus has learned. In the mid-eighties, when Dynapro announced a new product line of personal computers and software for use in manufacturing plants, customers immediately assumed that the firm's previous line was obsolete. "When the new product was announced, sales of the old product collapsed," says Brackhaus. Six months passed before the firm was able to get back on track. The incident did not halt ongoing innovation, but it did alter how they launch products. The firm has continued to design, manufacture, and market hardware and software for the industrial automation market, but now they know that when a new version is announced, they better be ready to supply what will almost certainly be immediate customer demand. Says Brackhaus, "You have to reinvent yourself and your products all the time."

Case study: Something out of nothing

Israeli-born Sam Gur provides an excellent example of how a high-tech company can be launched by one person and ride the wave of demand to success. Gur received a scholarship to study international economics under Robert Cox at York University and was surprised when he arrived in Toronto in the fall of 1985 to see the high public profile of one Bobby Cox. After a while, Gur realized that, although the names were the same, the coach of the Blue Jays was not his new prof. The team did provide the newly arrived immigrant from Israel with something else, however: a connection with his adopted country. "I knew nobody. I was lonely in the beginning. My first friends were the Blue Jays. Every night, I got together with my friends on TV. It would break a little bit of the silence of loneliness."

After three years at York, Gur had completed his course work leading towards a doctorate, but decided he'd had enough. "I was looking for a challenge. I was a lost soul looking for meaning in life," he says. Gur recalled with fondness the two years he spent in Paris earlier in the decade, the time between his BA degree and the start of his MA studies, when he worked as an assistant in the atelier of a kinetic sculptor. "Artists do art because they have to, they need to communicate. Art in the drawer is not art, it needs to be on the wall," says Gur. "Business is about communicating too. If you have the need within, you'll be prepared to sacrifice anything to achieve," he says.

Gur left York and visited his brother, who was working in the California computer industry. In California, Gur spent some time helping out a friend whose firm sold memory-storage devices. While the job lasted only a few months, Gur became fascinated by the velocity of change in the industry and the potential of new products coming onto the market. He returned to Toronto and launched DynaTek Automation Systems Inc. in November 1988, with one product, a removable device used to back up information stored on a hard drive. He launched the product, developed in partnership with a California company, DataMemory, at the Toronto computer show that month, accompanied by a cartoon pamphlet extolling its virtues.

Sales took off, reaching $2 million in the first year and tripling to $6 million in the second year, as Gur kept expanding operations in Downsview. He took a risk with the product, because all of his high-end storage products worked with what's known as small computer systems interface (SCSI), popularly known as "scuzzy." Initially, only Apple computers followed that protocol, but Gur was satisfied to go after that niche market and forget about compatibility with the products of other manufacturers. The other choice, to try and supply the larger market, made less sense. After all, there were already lots of companies in that field. He would have just been an also-ran, no matter how good he was. Instead, he took a contrarian view and followed the path that few others had – all the while knowing that chances of success were good. "You can't be everything to everybody or you'll end up being nobody," he says. "We positioned ourselves in a futuristic market before others were there."

Start-up tip: *The beauty of starting from scratch is that you don't have a lot to lose.*

As more computer manufacturers adopted the "scuzzy" system, DynaTek's product line expanded. The firm also began producing disk, optical, and tape products as well as CD-ROMs for all of the key computer operating systems, plus equipment for digital editing and recording. Typical of the firm's current new products is a CD-ROM library that operates like a jukebox, with robotics that lift the required CD into place. The basic unit costs $10,000, holds 250 CDs, and can be accessed by four users at any one time. The unit expands to hold up to 2,750 CDs, operating just like a book library by assembling information in a way that allows access by any networked computer. Companies find this product useful when they have many CD-ROM users and don't want all employees to demand individual copies of the same CD-ROM. This way, the companies need only one copy in the "library," rather than multiple copies of the same reference books on everyone's desk. "Most everything you've seen in computers, you've seen before," he says. "Scientific breakthroughs are not so easy; this is a scientific breakthrough."

Gur also set high standards of productivity, aiming for sales of $1 million per employee per year. "That's unachievable, but that's okay. If you don't have a dream that's unachievable, how do you get beyond the achievable?" At DynaTek, sales amount to about $700,000 per employee, or three times the industry average, as a result of setting tough targets. (By 1994, the firm had 145 employees and $100 million in sales.) Growing the company to that level involved moving. By 1992, DynaTek had reached $50 million in sales, and Gur was becoming discontent with manufacturing in the Toronto area. Although space costs were cheap because of the recession, he found the work force unstable, so the firm moved to Bedford, Nova Scotia, in 1993, taking over a 130,000-square-foot former Michelin Tire storage facility. There was a nationalistic aspect to the choice; he wanted to remain in Canada, even though U.S. jurisdictions beckoned.

The new location puts the company one time zone closer to Europe, where one-third of sales now occur. But there was another incentive, one that seems to be offered by different states and provinces to high-tech companies in particular, because they are perceived as "clean" companies. They don't require mining rights, won't pollute the air with their processes, and are perceived by taxpayers as likely to produce jobs. Nova Scotia offered an enticing deal financially. The rich package included: a $4-million long-term loan guarantee; a combined federal-provincial $3.4-million term loan at commercial rates for equipment purchase; a $4-million grant to renovate the premises; another $4-million grant to cover relocation expenses; and concessions that substantially reduce local business and property taxes. In return, DynaTek agreed to a five-year plan that includes job-creation targets. "They needed employment, we had jobs," says Gur. "We needed cash; they had it." He was able to use the loan guarantee, for example, to backstop a new $10-million line of credit with the Royal Bank.

Gur has found an improved quality of life in Bedford and says that the workers there are more loyal than in Toronto. Although some technical people were transferred from Toronto, two-thirds of the employees are local hires. DynaTek has also begun a co-op program with the Technical University of Nova Scotia to help train future employees. In addition to the Bedford plant, the firm has sales and distribution centres in

Toronto, Tel Aviv, and Winchester, England, to reach clients in forty countries.

DynaTek has decided to tackle other countries first before taking aim at the United States. One reason is that large American competitors are already well established there, but the second reason is that the nationality of a Canadian company is more helpful in Europe than in the United States. Canadians have achieved a good reputation in high tech, one on which other firms can piggyback. Moreover, the very nature of Canadians seems more acceptable in Europe generally. "In the United States, you are Canadian. In Europe, you're *not* an American although you are a North American," says Gur. "They prefer to work with Canadians because they don't arrive in Europe all full of themselves like the Americans do. If you want the core, go after the periphery. Let the Americans fight it out in their markets; you can build volume in the rest of the world."

Because high-tech firms are by their nature niche players, they can make deep inroads in specific markets. For example, DynaTek customers range from a $1-million (Australian) installation, connecting twenty thousand users across three hundred sites for the Australian Department of Social Security, to the likes of music producer Teddy Riley, who uses DynaTek's digital music equipment when he works with Michael Jackson or Heavy D and the Boyz. One high-profile endorsement came when the firm's music line was listed in the credits of the film *Lawnmower Man*, based on the Stephen King short story. Because high tech tends to be a word-of-mouth business, once you've had success with one company in a field, others will follow. A movie or music credit, for example, will very often mean that others chase after your product to mimic the style that succeeded.

High-tech firms cannot, however, rest on their laurels. You always have to make sure that the firm has a hand stretched out to the future. DynaTek is a member of the Optical Processing and Computing Consortium of Canada (OPCOM), a partnership with Digital Equipment of Canada, SPAR Aerospace, and the National Research Council. DynaTek's specific role will be to develop an ultra-high-performance data-storage system capable of transferring data at rates suitable for the processing speeds of optical computers used for applications like digital video and to search large databases.

The hybrid processor envisaged by OPCOM for development within five years would be a thousand times faster than current super computers and one million times faster than current desktop PCs. "The success of today should warn you about the failure of tomorrow," says Gur. "So many companies get cocky. You get thinking, 'I must be Midas.' Of course, that's just bullshit. Success is just driven by circumstances. When you're in a fast-changing industry, you have to have a fast-changing company. As a result, you have to be constantly listening to the heartbeat."

Start-up tip: *Comfort is your biggest enemy.*

For Sam Gur, the secret was creative positioning or preparing himself for the unknown. This is more than just niche marketing, this describes the right *kind* of thinking, the kind of high-octane strategic planning that helps you hit the moving target that is the future. Call this kind of thinking "creative positioning," for it prevents negativism inside an organization and keeps everyone focused on trends in the marketplace and innovations coming from others. But you cannot count on others to push you along to success, you need your own engineers, working on new developments, before others arrive at the same place. After all, technology *is* the market, technology defines the market. You don't need a large organization to do this. You can create the right technology with a very few people if they are the sort of people who don't think of themselves as using CAD/CAM, for example, but know instead that they are ultimately making a part of a larger whole.

That doesn't mean automatic acceptance for every new product. Canadian consumers can be wary of technology; that concern makes success tricky. "I've been on the bleeding edge several times," says Tom Moorehead, president of Mentor Networks Inc., a company that's working with Ottawa-area doctors in retraining programs that use interactive multimedia. "I've done pilots in the home. People love the stuff when it's free, but when they have to pay for it, it's another thing." As a result, you have to be careful to have a realistic view of the marketplace. Don't get so carried away by your work that you assume everyone wants it. With the right piece of software, however, one that buyers want, being on the "bleeding edge" is crucial. You have to stay ahead of the competition, because there isn't always much room for multiple producers of the same computer software to send faxes, for example. "Leadership is fleeting," says Moorehead. "You have to get to the market first."

Staying ahead

Right now, your competitor is probably on the verge of announcing new technology that will make yours obsolete. What are you doing to stay ahead? What are the characteristics of today's technology companies? They include:

- early obsolescence;
- highly technical products;
- intangible assets;
- large research-and-development expenditures;
- a workforce with superb skills; and
- fast sales growth, a high percentage of which are exports.

Research and development is another way of staying ahead, and ATS Aerospace offers an instructive example of how a firm used R&D grants, coupled with innovative thinking, for export success and growth at home. The firm's big break came in 1992 when ATS won a $5.2-million contract to supply a control-tower visual simulator for Vienna, Austria. The competition was global; the job was bigger than the ATS annual revenues at the time. Employment exploded from thirty-two people to eighty-four to produce the 360-degree tower simulator that delivers an image just like the real tower would, right down to the runways and skyline of Vienna.

To begin designing software before the necessary hardware is even on the horizon requires guts. "We took the leap of faith," says executive vice-president Amy Friend. ATS also succeeded in becoming a market leader in virtual-reality projects, because the firm spends 25 per cent of annual revenue on research and development, a level that Friend admits hurts. "It can be very painful, but if you keep R&D [spending] low, you're not going to hit that moving window of high technology."

In addition to radar simulators, ATS also builds air-defence targets for military training that simulate the infrared and radar signatures of modern aircraft and missiles. "The problem in peacetime is to present a realistic target and performance," says Friend. At $2 million a copy, Exocet missiles are a bit expensive for target practice. "This is a simple technology that supplies realism without blowing something up. The requirement for training goes on whether there's peace or war," she says.

Successful companies do not rely on popular tools and techniques to make their people faster, more productive, and innovative – instead, they fundamentally change the way they work and how they manage their people and resources. Gerry Meinzer, a partner in the Toronto-based merchant bank PMP Associates, worked at IBM and spent nineteen years as president of Real Time Datapro Ltd. He urges young firms to remember that "The Americans outdo us in one area – packaging and selling junk and improving the product as they go along. Know your marketplace and become part of it." In other words, if you wait for complete product excellence, you may never get it out the door. That's why most computer software products come out numbered, using various versions that are better than the previous ones. Consumers of these products have come to expect continuous improvement.

The Americans also outdo us in another talent: their capacity to accept home-grown success. At twenty-eight, Moya Cahill started MNC Group in 1989 in St. John's to market technology services to the increasing number of companies gathering there to develop Hibernia. During the first eighteen months, many of her clients were outside the province, and her office tended to be Air Canada business centres at airports, her only equipment a portable computer. As Hibernia nears its 1997 production date, the graduate engineer's firm has a dozen employees and bills more than $1 million a year doing a range of jobs from quality-assurance programs to structural inspections. "Newfoundlanders don't like other Newfoundlanders who succeed on Hibernia," she says. "I get along better with the boys from Chevron in New York than my fellow Newfoundlanders."

Maybe that's why many of the inventive entrepreneurs in Canada are relatively recent immigrants to Canada – they're not held back by their expectations of the culture nor by Canadian expectations of them. Emmie Leung of International Paper once followed another speaker at a conference who had talked about the difficulties other women face because North American culture has kept them in their place and under control. Said Leung in her opening remarks, "I'm an alien from outer space. I don't belong to this culture we've just talked about." On the one hand, immigrants don't know what can't be done; on the other hand, they battle hard for success and acceptance.

Case study: Stranger in a strange land

The story of Franz Plangger's success in Canada should serve to remind home-brewed citizens that sometimes we imagine barriers that don't exist. Without the knowledge of what you *cannot* do, sometimes you can achieve the unexpected. Plangger arrived in Canada in 1967 from Bregenz, Austria, and worked as chef for a year in Montreal, then cooked for three years at the Iron Ore Co. cafeteria in Labrador City. There, he finished his high-school education and studied university-credit courses from Memorial University via television broadcasting. As far as he was concerned, the chance to work in the far north and be educated at the same time was an opportunity he hadn't expected. "I couldn't believe my luck," he says.

He saved $9,000 during his stint, married a Québécoise teacher, and moved to the Gatineau region of Quebec. There, he bought a mobile home and attended Carleton University, where he received his BA followed by his master's degree in electrical engineering in 1976. As the winner of a National Research Council scholarship, Plangger worked at Bell-Northern Research, then moved to Jaytel Communication in the silicon valley area of Kanata, Ontario. In 1981, he joined a Carleton friend, David Choo, at CML Technologies Inc. of Hull, Quebec, the firm Choo had founded in 1979. (Plangger bought Choo out in 1989.)

During the eighties, CML changed from its beginnings as a scientific programming company to fill a new market niche: designing and manufacturing emergency communications and mobile radio-dispatch systems used by fire and police for 911 calls. Today CML has $9 million in sales and 115 employees. The firm also produces the Liberty Communications Console, which was developed by its own engineers, the external design done in concert with Gibson Product Design Inc., a firm Plangger found simply by looking in the Yellow Pages. The console provides display and control over radio, land lines, paging, and intercom functions in emergency situations. About 80 per cent of the firm's sales are in the United States; typical is a $5-million deal to supply a mobile radio console system with seventy-eight dispatch positions to the city of Chicago. "We're not the market leader, but we're the technology leader," says Plangger. "We want to be focused first, perform well in our niche, and not chase all over the place."

Patents pending

Because the market is chock-a-block with high-tech firms, you have to be certain that someone else hasn't already beaten you to your idea. If a patent has previously been issued, your progress could be blocked or you may need to enter into an agreement with that rival firm.

"Patents can be a critical component to shareholder value," says George Takach, a partner specializing in technology and software at the Toronto law firm of McCarthy, Tétrault. Takach has seen young firms do development work for years, only to discover someone else was there first. Takach quotes one incredulous businessman as saying, "You mean I spent $3 million and two years to find I have to pay a royalty [to another firm]?"

The answer is a $1,500 patent search that will let you work around a patent, if one already exists, or tell you that you need to head in a different direction. "In a start-up you have to treat it as a cost of business," Takach says. "Better to spend $1,500 on a patent search before you spend your evenings and weekends working on something that is already patented."

Case study: Rampant protectionism

Patents, however, don't offer automatic, hassle-free protection. Vas-Cath has twenty-eight different patents, most of them registered in several countries to protect the catheters made by the firm for medical purposes. "You patent everything you can to make a wall, not just what *you're* making, but also what others might come up with," says Vas-Cath's Geoff Martin. Since everyone is thinking the same way, bitter court battles ensue. Lawsuits are commonplace, as other companies try to build fences around their own business or knock a competitor out of the marketplace. Such fights are not only expensive, but they can also divert management attention from other aspects of the business in ways that become doubly hurtful.

Vas-Cath fought one patent case in Canada in 1987-88, spent $150,000 on legals, and lost at trial. That defeat was nothing compared to the next battle, against the same competitor, in the United States. This time, eight patents were involved, and Vas-Cath spent $750,000 by 1992 on legal costs, even before the matter went to trial. "The whole system seemed to be set up to make lawyers rich," says Martin. Vas-Cath had two of the eight allegations dismissed in the early going, but the rulings were reversed on appeal before initial decisions had even been handed down on the other six. "We were getting nowhere," says Martin, who decided to settle out of court rather than spend more money on legal fees in what his lawyers told him was becoming one of the most complicated cases in U.S. legal history.

Start-up tip: *When you're dealing with lawyers, the meter's always running. And you're paying.*

Meanwhile, Vas-Cath ran into other problems. The U.S. Food and Drug Administration (FDA) said the firm's products that were being exported to the United States failed to meet FDA rules. The Vas-Cath staff who were responsible for maintaining these high standards had assured the Martins, busy with the patent wars, that everything was fine, but suddenly in early 1993 Vas-Cath was hit with a ruling known as an "import alert." Overnight, U.S. sales of the firm's major product in the medical-devices market were halted. The first decision the firm took was not to pull back into a shell. "Too often, companies retreat," says Jane Martin.

The Martins suspected that, even though the Canada–U.S. Free Trade Agreement had been in place since 1989, Vas-Cath was the victim of protectionist action, engineered by a U.S. firm to protect the market against foreign competition. Certainly, treatment of American and Canadian firms can be completely different. A U.S. firm that has failed to meet one of the lengthy FDA criteria is notified of the failings and can work on improvements – while continuing to sell the item. Not only could Vas-Cath not sell the affected product, the firm could initially not even get a reading on what suddenly went wrong after it had received clean bills of health on every previous FDA inspection.

After a time, they were told that there was nothing wrong with the product itself, the potential problem was a packaging validation: would the package stay sterile and intact for the five-year shelf-life of the product? Vas-Cath argued that packaging passed muster but, just when Vas-Cath thought everything was okay, the FDA seemed to take a new position. Geoff Martin recalls one FDA inspector saying, "I was at a meeting last month and they've changed the rules." Vas-Cath couldn't seem to get firm dates set for inspection at its Mississauga plant to approve the packaging validation. Every time the FDA said an inspector would show up, the visit was postponed.

Meanwhile, although production had been chopped, Vas-Cath maintained employment levels, hoping that approvals would soon be in place, because the firm would need that expertise immediately to resume manufacturing for export. After seven months of export blockages, the firm finally let a dozen employees go in the summer of 1993. As Vas-Cath battled the FDA, the company tried to expand European sales, but the base was small and by September they had replaced only about 13 per cent of the U.S. business lost.

After the company had seen sales increases, on average, of about 35 per cent every year, it had come as quite a shock when sales in 1993 fell about one-third from 1992 levels. Vas-Cath had been number two in the U.S. market, with about 35 per cent of total sales, while the top firm had 50 per cent. With Vas-Cath barred, a number of smaller firms that shared the other 15 per cent became more aggressive. "The competition enjoyed it," says Geoff. "They had a field day."

Part of the problem with the U.S. regime is that patents are easier to obtain in the United States than in Canada. The U.S. patent office has taken the view that if there is *any* unique aspect to a product, it will issue a patent. The trouble is that more than one product may look and function exactly alike, and each of them may receive a patent number. Add such an easy-going attitude to the litigious nature of the United States, and lawsuits about patent infringement become part of daily business. The Martins made the strategic decision not to hire a Washington lobbyist to try and "fix" the problem on Capitol Hill. "I didn't want a political thing that takes years," says Jane. Instead, they retained a Canadian law firm, Gowling Strathy & Henderson, and also worked with officials at the Canadian Embassy in Washington. That combination finally caused the FDA to set an inspection date that the agency honoured. Approval quickly followed, and sales to the United States resumed at previous levels. "It doesn't sound like a big deal, but it was," says Jane. "We were in pain for nine months." But after suffering the sales setback in 1993, 1994 sales were back above 1992 levels by 30 per cent. Vas-Cath had recovered.

Partnerships for profit

Not everything you do will be based either on your own patents or proprietary software you have developed. Sometimes the best way to get ahead will be by working with other firms. Strategic alliances seem particularly necessary and productive among high-tech firms. Franz Plangger's CML Technologies has a strategic partner in GTE of Tampa, Florida. GTE distributes CML systems to certain customers, usually the independent phone companies. Such relationships can be pivotal, and they go beyond mere customer links to include equity investment, no-compete arrangements, and access to distribution systems you won't otherwise have. Alias Research, for example, almost went bankrupt at one point because of management's love affair with animation. Fortunately, Alias had a champion, General Motors, because Alias had sold six software systems to the giant automaker. Management was out of control, because they couldn't decide whether to go with their "champion" and produce practical applications, or go with their love, animated special-effects. Alias wisely decided to put aside love and focused on industrial design for Sony, Motorola, and Volvo. In six months, sales from these new customers moved cash in the bank from zero to $1.6 million. The coffers thus replenished, Alias was then able to return to animation. In 1995, Alias merged with Silicon Graphics Inc. of Mountain View, California, and Wavefront Technologies Inc. of Santa Barbara, California, in a deal worth $500 million to Alias.

Start-up tip: *A strategic alliance is like an orchestra; you need a conductor. You have to decide who's in charge, or you just end up with a cacophony.*

As the Alias deal proved, the lesson for any technology firm is to get involved with those companies synonymous with the best in the marketplace. Or, if they don't have the market cornered, at least those firms with the best distribution channels. The number-one criteria is to seek out management capability. "Ninety per cent of companies I look at have poor management or abysmal management," says merchant banker Loudon Owen. (Among Owen's most lucrative investments was $350,000 in Softimage in 1987, which was sold for $135 million to Microsoft half a dozen years later.) Management must possess talent and the capacity to work with others (including people outside the company), but most of all it must have guts, says Owen, "Because they're going to be scared out of their wits every two weeks." Management also needs a little luck to stay ahead of the competition. "You don't know who's developing what around the corner," says Owen. "Maintain your enthusiasm for life and realize that you can do well internationally."

For Dynapro's Karl Brackhaus, that helpful partnership came when Allen–Bradley Canada Inc. bought a 25-per-cent share in Dynapro in 1983 and became the firm's sole customer. In 1985, Allen–Bradley increased its ownership to 50 per cent (Brackhaus owns the other half). The strategic partnership brought both money for growth as well as increased sales to Allen–Bradley in the United States and Canada.

In 1991, Dynapro decided to diversify away from that sole client relationship by buying two former suppliers, John Fluke Manufacturing Co. of Everett, Washington, and a division of W. H. Brady Co. of Milwaukee, Wisconsin. Brackhaus closed Fluke and moved the firm's equipment to New Westminster, thus creating another assembly line that gave Dynapro a new family of touchscreen terminals and a larger customer base. A new plant in Milwaukee, along with the previous facility, meant that Dynapro could produce a full range of touchscreen terminals from as large as fifteen inches down to handheld versions measuring one inch by four inches. Financing of $3 million for the Wisconsin-based plant and equipment was helped by a bond guarantee given by Milwaukee that ensures long-term debt at 5.5 per cent. Dynapro has also been assisted in the past by the Canadian government's Western diversification fund.

Although all businesses have trouble convincing banks to lend money, high-tech firms have it particularly rough. Some entrepreneurs, however, are noticing that the glacier is melting. "There's a lot of interest now," says Toby Gilsig, president and CEO of M3i Systems Inc. of Longueuil, Quebec. "Banks have realized that bricks and mortar aren't as safe as they look. They're trying to get more knowledgeable [about high tech]." One of the ways that high-tech firms can respond is to make sure the revenue forecasts are accurate. In order to make those forecasts as predictable as possible, the firm's product should be sufficiently proprietary (yours alone), so that copying is difficult, but open and accessible enough so that the product doesn't frighten off buyers.

One of the first things you have to convince your banker about is this: high tech doesn't always equal high risk. For some bankers this is a more difficult concept than it is for others. Being near a high-tech centre helps. Because other firms in your field are concentrated there, banks are more likely to locate understanding bankers in the same region. "Because bankers are used to seeing and touching their collateral, many find it difficult to deal with the intangible aspect of knowledge-based assets," says TD Bank's Rick Lunny. "Without the tires to kick we are asked to finance air." Before he'll finance your "air" you'll need:

- a product with a good market acceptance or strong niche;
- strong financial controls and reporting systems;
- a reasonable level of existing cash flow; and
- patient, private capital from people who understand the business and give you your head.

Case study: You can bank on it

Back in the bad old days, when the bank's mainframe computer was so big that the machinery needed water-cooling, paying by credit card was a painful process. Choose an item in

the store, hand over the plastic, then wait while the clerk telephoned for approval of your credit standing. Even if everything was okay and you weren't over your limit, time dragged,
embarrassment heightened, and the lineup behind you turned
restive. Today, a simple swipe of that same card through a
point-of-sale device sends an electronic impulse to a contract
firm like Transact Data Services Inc. (TDSi) of Mississauga,
where, nanoseconds later, approval is authorized and the purchase is complete.

TDSi is the result of one man fleeing a large corporation to
found his own firm. John Rieschi, president and CEO of TDSi,
previously worked for NCR Canada Ltd., where, in 1982, he
launched a new service to handle credit-card authorization for
banks, oil companies, and retailers. By 1985, the data-capture
service was doing about thirty million transactions a year for a
bank and an oil company, thus truncating, or eliminating,
paper. Eaton's had a similar system, and the other banks were
beginning to look at how they should get into the field themselves rather than use a service firm like NCR. Although the
transaction-processing business was profitable for NCR, the firm
was losing interest and in 1985 chose to sell it.

Rieschi decided he'd do a management buyout and sought
a financial backer. The Federal Business Development Bank
introduced him to the Simkin family, four brothers who had
owned BACM Industries Ltd. of Winnipeg. They had grown
BACM to a $500-million land-development and construction
company with ten thousand employees before selling out to
Genstar in 1968. The family turned out to be familiar with
high-tech ventures. Gary Simkin, son of Abe and the youngest
of the four BACM brothers (the rest are now retired), was particularly knowledgeable about shared computer networks. The
family had already invested in an Atlanta-based firm called
Buypass, the System. As a result of being in that business, the
family knew the need for "neutrality" – the capability to work

with any firm's communications hardware rather than try to force one-size-fits-all solutions. "We were nimble," says Abe Simkin. "We offered total flexibility. Now, everyone is running to build networks. When we started, nobody was." What John Rieschi had in mind was very similar to the business that the Simkins were running in the United States. As a result, they needed very little convincing; they had already seen it work elsewhere.

With that family financial backing, Rieschi spent two months negotiating the sale of the transaction-processing business from NCR, working his way up the ladder and talking to officers at corporate headquarters in Dayton, Ohio. Finally, NCR decided not to sell after all. But by this time Rieschi had moved on in his mind beyond NCR; he knew he couldn't stay there, so he resigned and launched his own competing company, TDSi, in 1986. Since then, the Simkin family have put in $10 million through their firm, Heritage Investments Ltd. There has also been backing from Tim Casgrain at Hees International Bancorp, and Rieschi and four other senior managers have a "sweat equity" deal that gives them 10 per cent of TDSi over time as part of their compensation packages.

Rieschi launched TDSi from his home and lost money for the first two years. His strategy was not to insert the company between the hundreds of thousands of Canadian retailers and their respective banks but to try and become a silent provider to both sides. During the first few months, he focused on sales presentations and kept his costs down by working hundred-hour weeks from home and hiring only a part-time consultant. Leaving the safety of the corporate world and a regular paycheque was difficult. "For me, it was a major jump," says Rieschi. Moreover, he was dealing with a host of new problems, like leasing arrangements, capital needs, insurance requirements, and company bylaws.

Still, he had contacts from his NCR days, and he was finally able to convince the Bank of Montreal (which had no point-of-sale terminals of its own) to try a pilot project with one of its customers, a Beaver Lumber dealer. On the first day, TDSi successfully handled sixty transactions at the store, and the concept was rolled out to other stores in the chain. For the bank, there were cost reductions of twenty-five cents per transaction, because there was less paper to worry about and the transaction didn't need to be entered by hand into the system. Retailers, who paid for the terminal, benefited, because staff could get on with serving other customers, and the credit payment was guaranteed. Because he had seen how slowly a hierarchical organization like NCR responded, Rieschi wanted to create something different at TDSi. "We've built a team culture, a flat, dynamic organization. I love the entrepreneurial spirit."

The Bank of Nova Scotia also became a customer and, in 1988, TDSi broke even on $9 million in revenue and has been profitable every year since. "When we started, we weren't recognized as a major EDI [electronic data interchange] player," says Rieschi. "Today, we're *it*." Of the portion of the purchase price given up by the retailer when a credit card is used, twelve cents per sale goes to TDSi. TDSi's central Tandem computers are linked to forty-five thousand terminals and handle $20 million in retail sales daily (not just for banks but for service-station chains such as Sunoco). The firm employs 170 people and had revenue in 1994 of $32 million. TDSi also offers electronic authorization through SCAN Network Inc. for twelve million cheques used for retail purchases annually. Another division, TDNI Transport Data Network International Inc., provides cargo tracking and transaction processing for exporters and importers.

Start-up tip: *Service providers should work seamlessly between a client and that client's customers.*

The connection with Simkin proved to be more than just a money lifeline. Simkin introduced Rieschi to Great-West Life Assurance Co. of Winnipeg (Simkin is on the board of directors), and TDSi created SNS Shared Health Network Services Ltd. for Great-West and three other insurers. Shared Health connects twenty-five hundred pharmacists and twenty-two hundred dentists with insurance companies running health plans. An employee who is part of a company health plan presents a card to the pharmacist, who passes the card through a reading device, thereby informing the insurance firm electronically of the prescription purchase. Payment flows overnight to the pharmacist, and the three hundred thousand employees who are covered through this system are neither out of pocket nor do they have to wait weeks for reimbursement. Before the network existed, the per-claim cost for the insurer was $5 to $7 on a $21 prescription. Now it's $1, including twenty cents to TDSi.

For investor Simkin, the individual entrepreneur matters more than the idea, whether the person was a gung-ho engineer back at BACM who wanted to run a new division or Rieschi with his new technology. "Each guy was a king in his castle and we danced to his tune," says Simkin. "If you centralize, you stifle creativity." As a former corporate employee, Rieschi revels in his new life and his compensation depends upon the success of the firm. His annual salary is in excess of $150,000, plus a bonus that can be as much as 70 per cent of his base pay. That compensation package, along with his ownership position, means a substantial change from the past. Says Rieschi, "If I was still at NCR, I wouldn't potentially be a millionaire."

The information highway

Two years ago, no one had heard about the information highway. Now, the place is clogged with businesses trying to figure out how to make a profit on the Internet. North

America is still in the early stage of development, but money will certainly be made on the *infobahn*, as each month more people learn how to cruise the Net. Today, there are an estimated 50 million people with access to the electronic network of networks that makes up the Internet (perhaps 1.5 million of those in Canada) and, by the end of the century, the figure could be 1 billion. The closest parallel to the information highway may turn out to be the nineteenth-century railways. Investors and others took a chance in building railways across the country, expecting to make money from passengers and cargo. In fact, the real return on their investment flowed from the real estate that came with the rights-of-way.

The information superhighway may be like that; profits may be found in surprising areas that no one has yet considered. So far, even popular services don't create a broad enough base to pay for the initial investment, let alone turn a profit. Prodigy, owned by IBM and Sears and one of the best-known U.S. on-line information services, has been available in Canada since 1994. The commercial service cost U.S.$1 billion to build and has two million subscribers who exchange tens of thousands of messages daily – but it remains a money-loser. Prodigy also gives users access to the Internet, a loose affiliation of users who participate in a collection of international public forums that function as news networks on such diverse pursuits as religion, science, pets, hobbies, and UFOs. A typical "club" might include twenty-five thousand members who chat on-screen about birding, right down to current information like the particular warblers spotted today during migration at Cape May, New Jersey.

For all the problems, the Internet market potential is huge. Among some California aficionados, access to such gateways have become an integral part of any job package, just like a dental plan. For people who want to be part of the knowledge-intensive new economy and be wired to the world, one Canadian solution is CANARIE (the Canadian Network for

Advancement of Research, Industry and Education), the national scientific research network. The federal and most provincial governments are spending money to build networks, and CANARIE hopes to attract $1 billion from the public and private sectors by the year 2000 for the construction of an "electronic backbone" across Canada.

Individual businesses can use the Net to connect to potential clients around the globe. All that's required is a PC, a modem (which costs $300 to $500), and access. In addition to Prodigy (1-800-776-3449 for information), there is also GENie (1-800-638-9636), CompuServe, the largest of the four (1-800-848-8199), and America Online (1-800-827-6364). Each of these commercial networks costs about U.S.$10 a month for the basic Internet connect service, then bills for time used.

The Net can be a marketing and sales tool for your company if you have what's known as a "home page," or information site, which lists information about your firm. Setup costs can be $1,000 or more, and monthly fees could run around $150 to $200. Having a "home page," however, means that information about your firm can be accessed by potential customers you wouldn't otherwise have contacted. Duthie's, an independent bookseller in Vancouver, has already found the Internet a profitable way to sell books beyond its local market. Other firms are offering assistance in setting up home pages, among them The AdvantEdge Corp (see page 285).

Start-up tip: *If you're not on the Net, you may never get connected.*

Case studies: The road builders

A Toronto-based service, UUNET Canada Inc., isn't waiting for governments to get their acts together and sports this tell-all slogan: "Paving the information highway to you." "This is enabling technology that puts people in touch with each other," says Tom Glinos, UUNET vice-president. "Imagine the contents of a public library flowing daily. CANARIE wants to build the electronic backbone across the country, but that's not the problem," says Glinos. "The problem is the last mile." UUNET has already made the connection that spans that last mile to the user at home or in the office by charging a monthly fee to users.

Begun in 1992 by Glinos, along with partner and president Rayan Zachariassen, with $100,000 of their own money, UUNET grew in two years to three hundred subscribers and annual revenues of $750,000, and it expects to double those levels every year. Subscribers need an additional phone line and pay UUNET $50 a month plus $6 per hour for use. A dedicated business line can cost up to $1,200 a month. For that fee, a subscriber gets everything from the popular Internet features to items from the Library of Congress. "We supply access to the world," says Zachariassen. "We're like the phone system."

Well, not quite; there's no actual phone book – the system is expanding so rapidly. Most users don't know all that's available, because there are few clues beyond word of mouth or guidebooks published by others, such as *Zen and the Art of the Internet* (Prentice-Hall) and *Whole Internet User's Guide & Catalog* (O'Reilly and Associates).

But think of Internet as the early awakenings of the phone company. Decades ago you needed operator assistance to talk locally; now you make international calls directly. Party lines once meant no privacy; that problem has long since disappeared. Images are now possible on the Internet, but the quality is nothing like television quality, because there are many fewer frames per second than on TV. That's one area where entrepreneurs are busy working on what's become known as the five-hundred-channel universe. "I don't care how many channels you have beaming down to you, people only watch what they want to watch because they like it," says Syd Kessler of F/X Corp. "The more channels, the more product you've got to have, and there's not enough property out there."

Kessler plans to grow F/X from first-year sales of $8 million and forty employees to something much larger are nothing if they're not grand. "What I'm trying to create here is the new Warner Brothers, but in digital format. I want to create this big intellectual property-making or -buying company and have the kind of domination that Warner Brothers had in the forties. Not because I want to be large, but because with [size] comes the kind of efficiencies you can have so that people can afford your product. That's the issue in the new age. People have to get extraordinary value for their dollar."

F/X produces interactive training software, corporate presentations, and three-dimensional animation. Kessler has also bought a 50-per-cent interest in Canadian Sportfishing Communications Network. The network has an inventory of twenty-six hundred thirty-minute fishing shows, and he plans to produce more such outdoors entertainment, because fishing is an $8-billion-a-year industry in Canada. "Once you've sold a beer, you've sold a beer," says Kessler. "But with intellectual properties, you can sell to more than one person at a time."

Indeed, the prospects for software sales of all kinds are unlimited. A decade ago, the computer rule of thumb was $1 worth of software sold for every $10 spent on hardware. Five years ago that ratio began to even out, and it has now reversed, so that software outsells hardware ten to one. Changes in prices have been equally wild, and the acceleration has only just begun. Hardware that cost $50,000 in 1990 cost $5,000 in 1995, and will be worth $500 in 1997. The results have been equally breathtaking in the entertainment industry, where computer-generated visuals are becoming common. Sixty people worked for two and a half years for the four and a half minutes of special effects in *Terminator 2*. Only two years later,

Jurassic Park took another leap forward. Of the eighty-five shots of dinosaurs in the movie, sixty-eight were created by computer graphics.

"There are several different ways to get to the end point," says Robert Burgess of Alias Research. "We're dealing with several frontiers that are in chaos. Everything is changing so quickly that it creates the opportunity to be lucky."

Search for solutions

Keeping on top of new technology is so important at Phoenix International Life Sciences that all research-and-development managers meet every other week to share information. As a result of such constant communication, the firm is able to act quickly. In January 1993, for example, Phoenix heard about a new piece of testing equipment worth $600,000, and bought the machine within two days. The device was so accurate and swift that Phoenix bought four more during the year, part of the $5 million the firm has spent on new equipment and computers that year. Phoenix tests new drugs on healthy volunteers, using a thirty-thousand-name database from which to draw the three thousand persons that the firm uses annually. Screenings are so thorough that only six out of one hundred people qualify to participate in tests that pay from $200 to $2,000.

One of the ways some businesses solve the technology problem is by "outsourcing" and turning to companies like Bryker Data Systems, a mainframe service bureau with annual sales of about $15 million. "We've been the flavour-of-the-month for a year now. We want to leverage that," says president Bryan Kerdman, who knows companies have to jump on opportunities as they occur. Kerdman also knows that success can sometimes swell an entrepreneur's head. "My personal ego is as much in check as it can be for an owner-manager."

Canada Trust's new EasyLine home-banking service is a

typical Bryker client. When customers of the financial-
services firm pay a bill using the EasyLine at-home service,
Bryker electronically distributes the payments from Canada
Trust to the various recipients, such as phone companies or
utilities. Bryker writes the software program, runs the system,
and assumes the risk. "If it works, we'll make a profit and
they'll make a profit," says the owner-manager, who started
the business in 1976 after dropping out of the University of
Toronto. "Perhaps I was a visionary then, but everybody has
caught on now."

Start-up tip: *Pioneering doesn't always pay.*

"We're not on the bleeding edge," says Bryker. "Sometimes you can get cut by going too far beyond what your
client needs. We don't have to be first into the market." Yet
you have to be *ready* for the market. Firms prosper because
they begin developing software, even though the hardware
platforms to run such systems may not exist at the beginning
of the development cycle. Such risk-taking has paid off,
however. When the months of development are over, the
hardware and the needs have often been there when the software was ready.

Working with large firms provides both stability (that's
good) and dependency (that can be bad). Bryker does cash-
management and payroll services for the Bank of Nova Scotia.
The bank, obviously, is an excellent customer, pays on time,
and leads to other contracts, because potential clients are
impressed by such blue-ribbon work. There are, however, disadvantages. "We're just an ant on the backside of the ele-
phant," says Kerdman. "If they roll over, we're dead." As a
result, Kerdman tries to grow the firm slowly, aiming for an
8- to 15-per-cent increase in revenue each year. He claims to
have no profit targets, and is content "as long as the ink is

black, not red." On the bleeding edge, however, the colour red is all too common, as we shall see in the next chapter.

Summary:

1. Be realistic about your prospects. Don't do a business plan that predicts billions of dollars in high-tech sales.
2. Stay practical. Focus on a niche that you can fill.
3. Don't waste time. Technology changes quickly and you may lose your competitive advantage.
4. Find a strategic partner who can build on your knowledge and help get your product to market.
5. Retain your intellectual property, because it will outlast all else.

CHAPTER 11

High-Tech Wreck: The Rise and Fall of Remuera Corp.

"The biggest mistake Remuera made
was assuming past growth would continue."

– CFO Mike Fletcher

In 1993, Remuera Corp. of Ottawa employed sixty people and had $5 million in annual revenue. Viewed from the outside, it was a healthy high-tech success that had achieved prominence as a computer-services consultant to government. That December, Remuera was named by accounting firm Arthur Andersen & Co. and *The Financial Post* as one of the fifty best-managed privately owned companies in Canada.

Two months later, in February 1994, Remuera was bankrupt. "There was a void in the administrative element," says Mike Fletcher, who joined Remuera in February 1993 as chief financial officer (CFO). According to Fletcher, the firm was incapable of moving from the start-up, or entrepreneurial, phase to embrace a more professional management style. "The toughest thing for an entrepreneur to recognize is that, if you're a marketer, you need administrative backup. They just ran a little faster than their support systems."

Rather than develop what already existed and build on that solid base, Remuera leapt into a world occupied only by larger companies with greater management depth: it decided to buy, develop, and market a unique software product. That product required financial backing, engineering support, and sales skills that were well beyond the scope of Remuera. The time expended on the new product – away from consulting, the profitable core mission of the company – meant that Remuera did not deliver its client-service function as ably as before. At the same time, the new activity sucked away all profits from the core business in order to pay for development of something that was generating no revenue.

Moreover, Remuera found itself in a world about which it had precious little knowledge, a world of tax-driven partnership deals, offshore tax havens, and backers the firm barely knew. "The logistics were a combination of Steven Spielberg and Stephen King's basement," says president Peter Hyne. "I later realized that this was one of those lessons painfully learned when a company moves away from its core mission. It might have worked in the future, but we weren't strong enough at that point."

In fact, there was a long list of things that went terribly wrong for Remuera. Any young firm might successfully deal with some of them, but no firm could survive the toxic combination of events that overtook Remuera in the two-year downward spin that led to its eventual demise. The collapse of Remuera, then, is a cautionary tale of what can occur when any firm – start-up or otherwise – loses its corporate way in a thicket of its own making: excessive lifestyle spending, time-wasting partner disputes, poor financial controls, and an inability to execute its business plan.

When Charles Mawby and Michael Leahy decided to launch a computer-management firm in 1988, they racked their brains for a suitable corporate name. Various ideas they came up with were already taken, so finally Leahy suggested they simply adopt a name he'd already used for his personal consulting firm: Remuera. Leahy had travelled extensively, and the name had come from a golf course he'd played four years earlier in Auckland, New Zealand. They both agreed that Remuera – a Maori word meaning "burnt edge of a flax garment" – had just the cachet they wanted, and so Remuera Corp. it was. During the first few successful years, the framed scorecard from that namesake golf course hung in the firm's lobby, Leahy's score of ninety-nine discreetly covered.

Mawby, then age twenty-eight, and Leahy, age thirty-four, had met while working in Ottawa for the federal government team negotiating the Canada–U.S. Free Trade Agreement (FTA). Mawby was a geology graduate from Carleton University who was doing electronic data-processing work. Leahy's talent was project administration; his degree was in public administration from Queen's. Their time on the FTA gave them exposure to numerous Ottawa bureaucrats who advised on the pact and saw how the two, and a small support staff, were able to run a local area network (LAN) that supplied negotiators with the backup statistics they required on trade flows between the two countries and projected the impact of tariff changes proposed during the talks. "We realized we had a capital opportunity," says Mawby. "Everybody who went through there was impressed with the high level of service provided."

For Remuera's first year, Mawby and Leahy were the only salaried employees. Rather than hire full-time staff, they put half a dozen people on contract. That way, they thought, Remuera could grow slowly with very little overhead. They offered day-to-day oversight and technical support for computer networks at the premises of a lengthening list of clients, such as the Department of Regional and Industrial Expansion, Revenue Canada, and Health and Welfare. In the first fiscal year, ending August 31, 1989, revenue was a respectable $1 million. In 1990, revenue grew to $2 million, and in 1991, revenue hit $6.5 million, largely due to one lucrative contract relating to the introduction of the goods and services tax (GST).

In 1989, Mawby and Leahy hired as president Peter Hyne, another FTA colleague, who had spent fifteen years in the public service. It was Hyne who snagged the GST contract, and he served as project director of the computer-network installation that now manages GST collection, using a mainframe and desktop PCs across Canada. Although the Department of Supply and Services oversaw procurement, Remuera helped design the system architecture and directed three dozen companies that were providing resources and people. "I'm pleased to say that we were never part of the news," says Hyne, "and they began to collect the tax on time."

Getting there

Born in Australia in 1946 to an Aussie father and Canadian mother, Peter Hyne came to Canada with his family when he was two years old. His father's career moves and Hyne's lack of academic application meant that Hyne attended twenty-three high schools over a ten-year period and *still* didn't graduate. Hyne well recalls the parting words of his principal at Burlington Central High: "You'll be lucky if you can find the garbage, let alone make anything happen." For the next five years, Hyne worked at various companies, including his father's firm, Dominion Stores, then obtained a two-year diploma in business administration from Toronto's Humber College. In 1972, he graduated from Waterloo Lutheran University in English and philosophy. He then bounced around as a jail guard, psychotherapist, and parole officer, who finally found his niche in 1984-85 by learning about computers and becoming director of information-systems development for the Department of Correctional Services, where Michael Leahy also worked as a systems analyst.

Hyne and Leahy were reunited two years later when they both worked on the FTA. After that, Hyne went to the office of the auditor general, where he installed a network of laptop computers, then he joined Remuera at the same salary as he had received in government, $52,000. Bureaucracy had bored Hyne. "I was an entrepreneur in public servant's clothing," he says. Once Remuera had landed the GST contract, the firm began thinking big time. "We thought we knew what we were doing," says Leahy. "Everything we touched turned to gold."

In June 1991, U.S. communications giant AT&T made a hostile bid for rival NCR Corp. The transaction took several months to complete and, during that period, it became clear that neither all the NCR people nor all the firm's products would survive the takeover. NCR had been developing a software system in Columbia, South Carolina, called NetManager, which Remuera had first heard about that March as it searched for automated systems that could be sold to government departments. Only a few of the software systems had been installed, on what's known as a "beta," or test, basis, but clients trying the system – including Revenue Canada – were excited.

The system allowed firms to update thousands of personal computers installed in offices across the country on an overnight basis, simply by sending out the necessary instructions electronically from one central point. Such capacity to upgrade an entire system could save money, dramatically simplify processes, and give any organization remarkable control over its computer network. The system was just the thing for a financial-services company, for example, wanting to update programs, gather accounting information, or alter details about specific products without being concerned over security or worry about introducing the huge number of errors that would result if every workstation across the country were changed by individual operators.

Because AT&T had a similar system, called StarSentry, under development, NCR's system was dropped by the acquisitor. The NCR development team was suddenly in limbo, so all three Remuera shareholders agreed Remuera should buy NetManager. Explains Charles Mawby, "It was a way of making ourselves unique." From April to July, Remuera sent several teams to South Carolina to look at NetManager more closely. Although Mawby and other Remuera executives held the initial discussions with NCR about purchase price, it was Hyne who negotiated the final deal in August. Under an interest-free arrangement that was signed October 22, 1991, Remuera agreed to pay NCR U.S.$1.72 million over two years at the rate of approximately U.S.$250,000 per quarter. "You're optimistic about the time frame for getting money," says Leahy. "We saw it as a mature product from a known company that just needed some fine tuning. We thought we could make a quick hit and pay off our original payment." After all, 1990 had been Remuera's most profitable year ever – the company had an after-tax profit of $800,000. Moreover, NetManager would be kicking out profits quickly, wouldn't it?

The search for funds

On closer inspection, NetManager was less lucrative. There was still work to do on the network – even though NCR had begun development on the software in 1987. So, Hyne set out to find financing for development and marketing costs. He estimated he needed $2 million to $4 million for NetManager development, so he spent the next few months holding hopeful meetings in California hotel rooms, visiting New York financial houses, and telling his tale to venture-capital companies. He met a diverse range of investors, all the way from hotshots in Armani suits in bars to respectable pension-fund

managers in their boardrooms. Hyne quickly realized that
there were really two types of investors. The first group con-
sisted of serious money looking for good projects. Hyne was
interested in them, but found they could care less about him.
The relatively small amount of money he was looking for, in
their words, "Isn't worth our time." The second group, those
who *would* do the deal, didn't seem to have quite the same
level of respectability – plus they wanted majority ownership
of the firm in return.

While Hyne was searching for money, Mawby decided that,
if Remuera were going to develop NetManager further, they
should try to nab some of the NCR staff who knew NetManager.
Having the product was one thing, but the people mattered
too. They knew the quirks and passwords required for the
most-efficient operation. "Everybody said we had a great
product – keep on funding it," says Mawby. "We listened to
what we wanted to hear."

On January 6, 1992, Mawby established The Network Corp.
in Atlanta, Georgia, about a four hours' drive from Columbia,
put his father in charge of selling the product in the United
States, and set out to hire former NCR staff. Hyne was unhappy
with the move, arguing that Mawby's father, a former vice-
chairman of the U.S. subsidiary of Bombardier, The
Transportation Group Inc., had no experience with software,
but he acquiesced. "It was done with my knowledge and my
approval, but I was very uncomfortable with it. I didn't think
mixing in family was a very good idea," Hyne says. In the first
three months of 1992, Remuera spent about $300,000 on
rents, overhead, and salaries for seven or eight people in
Atlanta. NetManager was not much closer to market than previously, and no firm financing had been found, so the Atlanta
staff was let go in March and the office closed in April.
NetManager – meant to propel the company on to the next
corporate plateau – was becoming a drain.

At least the vendor was accommodating. Under the agreement with NCR, nonpayment of the quarterly U.S.$250,000 by Remuera meant the product had to be returned. But NCR was happy to have NetManager off the books and agreed that Remuera could postpone payments on the U.S.$1.72-million purchase price. Meanwhile, however, Remuera's other costs were beginning to climb.

The GST project had required Remuera to add staff. With the project finished, Remuera mistakenly kept them on salary. Of the hundred employees then at Remuera, twenty were doing nothing, waiting for the next project. In the parlance of the consulting industry, they were "on the beach" and not billing for their services. Salaries, however, averaging $40,000 to $50,000, were still being paid. Worse, salaries throughout the firm had risen higher than the three owners would have liked because of what Hyne calls "the Ottawa bubble." Since the public service pays well, and government contracts can be lucrative for individual self-employed consultants, private-sector companies like Remuera need to pay inflated compensation to keep quality people.

Rifts began to appear among the shareholders. Leahy wanted to cut back on overhead, but Hyne was opposed. Hyne argued that another contract like the GST was just around the corner, and "We're a $5-million company with the capacity to do $10 million" became a favourite Hyne phrase. "[Leahy] didn't see the momentum," says Hyne. "The bank loved Michael, he was conservative." Leahy was dubbed the corporate conscience. "It was a term I came to dislike," Leahy says. "People either tuned me out or Peter said, 'We'll make it back.'"

The three owners, however, were not scrimping on themselves. Mawby, Hyne, and Leahy increased their own annual salaries from $100,000 to $125,000. At Hyne's insistence, they had also traded their personal autos for spiffier vehicles leased for them by the company. "My two partners were showing up in jeans and backpacks as if they were trekking in India," says Hyne. "I was negotiating contracts with deputy ministers. I had to get them out of the basement." Mawby got a Previa van, and Leahy chose an Acura Legend. Hyne selected a 1986 black Mercedes-Benz 560SL convertible. All came courtesy of Remuera.

The Optimax connection

Hyne's search for financing had turned up only one likely prospect. In December 1991, Hyne met Mike McKie of Optimax Securities Corp. of Toronto, who said he could find backing, but thought the work required could take several months. McKie turned to Stephen Hall and his partner, Malcolm Rigby, who ran a Toronto-based company called TXN Solution Integrators, for an opinion on NetManager. Hall had twenty years' experience in systems and telecommunications and was a former vice-president with Wells Fargo Bank in San Francisco. Rigby had been marketing/project manager with INTERAC, the Canadian banks' electronic funds-transfer system, and was a former IBM executive. They liked NetManager too, and although TXN worked mainly with large mainframe computer systems, they agreed that TXN would be interested in distributing this product. McKie also tapped Pierre Vella-Zarb of First Investors Capital Corp., who had worked on other deals with McKie.

By that point, Hyne thought he needed $5 million to $7 million to cover the purchase costs and develop and market the software. McKie asked Hyne to prepare a more detailed business plan and obtain another outside evaluation of the software system for McKie's use in his presentations to potential investors. In a letter dated March 2, 1992, Protocols Standards and Communications Inc. of Ottawa said the software had been successfully demonstrated and concluded that the

"NetManager product presently offers a complete network and systems management solution for the Local Area Network and PC environment." Armed with this third-party endorsement, Remuera demonstrated NetManager to potential clients, including local software firm Cognos Inc., the Department of Supply and Services, and U.S. giants like Microsoft. Everyone was agog. There was nothing like NetManager on the market. Recalls Hyne, "No one asked the price. They all asked, 'When can we get it?'"

Malcolm Rigby told a fellow IBM alumnus – Lyn Bell – about Remuera and the product it was trying to develop. Lynwood Bell, age fifty-three, was born in Edmonton and worked with IBM from 1964 to 1977, latterly as systems marketing manager based in Toronto, where he was responsible for nine divisions. In 1981, Bell moved to the British Crown colony of Anguilla, a thirty-five-square-mile island that is part of the Leeward Islands, where he has residency while maintaining his Canadian passport.

Deals like Remuera were just to Bell's taste. He and his partners have financed about $250 million worth of deals for software, pharmaceutical, and waste-management companies. Bell employs fourteen people and takes the same attitude on such investments as a venture capitalist: for every ten deals he does, two succeed, two go in the tank, and six go sideways. Enough have done well for Bell (and partner Hope Ross, the local manager in Anguilla for accounting firm Deloitte & Touche) that Bell puts his personal net worth at $3 million. A widower, Bell is not a conspicuous consumer. He lives in a duplex and drives a Ford Tempo on the island. He travels six months of the year to market products in which he has interests and stays at inexpensive hotels. In London, for example, his favourite spot is the Norfolk Hotel, where his room costs a penny-pinching £43 per night. His only passion is dining. Bell's favourite restaurant in all the world is Georges Blanc, a

three-star Michelin establishment in Vonnas, France, where he
likes to dine two or three times a year.

"We try to find products like this that are in trouble or need
financing," says Bell. "I acquire them here in Anguilla, and our
intention is to exploit them around the world from this location, because it's a tax haven. Our contribution is to fund the
ongoing development, and, if there are acquisitions to be done,
they're often done with [promissory] notes. But, to be quite
honest, we're bottom-fishers in some respects. So [for] many of
the deals we've done we haven't paid a great deal at the front
end. We've rather just taken over the operation [and] allowed
the operation to continue functioning by supplying it with
working capital. As we get our financing in order, which is
often some time later, we would pay the original seller out."
Bottom-fisher is an interesting description. Bell saw Remuera,
even this early in the game, as all but finished. At Remuera,
they mistakenly thought they were just getting rolling.

On February 18, 1992, Hyne signed over the ownership of
the software – the intellectual property rights – from Remuera
to Estech Corp., an Anguillan company established by Bell.
Control of the future had slipped away from Remuera without
any money changing hands. Equally relevant was the fact that
Hyne did not inform Leahy or Mawby of his action, even
though all three were supposed to be equal partners.

Bell's relationship was with Rigby and Hall, not Remuera.
"They were really knocked out of the piece," says Bell of
Remuera. Remuera, however, had found a quiet backer
through a complicated corporate structure that was driven by
tax considerations. Anguilla's particular tax relationship with
Canada was established by Pierre Trudeau when he was prime
minister as a way of boosting local business in the Caribbean
and encouraging Canadian companies to market globally.
Anguilla is known as a "listed country" (Barbados is another),
where worldwide profits can be sent and attract no tax. In

turn, those profits can be paid, as dividends, to Canadian taxpayers who are resident in Canada – and attract no tax in their
hands. "It's extremely efficient," says Bell. "Quite a few large
Canadian companies have subsidiary operations set up in
countries like this for that very purpose, and they do all their
external marketing – even just in the United States – through
a listed country, rather than from Canada. There is not really a
wealth of knowledge about how to get into a business globally. People usually stagger into it, and sometimes spend far
more than they need to to get operations set up abroad. They
clearly always miss some of the significant tax incentives that
are there to help them do it well," says Bell.

As part of the corporate arrangements, a Wyoming-based
company called The Network Computer Corp. (Netco) was
incorporated to receive all Remuera's ownership rights of
what's known as the "source code," or the heart of the computer program in all forms, whether electronic or written. The
product was renamed TNC NetManager; Hall was named president and CEO of Netco, Rigby was vice-president. Beyond
Netco was Estech Corp.

For any company to cede ownership of a core product
seems like a terrible blunder. But Hyne says he didn't care
about ownership of the source code. "In exchange for 100 per
cent of the intellectual property, we would get a contract that
gave us worldwide exclusive marketing and engineering rights
for five years, for which we would be paid a prescribed
amount," says Hyne. "The reason why we would give up the
intellectual property was that, at the other end, at the end of
the five years, we would be so intrinsically tied to the product
in terms of our knowledge and expertise – and obviously the
sales had been successful – they would want to continue with
us. There was no goal to retain any ownership in the intellectual property whatsoever. That was something the investor
would be taking a risk with."

The sales effort

For any of this exotic organization to actually work, of course, there had to be NetManager sales that generated revenue. Remuera had hired David Abraham as vice-president of marketing and sales in January 1992. Abraham, who lived in Burlington, Ontario, had been in the computer business for twenty years and liked NetManager. "They were 100 per cent on the right track," he says. "They were ahead of the market." But he was also aware that the three owners were spending an inordinate amount of time arguing with each other. "Ownership disputes detracted from the ongoing business. The core business suffered," says Abraham, who was never able to make one sale of the product in the two years he spent under contract to Remuera.

With executive attention focused on wrangles rather than development, and a new product that wasn't bringing in any revenue, the firm was barely breaking even. There was just enough cash flow coming in from service contracts to cover bills that needed to be paid. Royal Bank account manager Brent Keating had had Remuera's business in his knowledge-based industry portfolio since May 1991, and he was becoming increasingly alarmed. When he took over the account, sales and profits were healthy, and the company had $500,000 in its account. Keating had been monitoring Hyne's unsuccessful search for financing for the NCR product, and had seen how spending was beginning to outpace revenue, as cash on hand in the account kept declining.

By February 1992, Remuera had spent about $350,000 that the firm hoped to have repaid once the financing was in place, so Remuera was carrying that amount on its books as a receivable. In March, Keating warned Hyne that overheads were increasing too quickly and told them they had to stop referring to the money that had been spent as a receivable. Instead, he said, it should be carried on the books as an expense. The effect of that accounting change meant that the bank would no longer lend money against the amount spent.

Remuera was also beginning to borrow fully on its operating line. Rather than have cash on hand, as it once did, the firm was moving towards the top limit of its $500,000 operating-line arrangement. The bank met several times through the spring with Remuera and, since the outside financing that would have gone to pay down the line did not arrive by the August fiscal year end, Remuera was forced to write off the money already spent on the NetManager system. Writing off the costs attributable to Atlanta, marketing, and the search for financing put the company in a $500,000-loss position for the fiscal year ending in August 1992. While the write-off did yield a tax break and lowered the tax owing, it also reduced the equity base of the company. As a result, when Remuera showed the books to potential outside investors, there were no retained earnings – and that hurt. "A nice clean balance sheet causes confidence," says Fletcher. "Everybody who saw the balance sheet saw a lot of red ink." At the same time, Remuera produced a business plan for the bank that said NetManager would be funded outside Remuera, with the result that Remuera would be profitable again in six months. Keating and the Royal were so satisfied with the response that the operating line was raised to $700,000.

Doing the deal

Meanwhile, outside experts continued to praise the product. Michael Ozerkevich of EMC Partners, a Toronto-based management-consulting firm, undertook an evaluation in 1992, and he concluded there was a market for the product and, if that market could be tapped, the product was worth $61 million. That was a huge amount, given the fact that NCR was selling it for U.S.$1.72 million, and it was an even more

daunting figure considering that Remuera had given away the
intellectual rights to the product. Most important, however,
the number would impress potential investors. Accounting
firm BDO Dunwoody Warn Mallette was also asked to run the
numbers, and came up with a $56-million value.

Using the $61-million estimate as a base, Mike McKie of
Optimax set out to sell a 50-per-cent ownership interest in the
program to investors for $30.5 million. Optimax established a
limited partnership, called Netman Partnership, and began
seeking investors by circulating a detailed ninety-eight-page
offering memo, dated September 18, 1992. The partnership
hoped to raise the $30.5 million by selling units worth $10,000
to individual investors, with $150,000 (or fifteen units) set as
the minimum investment per person. The prospectus predicted that sales of the product could hit $80 million over the next
five years.

Netman's deal was to buy the ownership position from
Netco, the Wyoming-based company, but that wasn't the end of
the corporate chain. In addition to Estech, Lyn Bell had also
created two more corporate entities, based in the Netherlands,
that were part of a deal signed September 4 by Hyne on behalf
of Remuera, Pierre Vella-Zarb for Netco, and Douglas Gough
for Netman. Those firms, Hansa Finance and Trust B.V. and
Dumatrust Management Services B.V., were established to help
market the software in Europe and Japan. The Anguillan-based
Estech Corp., however, remained the ultimate destination of
profits. Remuera had now not only given up the intellectual
property, but was also sharing marketing rights. Hyne signed
the September 4 deal, as he did the previous contract to convey
the software to Estech, without consulting his partners, Mawby
and Leahy, or getting their approval as directors.

NCR was becoming impatient for its money, and Hyne
wrote twice to Bell in 1992 before the partnership deal closed,
asking Estech to cover additional penalty costs amounting to

U.S.$111,000, payable to NCR because the closing on the Remuera–NCR deal needed to be extended.

When Estech struck the original deal with Remuera, Estech had agreed to pay the amount owing to NCR for the software. So, where was the money to come from to pay for the software Remuera had already passed along to Estech? Not from Estech or Bell or any of his corporate entities – he was too wise for that – but from a tax arrangement established by the Canadian government to encourage investment. Enter the Netman Partnership described in the offering memo. For investors, the partnership arrangement meant that not only was there potential for money down the road when NetManager began to throw off profits, there was also an immediate personal tax advantage.

Here's how it worked. To buy each $10,000 unit, an investor paid $1,800 in 1992 and a further $1,800 divided among four payments in 1993. Including interest at 7 per cent on the promissory note for the 1993 portion, the total per-unit investment in cash was $3,669. Each investor also signed a promissory note for the remaining $6,400 owing on each unit, but that note wasn't due until December 31, 2002. Income-tax write-offs (capital-cost allowance, soft costs, and interest) against the money actually invested – the $3,669 – totalled $10,318. Assuming that individual was in the 50-per-cent tax bracket, a deduction of $10,318 meant income-tax savings for the investor of $5,159 – an amount that was not only to cover the $3,669 investment but also to put $1,490 cash in the investor's pocket for every unit purchased. The minimum purchase allowed was fifteen units, so anyone in the 50-per-cent tax bracket who came in for that minimum purchase invested $3,669 per unit for a total of $55,035 and received a tax deduction totalling $154,770 that meant $77,385 in their pockets – enough to pay the actual cost of the fifteen units ($55,035) and put $22,350 in the hands of each investor!

Now, let's get this straight. The Canadian tax system and partnership arrangement not only provided enough money to pay off NCR, cover legals, and reimburse Optimax for its agent fees, but each investor also got an ownership position (and a claim on eventual profits) – and *a nice little bonus* of a minimum of $22,350 (some investors bought more than fifteen units). Since the total amount of money pledged – not raised, but pledged – was $20 million, this meant that two thousand units worth $10,000 each were sold. Each unit generated $1,490 cash in hand, so the two thousand units put $2,980,000 – almost $3 million – in the pockets of the fifty-nine investors. All out of thin air. Or, rather, from the tax system.

Even better, the other $6,400 owing per unit wasn't due for ten years. By that time, Remuera would be making money for the investors. Or, who knows, depending on the tax system at the time, maybe they could take another loss against income. Hall, Rigby, Mawby, Leahy, and Hyne, as well as two other Remuera employees, each bought $150,000 worth of units. McKie invested $450,000; Vella-Zarb, $400,000.

Originally the limited-partnership deal was scheduled to close in September 1992, but negotiations dragged on, and Netman Partnership was finally completed on December 31, 1992, the final day the members of the group could take advantage of that tax year. Stacks of paper were assembled in the Toronto boardroom of Borden & Elliot (the law firm representing the partnership), and the signing went on for hours. It went on so long, in fact, that Hyne almost didn't get back to Ottawa for New Year's Eve celebrations. He had invited two other couples to his home to spend the evening; Hyne finally arrived just before midnight.

Still, more than a year after the first meeting between Hyne and McKie, the deal was done. McKie was successful in lining up commitments for $20 million, the minimum amount he'd set as a goal, enough to buy slightly less than a one-third interest in the system from Netco. But the $20 million was the *promised* amount; in fact, there was only $7.2 million raised in cash, half collected in 1992, the other half in 1993. From the money raised, the U.S.$1.72-million purchase price (plus some carrying charges) was paid to NCR, and $1 million was paid to Optimax for its work as agent. Lawyers also collected their fees.

With the arrangement in place, Stephen Hall and Malcolm Rigby took up their active duties as president and vice-president respectively of Netco. Payment to them – from the money raised through personal-services contracts – was $1,500 a day for a minimum of four days a month. For that, Hall and Rigby were to oversee development of NetManager at Remuera on behalf of the investors. In addition, they received NetManager marketing rights in Canada for any potential client except Canadian-government sales, which would be handled by Remuera. Remuera's market had been whittled back again; a greater proportion of any future profits was going elsewhere. Neither Hall nor Rigby had had much exposure to Remuera to that point, but "We believed in the product," says Hall, "mainly in Mawby. He's as straight as a bear's dick and very impressive technically. It was on his enthusiasm that we based our enthusiasm."

The fights begin

Prior to closing, Netco had agreed to pay Remuera's expenses associated with marketing and developing NetManager during the last six months of 1992. When Mawby and Hyne met Hall and Rigby in January 1993 for the first "official" meeting, Remuera claimed $750,000 in expenses, for which it wanted repayment. Hall had not expected such a large amount, nor was he happy to hear that Remuera's work plan would spend all the money raised by Netman Partnership over the next twelve months. Hall pointed out that the money was supposed to fund development and marketing over a two- to three-year period. "We had control of the funds," says Hall. "We guarded that jealously. The money was raised to develop the product." In Hyne's view, however, the money had been raised for Remuera, and he should be able to spend the funds as he saw fit. Says Hall, "Hyne grew very testy."

"There was animosity from day one," says David Abraham, who attended meetings with Hyne, Hall, and Rigby.

"When Michael [Leahy] and I tried to talk to him about anything, he took it very personally," says Mawby of Hyne.

Netco refused to pay Remuera anything, and talks to solve the stalemate continued on and off through February. Under the terms of the agreement signed in December, Remuera was to send Netco a monthly invoice for development costs, such as the salaries of staff working on NetManager development. Remuera kept track of time spent, then marked up the salaries involved by 20 per cent as way of generating profit. Hall wanted to renegotiate the agreement, but Hyne was both frustrated and wary. He felt Netco's actions were tough on Remuera, but he didn't want to disrupt the flow of funds either. Remuera needed that cash flow. "I wanted to draw a line in the sand," he says, "but there was risk with these guys." But Hyne wasn't doing himself any good by arriving in Toronto, taking a two-floor suite at the Cambridge Suites Hotel, and holding meetings with Hall and Rigby in such splendid surroundings.

By March, Hall and Hyne were still deadlocked. Remuera had yet to receive any money. By mid-month, Hall was at the end of his tether. "I went to Ottawa in a very pissed-off mood, because I was prepared to remove the product from Remuera and take it to someone else," says Hall. Hyne's blood pressure was equally high. He not only refused to attend the meeting, he wouldn't even remain on the same floor where the session was being held. "It was at that point I started to have doubts about Peter Hyne's business acumen," says Hall.

Hall met with Mawby and Leahy instead, and they agreed to a specific month-by-month work plan for the year, which would bring NetManager to market. Netco agreed to reimburse Remuera for $250,000 of the $750,000 expenses incurred in 1992 and arranged a fixed-price invoice system for continuing costs. According to the new deal, Netco would pay Remuera a flat $137,500 each month to cover NetManager's engineering development costs. As for marketing costs (such as demonstrating the system to potential clients), any expenditures by Remuera were recoverable from Netco on a dollar-for-dollar basis. The monthly payment was retroactive to January; the first cheque was for $387,000 and covered $250,000 of 1992 expenses and January's payment. "He who has the money wins," says Abraham of the negotiations. "Remuera didn't have either the money or the product."

The flow of funds began just in time. Remuera had moved to fancy new digs. Previously, the firm had leased 4,500 square feet on Ottawa's Sparks Street Mall in a building owned by the Bank of Canada, but, in January 1993, Remuera also took over the eleventh floor. That top floor in the building, plus a mezzanine level that went with it, gave Remuera 20,000 square feet in which to spread out and expand. Rent skyrocketed – from $18,000 a month to $45,000 a month – an increase of $324,000 a year. Over the next six months, Remuera also spent $450,000 on renovations, interior-design features, office fit-ups, and furnishings. Under the terms of the lease, the Bank of Canada was supposed to repay Remuera up to $750,000 for such expenditures, but a dispute over what was actually covered by the lease meant that the bank paid only $170,000. Remuera was out almost $300,000 it had expected to collect. Remuera also spent money on a training centre before the firm even had clients who might use the well-equipped facility.

Hyne's office looked particularly lavish. He worked at a desk sculpted from a solid piece of white ash that he delighted in telling people was worth $30,000. On June 29, 1993, the *Ottawa Citizen* published a story about Hyne's grand plans to link with U.S. software firm Microsoft Corp. Hyne was called "quirky" by writer Alana Kainz, who quoted him as saying, "Anyone who sits behind this desk must have a massive ego." Another office adornment was a Persian rug he said was worth $100,000. In fact, Hyne's first wife bought the desk for him as a gift. Hyne claims she paid only $800. As for the rug, he'd inherited that from his grandfather, who'd paid $5,000 for it in 1929. But if people thought he *looked* successful, well, that was fine with him. For many observers in Ottawa, the "$30,000 desk" epitomized Remuera's runaway costs. As far as Hyne was concerned, riding high impressed clients and brought in new business. "I'm not going to hedge that overhead became an issue," says Hyne. "There was no place I could find a bench-mark for where our overhead should be. People in this town were living vicariously. They wanted us to grow." But Mawby admits, "It was a mistake."

The partners were no longer acting in concert. The March renegotiations with Netco divided Hyne from Mawby and Leahy. The three owners began to bicker about everything. "We were not functioning as a team," admits Hyne. "[The deal] very much diluted our energy." Relations among the three got so bad that, in May, Hyne offered to buy out his partners for $2 million each. Negotiations went on for six weeks, then bogged down. Hyne withdrew his offer and announced that he intended to act in future without bother-ing to consult either of them. "In areas, he's a genius, but he did not have the business experience to lead Remuera," says Mawby, who freely admits he couldn't run Remuera either and says he urged that they bring in someone else who could. "The relationship was strained," says Mawby. "Unanimity of purpose had long since gone." The feuding wasn't getting NetManager operational; nor was there much new business in the company's core area of systems management. Still, in the fiscal year ending August 1993, Remuera showed a modest profit of $11,000 on revenues of $7.8 million. The result was a welcome improvement over the year-earlier loss, but a long way from the salad days of 1990, when Remuera declared an after-tax profit of $800,000.

Dropping the ball

Remuera CFO Mike Fletcher had seen such roller-coaster rides before. He had worked in both the public and private sector as an assistant vice-president with the Federal Business Development Bank and as controller for Telemedia Publishing. According to Fletcher, management problems often arise with new companies in the $7-million sales range and are most likely to occur if growth is faster than 15 per cent annually. When sales growth is higher, companies get so caught up in heady success that they fail to build the infrastructure needed to support such growth. When a company signs a single contract like the GST deal that's as big as the previous year's sales, "You spend too much time on that contract," says Fletcher. "You want to make your name and you ignore administration. You wind up so totally focused on making sales that you drop the ball. You get distracted by the business that's coming at you."

Ego can also get in the way. Entrepreneurs make mistakes and don't admit them – and worse, they don't learn from their blunders, because they expect new sales will swell the coffers with cash that will solve any problems, current or pending. "You've created this baby, but it's grown up and you can't boss it around like you used to," says Fletcher. Too often, entrepreneurs dismiss the more conservative view of accountants or bankers who are trying to caution moderation. "Such advice is not just naysaying," says Fletcher. "Take it with a grain of salt, but don't ignore it." While every young company has a marketing arm and a product (or service) to offer, each firm needs a third aspect: finance and administration. "If two legs of a stool are solid, but the third is shaky, the laws of physics tell you that the stool could fall over. The laws of business are the same."

The instability was becoming obvious at Remuera. NetManager development was slow, and Hall was unhappy with progress and would delay payment of the monthly amounts owing. Perhaps he would question one item on the invoice, thus causing a halt on the full payment. Because revenue didn't meet ongoing needs, Remuera was increasingly forced to use the Royal Bank operating line to pay for salaries, the office fit-up costs, and other expenses. Such operating lines are supposed to be short-term agreements, meant to smooth out income and outflow. A firm expects payments from contracts to come in bulk amounts, but meanwhile it needs funds for daily expenses. The bank, aware that large sums are coming, lends a series of small payments, with the total repaid when a contract is completed. Usually a ceiling is established – in Remuera's case, $700,000 – and, as the amount owing reaches that level, the bank becomes more watchful and more nervous. By July 1993, Remuera had drawn down the full amount. The situation was rather like Canada's mounting deficits. Each passing month of losses added to the total debt. "Remuera based its overhead on projected revenues rather than realistic core revenues," says Mike Fletcher. "I couldn't get the shareholders to budge on any action plan to cut costs. Netco sustained that company from July on."

David Abraham, who was supposed to be selling the product, spent some of his time each month ferrying invoices to Netco and collecting the cheques issued. "Their ability to survive and recoup what they spent was 100 per cent in the hands of the NetManager product," says Abraham. Delivery of NetManager to his best sales prospect, accounting firm Coopers & Lybrand, kept being postponed by the Ottawa office.

Hyne tried to buttress Remuera management in August by hiring John Purdon as a new president for the Remuera NetManager division. Purdon had more than twenty years of high-tech experience, including twelve years at Cognos Inc., an Ottawa-based software company, latterly as vice-president of Americas/Pacific. Purdon's arrival brought a note of conservatism to Remuera, because he thought the firm's revenue projections were too aggressive. His specific task was to develop and bring the system to market. But Purdon also added new costs; his annual salary was $175,000. Moreover, Hall was not impressed by Purdon; he recommended against hiring him.

At the Royal Bank, Brent Keating was getting worried again. Remuera had hired accounting firm Deloitte & Touche to advise the firm, but costs were still outpacing revenue, and Remuera was using its full operating line. Keating didn't like the fact that Remuera had spent so much money so quickly on the office and training centre, and he asked the three shareholders to invest $150,000 of their own money in the company. They came up with $110,000 among them, money that reduced the amount owed on the operating line and was enough to satisfy the bank for the time being. Remuera also agreed to find more equity investment to strengthen the company's balance sheet and brought in another accounting firm, Ernst & Young, to conduct a management study and see if the company was viable.

Relations between Hall and Hyne grew more frosty. As far as Netco was concerned, Remuera was supposed to reach certain milestones each month – and they hadn't done that. Remuera seemed always to have another excuse. "From day one, we had a product to sell but not one bit of effort was given to sell that product," says Pierre Vella-Zarb, who helped Mike McKie put the tax deal together. Instead, Remuera seemed focused on improving and changing the product and selling that new version, rather than coming to market with the version Remuera bought from NCR. "We paid them for work they had not finished," said Vella-Zarb.

With the arrival of fall, Hall was expecting a finished product, but a new Remuera work plan seemed to push that off into 1994. Sales calls were going well, but as yet there were no clients and no revenue from NetManager. Investors in Netman Partnership, who made their final payment on October 1, were getting restless. In the spring, they'd heard an optimistic report from Mawby about the delivery schedule, and they were looking for results. Most of Hall's dealings were with Hyne and, to a lesser extent, with Charles Mawby, and Hall was becoming increasingly frustrated with delivery. Two days before the October 15 Coopers & Lybrand delivery date, Abraham had to tell the accounting firm that Remuera could not deliver for another six weeks.

Hall told Hyne that Remuera wasn't following the work plan agreed to in March, and withheld invoice payment in October. Hyne replied that such action would put Remuera out of business. Recalls Hall, "I told him, 'We're paying for services rendered. If you don't deliver, we won't pay.'" In a letter to Hall dated October 22, Hyne blamed Hall for the continuing problems, stating, "Operational discussions have been sparse [but] there has been abundant discussion of invoice payments, contract renegotiations, and future contract relationships. None of these activities, in my opinion, contributes to the success of this venture nor improves our Sales or Development effort in any way." Netco finally paid, and continued paying the invoices presented through December.

Going down

For the three shareholders, the final three months of Remuera's corporate existence were a fiasco. Mawby blamed Hyne and told Leahy they should get rid of Hyne, but Leahy dithered. "I couldn't make up my mind. It took me a while, but I concluded no," says Leahy, who now realizes that his hopes for improvement in the situation were naïve. "I thought we could get through the trouble we were in. I also thought, 'This can't be happening to me.'" Mawby then set out to raise enough money to buy Hyne's share. Meanwhile, Hyne was also looking for new money and found that Purdon and Harold Yule, also formerly of Cognos, were willing to put $500,000 into Remuera if Mawby and Leahy left. Mawby kept bumping into people from whom he was trying to raise money who had also been visited by Hyne for similar purposes.

On December 18, 1993, Remuera was listed in *The Financial Post* as one of Canada's fifty best-managed private companies. The announcement was the firm's last piece of good news. The fact that the firm was so near the end of its corporate days was not obvious to outside judgement; those inside still believed they could somehow skate across the thin ice to the safety of the far shore.

Finally, on December 31, 1993, Mawby and Leahy accepted Hyne's offer to buy them out. The deal meant that they would be absolved from the original personal guarantees they had signed to backstop bank loans and would get the loans repaid that they had signed in September when the bank asked for more money. Hyne had offered them $2 million apiece for their share at one point, yet Mawby and Leahy were now willing to walk away with nothing – as long as they didn't get stuck with any liabilities. Mawby and Leahy were unaware who was backing Hyne; they certainly had no idea that their colleague Purdon was involved. The deal was conditional on Hyne getting his financing organized by January 31, 1994. "What," Hyne asked Mawby and Leahy, "can go wrong?"

As it turned out, everything. In January, Hyne told Hall about his investors and said that he planned to take control of Remuera. "I considered it a disastrous plan," says Hall. "It was then I realized this company was going down the tubes. Hyne kept saying, 'You're going to put us out of business,' and I told him Netco was not in the business of keeping [his] company afloat." Hall was not going to pour any more money down a sinkhole; he refused to honour any more invoices presented.

"That," says Fletcher, "was the final nail in the coffin."

"In hindsight, I should have pulled the plug in October," says Hall.

Says Lyn Bell, "They just weren't doing the job for us, and we had to pull the plug."

In mid-January, Hyne informed Leahy that there was just one other wrinkle in his buyout offer. Leahy had personally signed the original application for American Express corporate credit cards to be used by employees who were charging expenses such as business lunches. As a result, in the eyes of Amex, Leahy was personally responsible for any debts, no matter who had incurred them. Hyne said Leahy would remain personally liable; the deal Hyne was offering did not involve removing Leahy's potential liability for Amex debts incurred by others. Leahy and Mawby, on advice from their lawyers, resigned as directors of Remuera, effective January 24. They remained as shareholders, but there was no deal with Hyne at month's end. His financing wasn't in place.

Ernst & Young produced a pessimistic report, dated January 7, 1994, about the prospects for Remuera. It said that there wasn't enough revenue to cover overhead, there was too much debt, and there was a need for a major equity injection. Once Netco refused to pay Remuera, cash flow was drying up, losses could only get worse, and NetManager seemed no closer to producing engineering and marketing revenue.

On February 3, 1994, Keating called a meeting at his bank office attended by Hyne, officials from Ernst & Young, plus legal counsel. Asked Keating: "Where are you going?" Replied Hyne: "Save your carfare." There was agreement on all sides that the $500,000 from Purdon and Yule would not be enough to reduce the amount owing on the operating line and get some working capital into the company. AT&T Global Information Solutions Canada Ltd. of Ottawa had already been in looking at Remuera for four weeks with a view to buying the core business of servicing government contracts. Netco, of course, already owned NetManager. Hyne suggested, and everyone agreed, that Remuera go into receivership and seek court protection to gain time to find a buyer. The company's debts totalled $2.7 million, including $787,000 to the Royal Bank, $208,000 to Revenue Canada, and $176,000 to each of the Bank of Canada and Customs and Excise.

"They made some classic business mistakes," says Keating. "Remuera tended to take on overheads and create infrastructure and then chase revenues rather than chase revenues first and then build an infrastructure. One of the reasons that we supported them as long as we did was because the core business was still very profitable. This was one of those companies where the assets walk out the door every night. It was important to keep the company operating to maintain its value."

Going into receivership did keep Remuera together, and over the next six weeks, under the protection of the Bankruptcy & Insolvency Act, AT&T negotiated the purchase of Remuera's core-service business and the office equipment, took over contracts and leases, and hired most of those Remuera staffers who billed out their time. About a dozen members of salaried management, such as Fletcher and Purdon, were let go. Hall and Rigby offered jobs to the dozen members of Remuera staff who had been developing NetManager. Mawby and two-thirds of that group signed on in March with a new corporate entity called Network Xcellence, owned by Hall and Rigby, to continue development of the product still owned by Netco. The Royal Bank got the money it was owed, and most creditors were repaid.

"Peter thought Remuera would be the Microsoft of

Canada," says Vella-Zarb. "He shot for the moon. You have to have some of that view, but you also need some realism. Entrepreneurs can think five years out, but they need people immediately below them who say, 'Here's what we're going to do today and here's where we're going to be in six months.'"

Remuera had tried to do too much; there were too many flaming torches in the air. In retrospect, nobody will admit fault, preferring to shift blame instead, but, as is usually the case with such failures – big and small – there was plenty of blame to go around. While Netco's refusal to pay the invoices precipitated the collapse, Netco's intransigence wasn't the sole cause of Remuera's demise. "I don't want to paint Remuera as a fiscally astute company," says Purdon. "Remuera got them-selves overextended." Salaries were too high, the firm had too much office space, and the surroundings were unnecessarily lavish. "That, more than anything, caused the problems. The company had problems whether Netco paid or not, [but] they started to depend on Netco's revenues."

"A large part of the blame can be laid at Peter's door," says Fletcher, who has known Hyne since university. "He has a good ten-year vision, but he's unable to do anything on a three- to six-month basis. It's hard to give up control and delegate authority. When you've been the jack-of-all-trades, it's difficult to back away, stop managing the details, and just do what you do well."

Moreover, the three shareholders really never did sort out their respective roles. "Peter wanted a big company, as big as he could get it," says Leahy. "He was older than us, and he wanted the company to outlast him so he could draw a pension." For his part, Leahy says he wanted security. Mawby had been stung in a previous partnership and didn't want any escape clauses, because he didn't want anyone bailing out on him. The three spent an inordinate amount of time during the first couple of years trying to devise a shareholders' agreement that would mean that they reported to each other but made Hyne president, because, in the words of Leahy, "Peter needed the prestige of presidency. . . . Our personalities got in the way."

After that, they seemed to spend the rest of their corporate lives together on different sides of every issue. On the face of it, their three different backgrounds – sales, administration, and technical – should have made for a good combination of talents. "It turned out to be the worst form of partnership. It was always two-to-one," says Leahy. "Ultimately we couldn't agree on anything." Leahy also knows now that he made a basic error in assuming that others would run things in his best interests. He had suffered through periods of unemployment in the past and thought that joining with others would offer protection against that happening again. "You have to be prepared to make all the decisions yourself," says Leahy, even in a partnership situation. "I thought some people would handle those for me. I thought if I did my part well, things would look after themselves."

There was also too little follow-through capability. "A lot of companies have brilliant technical people and bright ideas and sometimes even have contracts like these folks captured with NCR," says Bell. "That's quite common. But what we usually find is that the companies that we acquire from are either on their last legs or they have absolutely no wherewithal to complete any marketing or get the final bells and whistles put on the product and get it out the door. The technical fellow has run out of steam. He doesn't have the skills or the finances to take it any further. So, we can usually cut a fairly lucrative deal for ourselves at the front end, find a way to improve it, get some funding behind it – whether it be through the Canadian financing or our own. There are some where there are outrageous differentials between what we've paid and what we were ultimately able to conclude in the way of a final deal." One bankrupt company cost Bell $200,000, but eventually paid off "in the tens of millions," he says. "This one would not be all that different," says Bell of Remuera.

Indeed, Estech spent about $200,000 on the deal, but recovered most of that from the funds raised by the general partnership. In the end, the NetManager software that caused all the heartache – and could still pay off – is two-thirds owned by Estech. If there is a big winner in this, it will be Lyn Bell. At little cost to him. So far the only payment for those who were there at the beginning has come in the form of personal pain, shattered dreams, and lost jobs at the formerly high-flying Remuera Corp.

Epilogue

On a Saturday night in January 1995, almost a year after Remuera went down, thirty former Remuera employees held a reunion in a room at the National Arts Centre in Ottawa. For old times' sake, the group hired the same three-piece band that had played at the firm's final Christmas party thirteen months before. But the familiar music could not mask the might-have-been mood. Ten ex-Remuera employees who had been hired by acquisitor AT&T had just taken an early-retirement package the month before. The rest were worried about their future as AT&T downsized. Among those laid off by AT&T a month later was Peter Hyne. Michael Leahy remained unemployed until November 1994, when he was able to get some consulting work in Ottawa. A year after Remuera cratered, Leahy was still on the hook for $43,000 in Amex bills and was suing Mawby and Hyne to pay their share.

The only one of the three former owners who put in an appearance at the party was Charles Mawby of Network Xcellence. In March 1995, he was still working on the *first* NetManager deal – to the Saskatchewan Government Insurance Corp., where final approvals were pending. Revenue had yet to flow from the infamous software system that had dragged down Remuera.

John Purdon had gone off on another high-tech adventure as president and CEO of HavenTree Software Ltd. of Kingston, Ontario, and Mike Fletcher had joined Cablecom International in Ottawa as CFO. As for Stephen Hall and Malcolm Rigby, in December 1994, they took over a public company called BMB Compuscience Canada Ltd., renamed it Systems Xcellence Inc., and plan to roll their Network Xcellence ownership into the new entity based in Milton, Ontario. Hall and Rigby were advised in the deal by Pierre Vella-Zarb, who set up his own company, Falcon Corp., and no longer does deals with Mike McKie of Optimax.

"Remuera was a good and vibrant business if it had been managed properly. NetManager could have been a year ahead of where it is now," said Hall in early 1995. "I find Peter Hyne an interesting guy. I like him. Peter Hyne is a very valuable guy, but the problem is that he stays involved after his usefulness has been used up. Charles Mawby I hold guilty of being naïve. Michael Leahy just kind of turned turtle and acted like it would all go away. I gave Peter Hyne chance after chance to act on a businesslike basis."

The lessons to be drawn from the events at Remuera apply to any firm through the start-up period or as it grows in the early years. They include:

1. Don't move too far away from your core business.
2. Make sure development costs are in line and that the product or service you have in mind will begin producing revenue as quickly as possible.
3. Keep all overhead costs as low as possible.
4. Maintain up-to-date financial reporting.
5. Don't create a sales, training, development, or production infrastructure until you need to.

6. Be wary of tax-driven investment deals.

7. Devise a realistic business plan, then follow it.

8. Don't try to grow too quickly; 15 to 20 per cent is solid, anything beyond can be risky.

9. Resolve disputes with fellow owners quickly.

10. Dream big dreams, but make sure you have sound managers watching out for today.

11. Keep your ego in check.

CHAPTER 12

Going Public:
The Open Kimono

"There must be a sizzle to the story."

– Deborah Weinstein, Blake Cassels & Graydon

E ric Goodwin, president and CEO of Fulcrum
Technologies Inc. of Ottawa, was in the final stages of
launching his firm's new stock issue in 1993. After
having visited fourteen cities in thirteen days across four countries and two continents, the team doing the "road show" had
finally reached New York. Response everywhere had been
excellent; the issue looked as if it would be oversubscribed.
Still, this *was* Wall Street, and the fifty retail brokers assembled
at the standing-room-only meeting were essential to its
success. After the canned speeches and flashy video presentations came the all-important question-and-answer session.

A venerable gentleman began by asking why the parent firm
was selling shares. "What a dumb question," deadpanned
Goodwin. "They're dumping the stock." There was a baffled
silence in the room for a few seconds until everyone realized

Goodwin was joking, and then there was relieved laughter all round. The issue was a success at U.S.$11 per share and later hit a high of U.S.$14.75, a nice little flutter upward that meant the issue was well priced, and newly recruited shareholders could make a little money if they were nimble.

Most entrepreneurs who build companies eventually get to the point at which they consider taking their baby public. The decision is difficult. On the one hand, there's a compliment in having total strangers give you money to join in on what you've created. On the other hand, you suddenly have a whole new constituency to please. You started out a few years back to be your own boss and, instead, you have become responsible to thousands of shareholders.

In 1993, ninety-three Canadian firms went public, raising among them $3.9 billion. Half of the issues were relatively small, as firms raised under $100 million each. In 1994, the markets were not quite as active, but fifty-six issues raised $3.3 billion. Again, a goodly number were smaller companies: fifty of the firms going public raised less than $100 million each.

Firms thinking about taking the plunge into the public pool need to be sure that they can instill confidence in potential investors. Here's a basic checklist that describes what's required before a company should even think about going public:

- a minimum of $10 million to $15 million in annual sales;
- consistent annual earnings growth of 15 to 20 per cent;
- net tangible assets of $1 million, with profits of at least $100,000 before taxes and pretax cash flows of $400,000, or net tangible assets of $5 million and – if the firm is losing money – the likelihood of a return to profit;
- a strong board of directors that includes at least two outside directors;

• sound financial controls and five years of financial statements audited by one of the big accounting firms;
• industry leadership; and
• a management team of sufficient size so that some executives can spend the time necessary to launch an initial public offering (IPO), while other top managers mind the store. "People don't get a great deal of comfort from a one-man show," says Dan Hachey, vice-president of Midland Walwyn Capital Inc.

One of the most difficult new elements that an entrepreneur will face is making information public that was previously private. "I'm sure I won't enjoy reading about plunging profits in some quarter," said Colin Beasley, president of International Wallcoverings, before he took his company public in 1994. "But I'm not bothered by the information side."

For others, remaining a private company is the best choice. "I can take the longer view," says Bryan Kerdman of Bryker Data Systems. Rather than worry about keeping shareholders happy with consistent quarterly profit levels, Kerdman has been able to act exactly how and when he thinks the timing and opportunity is best. For example, there came a point a few years back when he decided to spend $1 million on 52,000 square feet of new floorspace. The undertaking was expensive, but it was one that he knew was right for the long term. He went ahead because there were no shareholders looking over his shoulder, wanting to maintain earnings-per-share so that the share values would rise.

While it can take three to five years to properly prepare a company to go public, once you've decided to take the plunge, the first step, taken six to nine months ahead of the prospective date, is to groom the market. Visit analysts, tour the trade shows, and make any other promotional visits you think will raise your profile as a possible investment. Some well-placed

Advantages to going public:

- access to capital;
- public-market valuation of the firm;
- issued stock that creates a currency other than cash for acquisitions;
- increased corporate visibility;
- options and other share incentive possibilities to attract and retain good employees; and
- liquidity for current shareholders.

Disadvantages include:

- increased public disclosure;
- more onerous reporting to provincial securities commissions;
- pressure to maintain growth;
- focus on quarterly results rather than the longer term;
- possible loss of control; and
- cost. In addition to the 6-per-cent cut the underwriter takes of the money raised, other costs (legals, auditors, printing, translation, marketing, etc.) can range from $250,000 to $750,000.

articles in the business press won't hurt. You want to find out the needs of potential investors, and alert them to your firm and to the opportunity down the road.

Start-up tip: *Focus on a few key people in the investment community; 10 per cent of the people influence the other 90 per cent.*

You need a competent second-in-command to run the business while you're spending time on the IPO. Even with that help, you'll work up to 40 per cent more hours than usual, trying to juggle both the offering process and the day-to-day business. The normal twelve- to fifteen-hour days of the entrepreneur become eighteen- to twenty-hour days. "You're going to have to think 'war room' to get above the noise," says Wanda Dorosz, president and CEO of Quorom Growth Inc. of Toronto and an author and lecturer on finance and venture capital.

Larry O'Brien, chairman and CEO of Calian Communications Systems Inc. of Kanata, Ontario, began working on the IPO a year before the stock went public, leaving day-to-day operations to other key colleagues during the stressful period of preparation. Running the business is important during the time immediately before the issue, because the quarterly results that follow the offering are crucial to maintaining share price. Only you can work on some aspects of the IPO, but you'll want to be sure that the business continues to be managed by your best associates. "Resist the temptation to sit in on every meeting," says Dorosz.

Fully 80 per cent of companies going public fall 10 per cent short of their projections for that first reporting period after the IPO, often because executives let the business get away from them while they were occupied with the launch. If the market doesn't like the numbers, the stock price can take a downturn, and the investors that you convinced to part with their money will be angry – and fast. In a company about to go public, everybody involved must try to maximize shareholder value and keep the business on track, says Rob Burgess of Alias Research. "Establish a common context and a lot of the smaller problems will go away," he adds.

Choosing the underwriting firm that will handle the deal requires you to think about the chemistry you have with the partners in the brokerage firm, that company's track record, and the likelihood of their ongoing commitment. When you're negotiating your original deal with the brokerage firm handling the IPO, get their commitment that the firm's analysts will follow your stock and issue regular reports after the company is public. If you go public, and none of the analysts watch you on an ongoing basis, your firm will slip into the market shadows. You want continuing attention, so that retail salespeople at brokerage firms are receiving a constant flow of material from their research departments about your firm.

Writing the prospectus

Every firm that goes public issues a prospectus, a thick document, often up to one hundred pages long, that details every aspect of the company. Drafting the key business-related parts of that prospectus is a job that only the CEO can handle, at least as far as the first draft is concerned. "No one will understand your business like you do," says Wanda Dorosz. "Go to a cheesy hotel for three or four days, send out for pizza and whatever drink you prefer, and don't stop until you have sixty pages of something." Among the aspects that should be included are benchmark analyses of other firms in your field, so prospective purchasers will be able to place your firm in a larger context.

Don't make wild projections about future sales. High-tech firms seem particularly prone to such claims. "Technology is years ahead of the ability to assimilate it," says Marcia Wisniewski, a technology analyst for Toronto Dominion Securities Inc., so expect revenue flow to be slow in coming, if the cash comes at all. "Remember artificial intelligence," she says. "I don't think anybody made money from that."

The sexier the story, the more the interest, agrees Michael Boyd, former senior vice-president and managing director of syndication at investment firm Marleau, Lemire Inc. "You've got to promise a lot if your numbers are small," he says. Wisniewski urges using key words in the prospectus. Although her examples might apply most readily to high tech, they give an idea of the sort of sizzle you should be attempting to describe. Wisniewski calls such words "an excitement list" – smaller, better, faster, easier, mobile, decision support, no technical boundaries, all in one. Stress the product's winning attributes: compact, lightweight, voice-activated, wireless, strategic partnerships, integrated. Ordinary people will be reading what you write, so don't use industry jargon understood only by insiders. "Don't be blinded by the science," she warns.

Everything in your prospectus must be carefully corroborated by a team of advisers, including lawyers and accountants, to ensure its accuracy. If shareholders are not happy with the investment at some future date, they'll comb the prospectus looking for promises that have not been kept so they can sue. The prospectus must disclose everything – whether it is favourable or not – that will enable potential investors to make a decision.

> **Start-up tip:** *The prospectus should contain full, plain, and accurate disclosure.*

The prospectus should also contain a complete legal and chronological history of the firm, five years of financial records, analysis about why revenues or expenses went up or down in a given year, details about lawsuits, both current and pending, all executive compensation figures, including salary, bonuses, and perks, plus information about material contracts. And that's just in what's known as the "preliminary" prospectus, which is submitted to the provincial securities commission for scrutiny. Within a month the commission will send you what's known as a "deficiency letter," which means that the prospectus requires further clarification and rewriting. Once those questions have been addressed, there may be another such letter from the commission before the prospectus is declared final and can be made public.

The toughest part to write will likely be the history and strategy of the company, which "You thought everybody agreed on," notes Harald Meuller of Eicon Technology Corp., a Montreal-based hardware and software company. When the time comes to put such aspects in black and white, there will be disputes among managers who see the firm's past and prospects differently than you do. Meanwhile, the meter for accounting, legal, and other fees continues to run.

Along the way, you'll have to tidy up some of those problems you've been putting off – like settling lawsuits. "The fewer questions, the better," says Wanda Dorosz. "There isn't a company that doesn't have a cluttered basement. Clean it out." You've also got to make good on everything you've told close associates over the years. "You've got to put on paper all the promises you've made to the people around you that you would do 'one day,'" she says. "That 'one day' has come."

Picking the exchange

In order to have securities listed and traded on a stock exchange, you'll need to file a listing application as well as the prospectus. (You can also sell securities in the unlisted, or over-the-counter (OTC), market, which is made up of securities dealers who trade using negotiated prices.) Listing arrangements for the Alberta and Vancouver exchanges offer lower hurdles than Toronto and Montreal. But, overall, securities that trade on a recognized exchange offer a greater guarantee that your firm's shares will have value and they will be more easily marketed than an OTC offering.

One of the advantages to a U.S. issue is that you can raise a smaller amount of money, like $5 million to $6 million, if that's all you're looking for. The threshold in Canada tends to be higher, in the $10-million range. But launching your IPO on a U.S. exchange like NASDAQ (National Association of Securities Dealers Automated Quotations) means that you face a higher risk of being sued than in Canada. Some U.S. law firms do nothing but look for businesses that have not met projections in their prospectuses and sue them on behalf of shareholders.

As a result, one firm in six on NASDAQ is sued. Even on the New York Stock Exchange, one firm in eight gets sued; in Silicon Valley, the ratio is one in three. Victory in such instances may mean you get legal costs reimbursed, but no one can ever reclaim the time wasted.

Individual corporate strategy will dictate which stock exchange is best for you. Ottawa-based Fulcrum Technology Inc.'s sales are largely in the United States, so the firm concluded that a listing where their customers were made the most sense. Peter Reid, CFO of the firm, which was launched in the eighties to supply text-retrieval systems, did his own research by visiting companies that had recently gone public, and he decided he would use two U.S. underwriting firms. He chose smaller firms, known as "boutique" firms, because they specialize in particular niches. Their size guaranteed that their senior people would work on the deal, rather than immediately fob the business off to juniors once the original contract had been concluded. Still, you are vying for attention, and, in a busy year, your firm will be only one of many competing for that attention. "You learn to be humble real quick," says Reid.

If you are considering going public in the United States, you may want to open a head office there first, in order to create attention. "Here, you're a big fish in a small pond," says Dan Hachey of Midland Walwyn. The United States is more volatile and, he says, "The Canadian market tends not to be as fickle."

Start-up tip: *Go when the markets are there for you; the market determines the price.*

You may also find a U.S. listing useful simply because no one in Canada is interested. Spectral Diagnostics, described in Chapter Nine, is run by Doug Ball and Dr. George Jackowski. Both of them are in their early forties, worked in the United

States, then chose to return to Canada, but here they have felt stifled by the conservative Canadian mindset. When Spectral sought financing to commercialize further the cardiac-test panel it invented, the firm hit a series of brick walls. Although Spectral had received early funding from the National Research Council, there really was no vehicle in Canada for the next step. Venture-capital companies demand majority ownership, the banks weren't interested, and no Canadian brokerage house would take on Spectral for a public-share offering. "The tendency of the Canadian investment community is to evaluate companies in the home market," says Ball. "Our market is the world."

The Canadian health community was equally unsupportive of Jackowski's work while he was at Toronto's Hospital for Sick Children. "I was regarded as a bit of a joke, because I wanted to win a Nobel Prize," says Jackowski.

Once Texas Securities Inc. of Fort Worth, Texas, signed on to do the initial public offering, however, Spectral might as well have received the papal imprimatur. Canadian brokerage firms quickly climbed aboard, too, and 70 per cent of the stock made available was sold in Canada. Spectral raised U.S.$4 million and investors did well. From an initial price of Cdn$7.53 for a unit consisting of a share and a warrant, the combined value sky-rocketed as high as Cdn$45.00 on the NASDAQ. (Jackowski owns 12 per cent of Spectral; Ball has 6 per cent).

Start-up tip: *There's nothing like a little respect in the United States to fuel interest in Canada.*

Other young companies may also find that foreign investors are often more prepared to take a chance on a Canadian company, even if they have little knowledge about the nation. "A lot of our investors don't even know where Canada is," says Loudon Owen, a partner in merchant bank McLean Watson. The difference between a Canadian investor and an American one, says Owen, is that the Canadian will focus on profit, the American will pay attention to growth. The former looks at historical financials, the latter at the future. The upside is that your company can come to the attention of U.S. research houses that recommend your stock to individual investors and institutions. Spectral has attracted wide stock-market attention from many on Wall Street, including Richard Yett, a vice-president at the New York research boutique of Monness, Crespi, Hardt & Co., who regularly visits emerging Canadian companies on behalf of his U.S. pension and mutual-fund clients. "I like [Spectral] a lot," says Yett. "I'm pleased the company is run by business-men and not scientists."

The last stage

Assuming that everything's a go, the next step is the "road show," when you take your preliminary prospectus, a corporate video, plus an upbeat speech, and visit half a dozen cities in as many days. In each community you'll meet institutional investors, such as pension-fund and mutual-fund managers, as well as retail sales staff from brokerage houses. Larry O'Brien of Calian Communications now says that his stock sold so well that he wonders if it was even necessary to have bothered with a road show, although most brokerage-house advisers would insist on some such selling. As it turned out, he spent only a modest $25,000. "We could have spent $300,000 without blinking an eye," he says.

Your stock issue has yet to be priced (that's the final step), but you're there at the road show to put on your best face, sell the company, and look like the next Microsoft, so institutional managers will buy shares or retail sales reps will tell individual buyers about your firm's prospects. The brokerage house taking you public will try to ensure a successful IPO by par-celling out a certain quota of shares to each local office, but you need to be pushing hard as well. With proper timing, there should be no problem. "If the market conditions are right, any good story will sell," says Peter Reid of Fulcrum.

When the time comes to set the share price, be careful and listen to advice. You may have a dollar figure in mind, but you also want a successful offering, so you have to make sure the market will agree. "The founder can get greedy," says Reid. "Leave some on the table and allow the stock to come up."

Some final warnings

Your attitude is important throughout the process, because, says Calian's Larry O'Brien, "You'll have a love-hate relationship" with the underwriters, lawyers, and auditors. That's because you'll be spending so much time with them and they'll appear to be so niggling about details. If you're a freewheeling deal-maker, you won't be happy having to pay attention to audits, specific forecasts, negative variances, board minutes, and all the other picky details, such as lengthy résumés about everyone.

Above all, you must be in control of everything. "Don't assume just because you haven't done this before that you shouldn't be in charge," says Deborah Weinstein of Blake Cassels & Graydon. "Ensure you control the process. It's your company." At the same time, remember, maintaining your previous level of business growth while this is going on is critical.

After all that effort, at the last minute your underwriter may suddenly decide not to go ahead, arguing that the market has taken a turn for the worse. The firm that convinced you going public was a great idea may exercise the "out clause" in the agreement and leave you gasping for air like a beached whale.

Presuming the deal proceeds, be prepared for a massive change in your own life and in your perception of yourself. "You don't own the company anymore. It's no longer your fiefdom," says David Gurney, chairman and CEO of SoftQuad Inc., a software and services vendor based in Toronto. "It's a huge and fundamental shift to how you run your life and manage your business." Also, world events that you previously didn't care much about suddenly take on new meaning. Gurney was involved in an IPO in the final phase, setting the share price, when Boris Yeltsin was coming to power in Russia and there was shooting in the streets of Moscow. "I sat down for three hours and tried to figure out how the Russians shooting at themselves would affect the issue I was trying to price."

"Make sure you're going public for the right reason," says Larry O'Brien. "Make sure you need the cash. After the IPO, the world changes." Quality and sustainability of earnings matter, and a public company has an entirely different profile. You'll get telephone calls from strangers who are also shareholders, demanding to know why the stock price hasn't doubled. The board now sees its role as keeping management on their toes. "[The board] can be downright hostile, because they represent the shareholder," O'Brien says.

While the additional capital raised can make employees feel more secure about the company's long-term health, information revealed in the prospectus may also make those same employees realize that the firm has been playing favourites, through ownership positions or other sweetheart deals. "Your employees very quickly understand who are the haves and the have nots," says Harald Meuller of Eicon. "There will be emotional and mental casualties along the way." Moreover, if management claimed in the past that cash-strapped conditions prevented certain steps, that excuse may evaporate once everyone knows what's in the treasury.

Yet doing the deal has a surprise payback. Garry Foster of auditing firm Deloitte & Touche relates the story of a company that went public because the bank wouldn't approve any more debt. Once the firm was public, shares were available to acquire a U.S. firm in a $100-million "paper" deal. Says Foster, "Now the bankers are knocking on their door to get them to take some money."

Offsetting that different – and positive – market perception is the constant pressure to maintain growth. But, hey, you pulled it off. The world has acknowledged and affirmed your success by buying in. For the first time, you'll be debt free, have access to cash, get the bankers off your back, and have no more need to sign all those irritating personal guarantees. You can issue stock options to key staff as incentives and rewards for their contribution, past and future. You now have both the financial strength and the public profile to be able to move ahead of the competition. You may even run your business better. "The scrutiny is good for you," says David Gurney of SoftQuad. "Quarterly reporting and due diligence ensures that you and your management are focused."

Not to mention the financial reward. Says Michael Boyd of Marleau, Lemire, "At closing, when the CEO gets a cheque for $10, $20, or $30 million, the process is very worthwhile." Says Meuller, "The rush is extremely rewarding." That fire in your belly when you launched the business has finally paid off in the pocket.

Summary:

1. Realize that going public means many of your corporate secrets will be made public.
2. Pick your underwriter and other advisers carefully; you'll be spending months in their presence.
3. Write a first draft of the business parts of the prospectus yourself; no one knows the firm like you do.
4. Before the IPO, solve strategic-direction dilemmas and use the IPO to reward longtime backers.
5. Enjoy your newfound wealth. You might even use some of those funds to back another start-up situation. After all, you know a thing or two about business.

CHAPTER 13

Farewell Thoughts

Just as baseball players are superstitious because they don't know where their power comes from, businesspeople often find inner strength and meaning from something outside themselves – religion. Jack Stultz, president of Apex Industries Ltd. of Moncton, New Brunswick, has been a born-again Christian since attending a Youth for Christ meeting as a thirteen-year-old boy. "The Christian faith is very important in a free-enterprise system, because it is the conscience or balancing factor to the unfettered drive of capitalism," says Stultz. "We don't do all things right. We're sinners saved by the grace of God. He's the guiding light, and whatever I do I want to give Him credit." Stultz has included his personal religious belief in the mission statement of Apex, a $23-million company with sales in a wide range of products and services including cranes, doors, and land surveys. The page-long printed version of the vision concludes: "The work of our company should be an honourable offering onto God."

Syd Kessler of F/X Corp. draws his inner peace and power from the ancient Jewish manuscript called the Kabbalah. While Kessler is well aware that corporate infrastructure, management skills, and financial backing are each important for professional success, mystical Judaism has become Kessler's driving spiritual and personal force. According to Kessler, the Kabbalah teaches that, when you see a tree, you ask, Wherein is contained the potential of the whole tree? The answer, of course, is in the seed. "So when I plant my personal and business seeds, I inject into that seed that which I want to come out of it," he says.

In the past, Kessler took a *laissez-faire* attitude towards greed in others. "I knew they were greedy, but I figured, if they've got a good idea, a good product, or a good service, I'll do a deal with them. Well, guess what? In the short run, I always made money, but in the long run I didn't, because those people were just greedy. They were just going to screw me." Applying the Kabbalah to everyday life changed all that wrong-headed thinking. "I started to be more sharing with people. When I started planting my seeds that way, the flowers I was getting were more consistent. I know it sounds stupid, but it was a major revelation for me."

For Kessler, the philosophy has yielded positive results in his business life. He journeyed to Japan in 1994 to negotiate a deal that everyone said would require a six-month effort. Time required was, in fact, ten days. All Kessler did was ask the Japanese, "What do you need for your company that will make this a positive sale for you?" Not only did that approach speed up the process, but the purchase price Kessler paid was half what a U.S. firm spent to cut a similar deal with the same party. "It was extraordinary for me," he says. "Things react to us the way we want them to react."

That's a thought worth repeating: *Things react to us the way we want them to react.* If you have a burning desire within, a fire in your belly, about starting a business, don't procrastinate. Reach inside yourself for the will and look outside as well for inspiration but, above all, get started. Maintain a positive attitude and, as Rick Padulo says in Chapter One, have a little faith in yourself. Apply some of the secrets of success shared by the businesspeople quoted in this book, but don't forget that you can launch a business your own way too. You can be creative and innovative; you don't need to follow someone else's specific step-by-step pattern. Why? Because the way business has functioned in the past is finished. Command and control no longer works. Team-based solutions do.

In the future, employees are going to be more mobile and less loyal. The most successful firms will be those that demonstrate the characteristics of the virtual corporation, where entire business functions are conducted outside the walls of an organization, as contract work and outsourcing become more commonplace. Compensation will be important, but so will a sense of belonging, of contributing to an overall effort. Key colleagues will be paid based on their performance and will participate in ownership of the business. As a result, you'll hire fewer people and train them better. Networking with other firms and using computer groupware at your firm will mean that people who work with you or for you don't need to be under the same roof, in the same city, or even the same country. Call it virtual co-location.

There's already a pilot project called Virtual Presence running in Toronto and Ottawa, a video hookup that allows you to "roam" visually into a number of offices to see if a colleague is there with whom you might want to consult – immediately. What's happening is that technology is extending the normal reach of human endeavour. You can "walk" down the hall to brainstorm with someone, even if that person is miles away. In the future, these sorts of extended partnerships in the virtual corporation will expand to include suppliers and competitors who will share with you and with each other the kind of information that might in the past have been considered competitive or privileged. Call it co-opetition.

Another element of the virtual corporation will be the

capacity to do in parallel what has traditionally been done in sequence. How many products today are made the old way, using some rigorous step-by-step process, with workers waiting for someone else to complete one aspect of the task before the next action can occur? Look how automotive production has changed. Henry Ford invented the assembly line and the concept worked, more or less, for fifty years. Then somebody got the bright idea to turn the car sideways, put it on a mobile platform, and take the vehicle right to the work teams. Have you been in an auto plant lately? Now the robotics and other assembly operations are attached to the units bearing the vehicles as they move about the plant. The factory is alive. Call it concurrency.

The Internet is changing the way companies communicate with each other and their customers. But what really matters for your start-up business is not concurrency, virtual reality, re-engineering, or any of the other business-process buzzwords. What matters is people – managing them and achieving goals together. Quality products and excellent service are key, but leadership is what counts for success – leadership that comes from you. "The only reality is action," said French philosopher Jean-Paul Sartre. "Man is nothing other than what he does." What's needed to take that action is a personal vision, coupled with the capacity to nurture talent and the ability to harness knowledge – both in yourself and in others.

A leader, according to Napoleon, is a dealer in hope. You, too, can be such a dealer in hope – by starting your own business. With the arrival of today's more affordable technology, everyone is on an equal footing, because what matters now is knowledge. Big companies used to have the advantage, because they had economies of scale; cartels dominated entire sectors and controlled supply, pricing, and entry. Today, the cost of starting up a business can be as little as you want. Look around you, individuals are beginning to think more for themselves and rely less on commentators, politicians, and regulators to interpret events for them. The mass media is losing much of its power as an agenda-setter and moulder of public opinion. Any individual is able to obtain all the information needed to assess situations clearly and apply that knowledge to their own situation and solution.

Change has become a permanent feature of life. Fragmentation of the marketplace will accelerate. Niches will become even more focused. Institutions will continue to crumble. Just as the old organizational structure has become obsolete, so have the requirements for institutional leadership. For some, this lack of structure and direction is worrisome. For you, the tectonic shift that's occurring in society can be an opportunity to achieve the dream that burns within. That's because, in the new economy, leadership can arise from anywhere. The person at the top can no longer learn for the entire organization. You can participate, by transforming yourself, or you can risk being swept away. Canada must become a nation of nomads, a people always on the run.

Here are the three challenges for any enterprise in the new economy:

- First, the focus for the enterprise should not be on streamlining or cost reduction, it must be on innovation and value added. The focus of change will be on the fusion of processes and people.
- Second, the enterprise will have to embrace and provide all the creative communication-oriented and multimedia tools (CD-ROMs and Internet access, for example) required by what management guru Peter Drucker calls "brain capital."
- Third, solutions can no longer be decided by a few folks, who then dispatch the word top-down. Strategies for success must grow out of a team-based organization.

The enterprises that prosper in the future will be those that nurture individuals and encourage them to use all their talents. The businesses that soar on strong wings will be those that let every person realize the dreams within, just as you are about to realize yours.

And remember, success comes to those who achieve what they dream . . . but happiness only arrives when you want what you get.

Let that fire in your belly set the hills ablaze. After all, you are Canada's last, best hope.

accounts receivable: Money owed to you, of which there is usually a scarcity.

accounts payable: Money owed by you; always too high a total.

angel: Someone who lends you money when no one else will.

appraised value: An expert's opinion of the value of assets. Market value is what someone will actually pay.

assets: Items you have with value or net worth after debts against them are paid off.

capital investment: Money that goes to buy items that last, like equipment.

cash flow: Money moving into the business from customers and clients.

chattel mortgage: A pledge on a vehicle or a mortgage on your house; if loan payments are not up-to-date, the goods can be seized.

collateral: More of the same; bankers are very cautious about these things, so they have several terms for the same handcuffs.

debt: What you owe (not to be confused with bad debt, which is money owed to you for too long).

debt/equity ratio: Debt divided by equity; a measure of financial health.

default: When you've missed a loan payment, you're in default; like being in deep doo-doo.

demand loan: A loan that can be called by the bank; they "demand" full and immediate payment. Often happens when you least expect it.

equity: Net worth; what the business is worth once all debts have been paid; what you would pocket if you sold out; the value of what you've built.

failure: Not a word that's found in your vocabulary.

franchisee: You, the one who buys the franchise.

franchiser: The owner of the master franchise with whom you share profits.

gross profit margin: Markup; the difference between what you pay for goods and what you can sell them for.

interest: The cost of borrowed money; often expressed as prime plus one or two, meaning one or two percentage points over the prime rate.

inventory: Goods on hand.

lessee: You, the one who rents the space.

lessor: The landlord.

line of credit: An amount of money (with a specified ceiling) that your bank has agreed to let you draw from in order to smooth out the peaks and valleys of cash flow. When you need cash for the payroll, you draw down the line; when money owed by a client arrives, you repay the line.

operating loan: Unlike a term loan, this money is used for day-to-day needs, like overhead.

overhead: Fixed costs required just to keep the doors open, whether you make a sale or not: taxes, heat, hydro, rent, payroll, production.

personal pledge or guarantee: The final ounce of blood demanded by the bank, when you agree to pledge personal assets, such as your house, in order to get a business loan.

prime rate, or prime interest rate: The interest rate set by the bank for its best corporate customers, like Conrad Black; you will pay two or three percentage points more.

principal: What you owe, the loan amount; interest is on top.

profit-and-loss statement: Known in accounting shorthand as the P&L, this annual snapshot prepared by your accountant gives details of your assets, liabilities, and – as the name implies – profit or loss, and describes the sort of year you've had.

promissory note: A signed agreement by you to pay a certain amount to the holder of the note by a specific date.

return on investment: A ratio used by financial backers to measure the annual payback against the cash put into your business.

securities: Stocks and bonds you hold as investments that can be sold to obtain start-up funds or used as loan collateral.

security: Like collateral; more backstop for loans. The building you buy with borrowed money is pledged to the bank as security in case you default. If it doesn't get your cash, it takes what you spent the money on.

skus: Stock-keeping units; individual items carried by a retail outlet.

taxes: Unavoidable.

term loan: Money borrowed over a long term, such as five years, to purchase a building or machinery.

venture capital: Money from sources willing to take greater risks than banks; they usually charge higher interest rates and require a stake in your business.

vulture capital: Investors who come looking for sweet deals when your business is on its last legs.

The Big Idea, a PC-compatible disk that offers a template for writing a business plan. Available free from any business branch-banking centre of the Royal Bank.

Business Start-up Kit and How to Prepare a Business Plan. Available free from national accounting firm BDO Dunwoody Ward Mallette. Phone: (416) 369-3115.

Business Survival Guide, by Andy Farvolden, published by Key Porter Books, Toronto: 1992, $16.95.

Canada's Postal Code Directory lists every postal code in Canada, available for $11 plus taxes from the National Philatelic Centre, Canada Post Corporation, Station 1, Antigonish, Nova Scotia, B2G 2R8. Phone: 1-800-565-4362.

CanadExport, a twice-monthly newsletter aimed at exporters, and *Road Map to Exporting and Export Financing*, a pamphlet, both from CanadExport, Department of Foreign Affairs and International Trade, 125 Sussex Dr., Ottawa, Ontario, K1A 0G2.

Cover Your Assets: The Creditors' and Debtors' Guide to Survival and Success, by Bernard R. Wilson. Free from Price Waterhouse,

20 Queen St. W., Suite 300, Box 75, Toronto, Ontario, M5H 3V7. Fax requests: (416) 979-4631.

Financing a Small Business – Working with Your Bank. Available free from the Canadian Bankers' Association. Phone: 1-800-263-0231, Fax: (416) 362-7705, or write to: Suite 600, The Exchange Tower, P.O. Box 348, 2 First Canadian Place, Toronto, Ontario, M5X 1E1. Offices across Canada. The CBA also runs business-plan seminars.

Getting Ready; *Getting Started*; *Getting Money*; and *Getting Sales*, by Dan Kennedy, Self-Counsel Press, Toronto: 1991. Four practical books at $7.95 each, available from 1481 Charlotte Rd., North Vancouver, British Columbia, V7J 1H1, or 8-2283 Argentia Rd., Mississauga, Ontario, L5N 5Z2.

The Going Public Decision, from any office of accounting firm Ernst & Young.

Government Assistance Programs in Canada, by KPMG Peat Marwick Thorne, a 620-page book for $32.95 published by CCH Canada, Toronto. Phone: (416) 441-2992 or 1-800-268-4522, ext. 386.

Guide to Business Planning. Available free from any commercial branch of the Canadian Imperial Bank of Commerce. Phone: 1-800-465-2422 for nearest location.

Making Technology Happen, by D. J. Doyle, $20, available from Doyletech Corp., 362 Terry Fox Dr., Kanata, Ontario, K2K 2P5.

Outline for a Business Plan, free from Ernst & Young, P.O. Box 62202, Stn. B, Toronto, Ontario, M7Y 2T1. The accounting firm also publishes a quarterly newsletter for entrepreneurs called "The Enterpriser," a bulletin about the economic environment and tax information, all from the same address. Also available is financial and tax-policy information, including analysis of federal and provincial budgets within hours of release, on the World Wide Web. The Internet address is http://tax.ey.ca/ey

Plan A, a business, marketing, and advertising plan on computer disk, and a book called *How to Think Like an Entrepreneur*, $95, from The Mighty Information Co. Inc., Nun's Island, Quebec.

Raising Money: The Canadian Entrepreneur's Guide to Successful Business Financing, by Douglas Gray and Brian Natrass, McGraw-Hill Ryerson, Toronto: 1992, $22.95.

Raving Fans: A Revolutionary Approach to Customer Service, by Ken Blanchard and Sheldon Bowles, William Morrow, 1994, $26.95.

The Solvency Solution: Save Your Business from Bankruptcy, by Martin Turner, Key Porter Books, Toronto: 1994, $19.95.

Starting a Business: A Complete Guide to Starting and Managing Your Own Company, by Gordon Brockhouse, Key Porter Books, Toronto: 1994, $19.95.

Starting a New Business: A Guide to the Financial, Tax and Accounting Considerations, free from Beallor, Beallor, Burns, 28 Overlea Blvd., Toronto, Ontario, M4H 1B6. Phone: (416) 423-0707, Fax: (416) 423-7000.

Strategies for Success: A Profile of Growing Small and Medium-sized Enterprises in Canada, $15 per issue from Marketing Division, Sales and Service, Statistics Canada, Ottawa, Ontario, K1A 0T6.

Succeeding in Small Business: The 101 Toughest Problems and How to Solve Them, by Jane Applegate, Penguin Books, Toronto: 1992, $14.99.

The Succession Plan, free from any office of accounting firm Deloitte & Touche.

Venture Capital in Canada, free from The Association of Canadian Venture Capital Companies, 1881 Yonge St., Suite 600, Toronto, Ontario, M4S 1Y6. Phone: (416) 487-0519.

Your Business Matters, four-volume series of guidebooks on financial aspects of small business, free from the Royal Bank.

The AdvantEdge Corp., 69 Yonge St., Toronto, Ontario, M5E 1K3. Phone: (416) 955-0126, Fax: (416) 955-0271. Creates Internet home pages and CD-ROMs.

Association of Collegiate Entrepreneurs, 140 Renfrew Dr., Suite 205, Markham, Ontario, L3R 6B3. Phone: (905) 470-5193 or 1-800-766-8169, Fax: (905) 470-8512. Has local chapters, international programs, and seminars.

Business Centurions, 1 St. Clair Ave. E., Suite 505, Toronto, Ontario, M4T 2V7. Phone: (416) 969-1155, Fax: (416) 969-1154. Venture capital and advice.

Business Development Bank: for information on seminars and programs such as Step-In for beginning entrepreneurs and Step-Up, a mentoring program for women who are ready to expand their businesses, as well as working-capital loans through seventy-eight branches nationwide call 1-800-361-2126.

Canadian Association of Family Enterprise, 63-B Church St., Markham, Ontario, L3P 2M1. Phone: (905) 472-0546 or Fax: (905) 294-2983 for workshops and seminar locations and times across Canada.

Canadian Business Centre, Ejercito Nacional #926, Mexico D.F. 11540, Mexico. Phone: (011-525)580-1176, Fax: (011-525)580-4494. Canadian government-supplied office and exhibition space, communications and conference rooms, business support.

Canadian Franchise Association, 5045 Orbitor Dr., Bldg. Twelve, Suite 201, Mississauga, Ontario, L4W 4Y4. Phone: (905) 625-2896, Fax: (905) 625-9076. Has a dozen guides and handbooks as well as a $24.95 information kit that includes a booklet called "Investigate Before Investing," a directory of association members, as well as various articles and helpful checklists.

Canadian Federation of Independent Business, 4141 Yonge St., Suite 401, Willowdale, Ontario, M2P 2A6. Phone: (416) 222-8022.

Canadian Foundation for Economic Education, 2 St. Clair Ave W., Suite 501, Toronto, Ontario, M4V 1K7. Phone: (416) 968-2236, Fax: (416) 968-0488. Has a motivational six-lesson video program for entrepreneurs at $250, or separate user's guide for $20.

Canadian Organization of Small Business, 3555 Don Mills Rd., Unit 6-105, Willowdale, Ontario, M2H 3N3. Phone: (416) 534-7324, Fax: (416) 537-2545.

Canadian Professional Sales Association, Phone: (416) 408-2685 (Toronto) or 1-800-268-3794, Fax: (416) 408-2684.

Export Development Corp., 151 O'Connor St., Ottawa, Ontario, K1A 1K3. Phone: (613) 598-2500, Fax: (613) 598-2960. Offices in Vancouver, Calgary, Winnipeg, Toronto, London, Ottawa, Montreal, and Halifax.

InfoCentre (formerly InfoExport), Phone: (613) 944-4000 (Ottawa) or 1-800-267-8376. A counselling service for Canadian exporters.

Network International Inc., 120 Guelph Street, Georgetown, Ontario, L7G 4A4. Phone: (905) 877-8668 or 1-800-465-6006, Fax: (905) 877-8901. A data bank of potential investors.

Ontario Investment and Employee Ownership Program, English inquiries: 1-800-263-7466, French inquiries: 1-800-668-5821.

Open Bidding System and **Bid Request Line** for federal government contracts: 1-800-361-4637 or, in Ottawa: (613) 737-3374.

Retail Council of Canada, Phone: (416) 598-4684, Fax: (416) 598-3707.

Society of Plastics Industry of Canada, 5925 Airport Road, Suite 500, Mississauga, Ontario, L4V 1W1. Phone: (905) 678-7748, Fax: (905) 678-0774.

The Women Inventors Project, 1 Greensborough Drive, Suite 302, Etobicoke, Ontario, M9W 1C8. Phone: (416) 243-0668, Fax: (416) 243-0688. A nonprofit organization offering courses and workshops, videos, and publications.

YMCA Enterprise Centres offer business courses across Canada. Phone: (416) 651-0010 for local and regional information.

INDEX